★VALUES iN ACTION®

LIFE STORIES OF

100 FAMOUS WOMEN

ddams • Madeleine Albright • Louisa May Alcott • Marian Ande
n • Sarah Bernhardt • Mary McLeod Bethune • Shirley Temple Bl
ë and Emily Brontë • Rachel Carson • Mary Cassatt • Catherine tl
• Diana, Princess of Wales • Emily Dickinson • Isadora Duncan • /
ne Frank • Betty Friedan • Indira Gandhi • Judy Garland • Althe
• Fannie Lou Hamer • Dorothy Hamill • Lillian Hellman • Audrey
• Helen Keller • Billie Jean King • Mary Leakey • Annie Leibovitz
herine de Médicis • Golda Meir • Edna St. Vincent Millay • Maril
tilova • Nefertiti • Florence Nightingale • Annie Oakley • Sandr
dy Onassis • Rosa Parks • Eva Perón • Pocahontas • Beatrix Pott
lph • Sacagawea • Margaret Sanger • Elizabeth Cady Stanton • (
Teresa • Margaret Thatcher • Sojourner Truth • Harriet Tubman •
ngalls Wilder • Oprah Winfrey • Babe Didrikson Zaharias • Jane /
gelou • Susan B. Anthony • Jane Austen • Lucille Ball • Clara Ba
th Blackwell • Nellie Bly • Margaret Bourke-White • Charlotte Bi
opatra VII • Hillary Rodham Clinton • Nadia Comaneci • Marie Cu
t • Elizabeth I • Ella Fitzgerald • Margot Fonteyn • Dian Fossey •
Goodall • Martha Graham • Ella Grasso • Florence Griffith Joyne
Holiday • Mae Jemison • Joan of Arc • Mother Jones • Frida Kah
• Belva Lockwood • Dolley Madison • Madonna • Margaret Mead
e • Maria Montessori • Toni Morrison • Grandma Moses • Martina
nnor • Rosie O'Donnell • Georgia O'Keeffe • Jacqueline Bouvier
tte Rankin • Janet Reno • Sally Ride • Eleanor Roosevelt • Wilm
inem • Martha Stewart • Harriet Beecher Stowe • Ida M. Tarbell •
ia • Sarah Breedlove Walker • Barbara Walters • Ida B. Wells-Barn
dams • Madeleine Albright • Louisa May Alcott • Marian Anderso
n • Sarah Bernhardt • Mary McLeod Bethune • Shirley Temple Bl
ë and Emily Brontë • Rachel Carson • Mary Cassatt • Catherine tl
• Diana, Princess of Wales • Emily Dickinson • Isadora Duncan • •
ne Frank • Betty Friedan • Indira Gandhi • Judy Garland • Althe
• Fannie Lou Hamer • Dorothy Hamill • Lillian Hellman • Audrey
• Helen Keller • Billie Jean King • Mary Leakey • Annie Leibovitz

Maya Angelou • Susan B. Anthony • Jane Austen • Lucille Ball •
Elizabeth Blackwell • Nellie Bly • Margaret Bourke-White • Charlo
at • Cleopatra VII • Hillary Rodham Clinton • Nadia Comaneci • A
Earhart • Elizabeth I • Ella Fitzgerald • Margot Fonteyn • Dian Fo
on • Jane Goodall • Martha Graham • Ella Grasso • Florence Grif
urn • Billie Holiday • Mae Jemison • Joan of Arc • Mother Jones •
a Lin • Belva Lockwood • Dolley Madison • Madonna • Margaret
nroe • Maria Montessori • Toni Morrison • Grandma Moses • Mar
O'Connor • Rosie O'Donnell • Georgia O'Keeffe • Jacqueline Bou
eannette Rankin • Janet Reno • Sally Ride • Eleanor Roosevelt • '
Steinem • Martha Stewart • Harriet Beecher Stowe • Ida M. Tarbe
oria • Sarah Breedlove Walker • Barbara Walters • Ida B. Wells-Bar
ns • Madeleine Albright • Louisa May Alcott • Marian Anderson • '
Sarah Bernhardt • Mary McLeod Bethune • Shirley Temple Black
and Emily Brontë • Rachel Carson • Mary Cassatt • Catherine the
Diana, Princess of Wales • Emily Dickinson • Isadora Duncan • An
Frank • Betty Friedan • Indira Gandhi • Judy Garland • Althea G
nnie Lou Hamer • Dorothy Hamill • Lillian Hellman • Audrey Hepl
lelen Keller • Billie Jean King • Mary Leakey • Annie Leibovitz • /
therine de Médicis • Golda Meir • Edna St. Vincent Millay • Maril
atilova • Nefertiti • Florence Nightingale • Annie Oakley • Sandr
edy Onassis • Rosa Parks • Eva Perón • Pocahontas • Beatrix Pot
olph • Sacagawea • Margaret Sanger • Elizabeth Cady Stanton • '
her Teresa • Margaret Thatcher • Sojourner Truth • Harriet Tubmar
Laura Ingalls Wilder • Oprah Winfrey • Babe Didrikson Zaharias • '
aya Angelou • Susan B. Anthony • Jane Austen • Lucille Ball • Cl
Elizabeth Blackwell • Nellie Bly • Margaret Bourke-White • Charl
eat • Cleopatra VII • Hillary Rodham Clinton • Nadia Comaneci • A
a Earhart • Elizabeth I • Ella Fitzgerald • Margot Fonteyn • Dian F
son • Jane Goodall • Martha Graham • Ella Grasso • Florence Grif
urn • Billie Holiday • Mae Jemison • Joan of Arc • Mother Jones
a Lin • Belva Lockwood • Dolley Madison • Madonna • Margaret

★VALUES ﬁNACTION®

LIFE STORIES OF
100 FAMOUS WOMEN

by
Susan E. Edgar
and
Kathleen J. Edgar

kidsbooks®

PHOTO CREDITS

AP/Wide World: pp. 18, 28, 33, 36, 39, 68, 74, 91, 108, 124, 129, 135, 157, 160, 180, 186, 198, 204, 209, 215, 221, 231, 237, 243, 254, 260, 265, 281, 297, 303, 309, 326, 332, 344, 349, 355, 365, 368, 370, 399, 401, 405, 411, 417, 422, 425, 428, 450, 456, 467, 489, 495, 517, 512, 564, 569, 572 • **Archive Photos:** pp. 51, 141, 170, 175, 376, 483, 547 • **The Granger Collection:** pp. 81, 85, 248, 276, 291 382, 433, 439, 473, 500, 529, 541, 559 • **Rachel Carson History Project:** p. 102 • **Library of Congress, Prints and Photography Division:** pp. 192, 315, 360, 478, 506, 553 • **Corbis/Bettmann:** p. 271

On the cover, left to right:

Top row—Diana, Princess of Wales (Archive Photos) • Sacagawea (The Granger Collection) • Amelia Earhart (The Granger Collection)

Center row—Eleanor Roosevelt (The Granger Collection) • Elizabeth I (The Granger Collection) • Wilma Rudolph (AP/Wide World)

Bottom row—Jane Goodall (Penelope Breese/The Liaison Network) • Oprah Winfrey (AP/Wide World) • Mother Teresa (Santosh Basak/Gamma)

Visit us at **www.kidsbooks.com**

Contents

A Library of Life's Lessons

If actions speak louder than words, role models speak volumes on values. In these short biographies, 100 famous women put their determination, compassion, hard work, courage, imagination, and many other values into action. These inspiring figures faced challenges, overcame adversity, and often accomplished what no woman, or man, ever had before.

Harriet Tubman was determined to escape from her life as a slave, and to help other slaves escape as well. She risked her life again and again, because she knew that what she was doing was right.

When Sandra Day O'Connor could not get work at a law firm because of her gender, she started a firm of her own. She went on to become the first woman appointed to the U.S. Supreme Court, proving to the nation that gender does not determine a person's worth.

Closely watched by the government in her native Czechoslovakia, Martina Navratilova risked her life and career when she defected to the United States. Once free, Navratilova smashed women's tennis records and influenced the sports world's ideas about fitness and health.

Role models inspire us to aim high, do our best, and try again and again when we fail. A library of life's lessons, this collection of biographies will introduce young readers to people from whom they can learn and whose values they can respect.

Jane Addams
Social Reformer and World Peace Activist
(born 1860 • died 1935)

During the late 1800s, hundreds of thousands of immigrants from Europe and Asia came to America's shores. As the population of the U.S. increased, jobs became scarce, leaving many of the newcomers poor and homeless. In response, Jane Addams worked to help the poor make better lives for themselves. She was a pioneer of the social reform movement and urged society to change for the better.

A Social Reformer Is Born

Born on September 6, 1860, in Cedarville, Illinois, Jane was one of nine children. Her father was a state senator and a friend of President Abraham Lincoln.

Jane attended Rockford Female Seminary and Women's Medical College, but was unsure what she wanted to do with her life. When she was 27, Jane Addams traveled to Europe with her friend Ellen Starr.

While in England, she visited Toynbee Hall, a settlement house in London. Settlement houses offered cultural and educational programs to poor families in an effort to bring new life to communities. Addams and Starr were impressed by this idea and returned home with plans to create a settlement house in Chicago.

Hull House

First, Jane Addams and Ellen Starr purchased the Hull estate, a large, run-down mansion in a poor section of Chicago. After making some repairs, the two women opened Hull House in 1889. Modeled after Toynbee Hall in London, Hull House helped needy families. It also offered educational programs for immigrants, and day care for the children of working parents.

> "Private beneficence is totally inadequate to deal with the vast numbers of the city's disinherited."
> —Jane Addams

During the next several years, 12 more buildings were added, making Hull House one of the largest centers of its kind in the United States. Private citizens and other charity groups donated funds to keep the settlement growing. Hull House also offered training programs for people who wanted jobs as social workers.

Following the success of Hull House, Addams turned her talents to social and labor issues. Speaking out on topics such as public education, labor reform, and the rights of immigrants, Addams worked to create laws to help average people. These laws included limiting work to eight hours each day, providing wages to workers who got hurt on the job, and making sure factories were safe.

Pleading for Peace

In 1914, World War I broke out in Europe. Addams believed that people should live peacefully and not harm each other. In 1915, she traveled to the Netherlands to join more than 1,000 women from Europe and North America to discuss putting an end to the war. Known as the International Congress of Women, the group wanted to meet with government officials from the warring nations in "protest against the madness and horror of war." Addams was elected president of the Congress.

The Congress chose 30 women to travel through Europe. As president of the group, Addams represented women who had lost loved ones in the war. The group insisted that average citizens and prisoners of war be treated fairly. They also suggested that a Society of Nations be established to act as a world-

TOPICAL TIDBIT

The United Nations

The United Nations (UN) is an international organization dedicated to maintaining peace throughout the world. Based on a proposal drafted by the International Congress of Women in 1915, the United Nations Charter was signed by representatives from 51 nations on June 26, 1945, in San Francisco, California. (A *charter* is an official document that creates an organization and spells out its rules and regulations.)

wide governing body. World War I lasted until November 1918, but government officials did adopt many of the ideas presented by the International Congress of Women—especially those regarding the treatment of prisoners of war.

After the war, Addams kept working for reforms. In 1920, she helped found the American Civil Liberties Union (ACLU), which is still active today. In 1931, she was awarded the Nobel Peace Prize for her efforts in social work and pleading for peace throughout the world.

Worthy of Remembrance

Jane Addams died on May 21, 1935, in Chicago. Hull House, now a museum, remains as a monument to Addams, one of the greatest social reformers in U.S. history. ◇

LIFE EVENTS

1860
Jane Addams is born in Cedarville, Illinois.

1889
Impressed with a successful settlement house in London, Addams and her friend Ellen Starr open Hull House in Chicago.

1910
Addams's auto-biography, entitled *Twenty Years at Hull House*, is published.

1919-1935
Addams helps found, and serves as president of, the Women's International League for Peace and Freedom.

1931
Addams is awarded the Nobel Peace Prize in recognition of her efforts in social work and reform.

Madeleine Albright
U.S. Secretary of State
(born 1937)

Thomas Jefferson made history more than 200 years ago when he was sworn in as the first U.S. Secretary of State. History was made again on January 23, 1997, as the 64th—and first female—Secretary of State took office. On that day, Madeleine Korbel Albright became the highest-ranking woman in the United States.

Coming to America

Marie Jana Korbel was born on May 15, 1937, in Prague, Czechoslovakia (now the Czech Republic). She was called Madeleine by her family. Just a year later, the Nazis invaded Czechoslovakia and Madeleine's family fled. The Korbels moved to London, where they stayed during World War II (1939-1945). During that time, Madeleine's grandparents were forced into concentration camps because they

were Jewish. They died in the camps. After the war, the Korbels returned to Prague, but had to leave again 10 years later—this time, because of the Communist takeover. They settled in the U.S., in Denver, Colorado, where Madeleine became a U.S. citizen.

Becoming a Diplomat

Madeleine's father had been a diplomat for the Czechoslovakian government. When she was growing up, Madeleine learned to speak several languages, including French and Russian. She began her career in international relations when she was very young, as she often greeted government officials in their own language when they came to the Korbel home.

After graduating from college, Madeleine married Joseph Albright, and they had three daughters. Joseph's family owned the *New York Daily News* and *Newsday* newspapers. Madeleine had hopes of becoming a journalist. Instead, however, she continued her education in international relations while raising her daughters. After 23 years of marriage, the Albrights divorced. Madeleine Albright began teaching classes in foreign policy, politics, and international relations at the School of Foreign Service at Georgetown University. She also acted as the director of Women in Foreign Service, teaching women to become foreign ministers, ambassadors, and staff for the U.S. diplomatic corps.

> "We are not always right in our actions and judgments, but I know from the experience of my own life the importance and rightness of America's ideals."
>
> —Madeleine Albright

In 1993, things changed for Madeleine Albright. She was appointed by President Bill Clinton as the

U.S. ambassador to the United Nations. She was chosen for the job because of her vast knowledge of international relations and foreign affairs.

Rising to the Top

Four years later, in 1997, Albright was sworn in as U.S. Secretary of State—the first woman in U.S. history to hold this high position. From 1997 until 2001, Albright represented the United States in matters such as the banning of chemical and biological weapons, supplying aid to emerging nations, calling for human rights throughout the world, and issuing orders for U.S. military involvement in Bosnia. She also was active in keeping peace in the Middle East, as tensions rose between the Israeli and Arab nations.

Government officials are often criticized for making tough decisions. Like other secretaries of state in the

TOPICAL TIDBIT

Secretary of State

The Secretary of State's duties are outlined in the U.S. Constitution. The duties include serving as the president's adviser on foreign policy, advising the president on the appointment of ambassadors, negotiating international treaties and helping put them into effect, and protecting U.S. citizens while they are in other countries throughout the world.

past, Albright had critics. She was sometimes said to be too outspoken or not very diplomatic because she said what she thought. However, Albright often showed that she had a sense of humor. After one foreign official called her a serpent, Albright began wearing a golden snake pin on the lapel of her suit. She also was seen wearing a pin shaped like a broom after someone else called her a witch.

Albright promised that, as Secretary of State, she would do what she could to help keep peace in the world, even if it meant calling upon the U.S. military to do so.

Opening Doors

Through hard work, Madeleine Albright helped change the role of women in international relations and foreign affairs, opening doors for women to enter the diplomatic corps. Albright once said, "Today's world needs the skills and experience that women bring to diplomacy." ◇

LIFE EVENTS

1937
Marie Jana Korbel is born in Prague, Czechoslovakia (now the Czech Republic).

1948
The Korbel family immigrates to the U.S.

1993
Madeleine Albright is appointed U.S. ambassador to the United Nations by President Clinton.

1997
Albright is sworn in as the first female U.S. Secretary of State.

Louisa May Alcott
Author
(born 1832 • died 1888)

One of the most popular children's books of all time is *Little Women* by Louisa May Alcott. Over the course of her life, Alcott wrote more than 250 pieces, including books, poems, short stories, and articles.

Always a Writer

Born on November 29, 1832, in Germantown, Pennsylvania, Louisa May Alcott was raised in the Christian faith. She was the second of four daughters. Her parents, Bronson and Abigail May Alcott, encouraged the girls to be independent and believed strongly in abolition (ending slavery). At one point, the family hid a runaway slave.

The Alcott family had little money, so Louisa and her sisters Anna, Elizabeth, and May had to make do without fancy clothes and toys. They relied on each other for entertainment. Louisa liked to create stories and perform them with her sisters. She was a tomboy, and always played the villains and bandits in her plays.

Louisa's father rarely had a steady job. He was a teacher with unusual ideas about education. Louisa received her schooling from her father and distinguished family friends, such as authors Henry David Thoreau and Ralph Waldo Emerson.

Unusual Childhood

Louisa grew up in Massachusetts, first in Boston, then in Concord. In Boston, she attended Temple School, which was founded by her father. He thought that school should be fun, and he taught his students to learn through conversation. Other schools of the day were very strict.

Several years after the school closed, the Alcotts moved to Fruitlands, a community started by Louisa's father. There, like-minded people lived and worked together, sharing resources. After Fruitlands closed, Louisa worried about the family's debts. She wanted to lessen the burden, so she worked as a teacher, nanny, and servant. She also became a writer.

Finding Fame

In 1852, Louisa May Alcott published her first story, "The Rival Painters." She followed with a book in 1855 called *Flower Fables*. Much of her early writing included suspenseful tales and mysteries. She wrote them under the fake name A. M. Barnard, since in those days many people would not read such stories if they were written by a woman.

TOPICAL TIDBIT

The Wayside

Author Nathaniel Hawthorne also lived in Concord, Massachusetts. In fact, he bought the Alcotts' house. While Louisa lived there, the Alcotts called it "Hillside." Nathaniel Hawthorne, who wrote *The Scarlet Letter*, named it "The Wayside." Today, it is a National Historic Landmark.

In the mid-1850s, Alcott's sister Elizabeth died of scarlet fever. Then, beginning in 1861, the nation was thrust into a civil war. These were tough times for the Alcotts. Louisa May Alcott went to work in Washington, D.C., as a nurse, but came down with typhoid fever.

While working as a nurse, Alcott had written many letters to her family. After she returned, she published them in a book called *Hospital Sketches*. People enjoyed reading about her experiences; many copies of the book were sold. The success of *Hospital Sketches* opened more doors for Alcott. She was glad, because it meant that she could help her family more.

> "The truest words are often the simplest, and when wisdom and virtue go hand in hand, none need fear to listen, learn, and love."
> —Louisa May Alcott

Little Women

In the late 1860s, while writing stories for *The Atlantic Monthly* magazine, Alcott wrote *Little Women*. She modeled the book on her own experiences with her sisters, including acting out plays in the family's barn, borrowing books from Ralph Waldo Emerson, and learning about nature with Henry David Thoreau.

The book was a huge success, which led to financial security for Alcott and her family.

Alcott continued writing books, including *Little Men* and *Jo's Boys*. In *Little Men*, the characters learn lessons such as those Alcott's father taught in his school: to love nature, to be independent, and to express oneself. Alcott died on March 6, 1888, in Boston.

A Hero for Generations of Girls

Louisa May Alcott is one of the most famous American authors of the 20th century. Her character Jo in *Little Women* is a popular role model for young girls. Jo was unusual for the times because she was strong-willed and independent—like her creator, Louisa May Alcott. ◇

LIFE EVENTS

1832
Louisa May Alcott is born in Germantown, Pennsylvania.

1851
Alcott's poem "Sunlight" is published.

1852
Using the pen name A. M. Barnard, Alcott publishes her first story.

1862
Alcott serves as a Civil War nurse in Washington, D.C.

1867
Alcott becomes editor of *Merry's Museum*, a children's magazine.

1868
Alcott publishes *Little Women*.

1888
Louisa May Alcott dies in Boston, Massachusetts.

Marian Anderson
Singer and Diplomat
(born 1897 • died 1993)

When Marian Anderson was a little girl, she displayed an incredible talent for singing. People who heard her perform knew that she would be famous one day. As an African American woman, she faced many obstacles. To escape the rampant racism in the U.S., Anderson decided to perform in Europe. She became a success abroad long before her talents were recognized in her own country.

The Gift of Voice

Marian Anderson was born on February 27, 1897, in Philadelphia, Pennsylvania. (Some records list her birth year as 1902.) Her parents had little money, so Marian helped out by doing odd jobs, such as scrubbing floors. The family could not afford singing lessons, so Marian joined her church choir.

In time, friends, family, and church members realized that Marian was a gifted singer. They raised money to send her to music school. The music

Marian Anderson prepares to sing on the steps of the
Lincoln Memorial, April 9, 1939.

school, however, was segregated, and would not
admit Marian because she was black. Marian's
voice would not be silenced. She used the money
for singing lessons.

Marian Anderson's big break came in 1925, when
she won a talent contest. She was 28 years old. The
prize was to sing in a concert with the famous New
York Philharmonic Orchestra.

Prejudice at Home

In America of the 1930s, people were denied things based on their gender and race. African Americans were refused service in restaurants and denied jobs. As an African American woman, Anderson faced prejudice every day. And her career was affected because she was only allowed to perform in black concert halls in the United States. Other venues were strictly off-limits to her.

In Europe, there were fewer restrictions for blacks. Anderson first performed in Europe in 1930, and gave many concerts there during the next five years. She attracted a huge following and received several scholarships to continue her education in Europe.

> "As long as you keep a person down, some part of you has to be down there to hold him down, so it means you cannot soar as you otherwise might."
>
> —Marian Anderson

In 1935, Anderson returned to the U.S. to make her official New York concert debut. Four years later, she wanted to perform at Constitutional Hall in Washington D.C. When she tried to book the hall, however, she was turned away because she was black.

Constitution Hall was owned by the Daughters of the American Revolution (DAR)—an organization of prominent women who were descendents of the country's founding fathers. The group had not allowed African Americans to perform at the hall since 1932.

Marian Anderson Shines Through

One of the most famous members of the DAR was First Lady Eleanor Roosevelt. When Roosevelt found out why Anderson could not rent the hall, she was outraged, and resigned from the DAR in protest. Many other DAR members did, too. The White House made arrangements for Anderson to sing at the Lincoln Memorial instead, and about 75,000 people went to hear the concert.

As Anderson sang that day, it was obvious that thousands of people in the U.S. supported her remarkable talent. In her autobiography, *My Lord, What a Morning*, she remembered how she felt during that concert. "I had a feeling that a great wave of goodwill

TOPICAL TIDBIT

Contra What?

Marian Anderson was among the best contraltos ever heard. A *contralto* is a singer who can hit a wide range of notes. Anderson could sing lower tenor parts and higher mezzo (mid) soprano parts. As a result, she could perform many types of music.

poured out from these people."

Anderson again made headlines in 1955, when she became the first black performer to sing with the Metropolitan Opera. Several years later, she expanded her career to include diplomatic work: In 1958, she was appointed as a delegate to the United Nations. Shortly before her death on April 8, 1993, Anderson was honored with a Grammy Award for Lifetime Achievement.

A World-renowned Voice

Marian Anderson overcame prejudice to become a world-renowned singer. Her voice won over audiences throughout the world. She received many awards, including the Presidential Medal of Freedom, which she received in 1963 from President Lyndon B. Johnson. In 1973, she was inducted into the National Women's Hall of Fame. ◇

LIFE EVENTS

1897
Marian Anderson is born in Philadelphia, Pennsylvania.

1939
Denied the right to sing at Constitution Hall in Washington, D.C., Anderson sings at the Lincoln Memorial.

1955
Anderson makes her debut at the New York Metropolitan Opera House.

1956
Anderson publishes her autobiography, *My Lord, What a Morning.*

1984
Anderson is the first recipient of New York City's Human Rights Award.

1993
Marian Anderson dies.

Maya Angelou
Author, Poet, Actor
(born 1928)

The life of Maya Angelou is an example of how someone can rise above major hardships and succeed in life. After a traumatic experience as a child left her unable to speak for several years, Maya Angelou eventually found her voice and now uses it to inspire others. As a popular author, poet, and entertainer, Angelou encourages other people to move past the difficulties in their lives and work toward achieving their goals.

Experiencing Trauma

Maya Angelou was born Marguerite Johnson on April 4, 1928, in St. Louis, Missouri. Her older brother, Bailey, called her Maya. In the 1930s and 1940s, Maya grew up in a segregated world. As an African American, she faced prejudice and discrimination every day.

In addition to segregation, Maya experienced the breakup of her parents' marriage when she was very

young. For a while, Maya and Bailey were sent to live with their grandmother in rural Arkansas. After they rejoined their mother in St. Louis, Maya entered one of the most difficult periods in her life.

When Maya was about seven or eight years old, she

was physically abused by her mother's boyfriend. Although dealing with the abuse was difficult enough, Maya then testified at the man's trial.

Finding Her Voice

Such events took a toll on little Maya, and she stopped speaking for five years. The children returned to Arkansas. Through the encouragement of her grandmother, Maya learned to love literature and the arts. She also found her voice again and began to speak. Later, she went to live with her mother in San Francisco.

Maya continued to face challenges. She became a single mother when she was about 16. Despite her pregnancy, Maya still

> "Without courage, you cannot practice any other virtue."
>
> —Maya Angelou

graduated from high school. In the 1950s, she became an entertainer, working as a dancer, singer, and actor under the name Maya Angelou. She studied dance with Martha Graham, a world-famous dancer and choreographer. Angelou had the opportunity to see various parts of the world when she toured with the opera *Porgy and Bess*.

Angelou also became a civil-rights activist. In the early 1960s, civil rights leader Dr. Martin Luther King Jr. asked her to serve as the northern coordinator for the Southern Christian Leadership Conference (SCLC). Later, she lived in Africa for several years, working as an associate editor for the *Arab Observer* in Cairo, Egypt, and later as a feature editor for the *African Review* in Ghana.

Writing What She Knows Best

After returning to the U.S., Angelou began to write books based on her life. Her first autobiography, *I Know Why the Caged Bird Sings* (1970), continues to be a best-seller. Later autobiographies include *The Heart of a Woman* (1981) and *All God's Children Need Traveling Shoes* (1986).

Angelou also established a reputation as a poet. Among her popular books of poetry are *Just Give Me a Cool Drink of Water 'fore I Diiie* and *And Still I Rise.*

TOPICAL TIDBIT

Woman of Many Talents

Maya Angelou has written several books for children. Among them are *Life Doesn't Frighten Me* and *My Painted House, My Friendly Chicken and Me.* She also wrote and produced *Three-Way Choice*, a five-part miniseries for television, and has produced several documentaries such as *Afro-Americans in the Arts.*

In 1993, she read her poem "On the Pulse of Morning" during President Bill Clinton's first inauguration ceremony.

As well as working as an actor on television (*Roots*) and in films (*How to Make an American Quilt*), Angelou also became the first female African American director in Hollywood. She wrote the screenplay and musical score for the film *Georgia*,

Georgia; produced and directed *Cabaret for Freedom* for the stage; and created several works for television. In addition to her writing and entertainment pursuits, Angelou also serves as a professor at Wake Forest University. She has been married several times.

An Inspiration to Others

Maya Angelou's story has inspired many people, especially African Americans and women. Angelou shows how her belief in God has helped her conquer life's difficulties. She is known for the characters she creates, particularly black women, who show incredible strength and determination.

In addition to receiving many honorary degrees and awards, Angelou was inducted into the National Women's Hall of Fame in 1998. ◇

LIFE EVENTS

1928
Maya Angelou is born Marguerite Johnson in St. Louis, Missouri.

1960
Angelou writes a revue called *Cabaret for Freedom*, which she produces, directs, and stars in with her friend Godfrey Cambridge.

1970
Angelou publishes her first autobiography, *I Know Why the Caged Bird Sings*.

1971
Angelou is nominated for a Pulitzer Prize.

1995
Angelou reads her poem "A Brave and Startling Truth" at the 50th-anniversary celebration of the United Nations.

Susan B. Anthony
Women's Rights Leader
(born 1820 • died 1906)

Susan B. Anthony and Elizabeth Cady Stanton led the crusade for women's rights in the U.S. during the second half of the 19th century. For more than 50 years, they worked together to change the way women were treated in America. Because of their efforts, women were eventually granted the right to vote. Anthony and Stanton worked well together—Anthony organized, while Stanton wrote pamphlets and articles for the cause.

Fighting for the Cause

Susan Brownell Anthony was born on February 15, 1820, in Adams, Massachusetts. She was one of eight children. Susan's father, the owner of a cotton mill, encouraged his children to get a good education. Susan was a bright child who learned to read and write when she was just three years old. She did very well in school and became a teacher when she was only 15.

Susan B. Anthony had strong ideas about the way people should treat one another. She was an abolition-ist—someone who believed that slavery should be out-lawed. She believed that all people should be treated equally and fairly, and that no one had the right to own another person. She then became active in the temperance movement, which was designed to stamp out drunkenness and the use of alcohol. She also became involved in the women's rights movement.

The Revolution

In 1850, Susan B. Anthony met Elizabeth Cady Stanton, one of the founders of the women's rights movement. The two women became instant friends, as both had the same ideas: Slavery and liquor were wrong and should be abolished. However, they believed that their views on alcohol and slavery would not be taken seriously while the laws in the U.S. treated women as second-class citizens. They both agreed that there was only one way to influence people to their way of thinking—to become voting citizens. Anthony and Stanton united themselves to the cause of women's suffrage—the right to vote.

> "Men, their rights and nothing more; women, their rights and nothing less."
> —Susan B. Anthony

For the next 50 years, the two women devoted their time and energy to that cause. In the late 1860s, they formed the National Woman Suffrage Association (NWSA) and published *The Revolution*, a newspaper dedicated to women's voting issues.

Jailed for Freedom

In 1872 Anthony broke the law by voting in the presidential election. She went to the polls in her hometown of Rochester, New York, along with 12 of her supporters. The women persuaded the election inspectors to let them vote. Two weeks later, all of them—the women and the inspectors—were arrested and put on trial. During the trial, the judge feared that the jury might let the women go, so he dismissed the jury and found Anthony guilty. She refused to pay the fine of $100, but the judge let the case drop. The inspectors were also fined, although none of the other women were.

For many years after, Anthony traveled across the country, inviting men and women to join the suffrage movement. She gave speeches on street corners and in lecture halls about a woman's right to vote. Anthony was not a dynamic public speaker. However,

TOPICAL TIDBIT

Not for Ourselves Alone

In the late 1990s, filmmakers and historians Ken Burns and Geoffrey C. Ward chronicled the history of the women's suffrage movement in a documentary film and book, *Not for Ourselves Alone: The Story of Elizabeth Cady Stanton and Susan B. Anthony.*

the words in the speeches, written by Elizabeth Cady Stanton, still had a great impact on her audiences.

In 1878, Anthony appeared before the U.S. Congress and proposed an amendment, or change, to the U.S. Constitution. Written by Stanton, the amendment called for the government to grant women the right to vote. The amendment failed, but that did not stop Anthony. She appeared before Congress each year until her death, hoping that the amendment would someday pass.

Lasting Influence

When Susan B. Anthony died on March 13, 1906, in Rochester, New York, the amendment had not become law. Other suffragists followed in Anthony's place, however, and, in 1920, the states approved the 19th Amendment to the U.S. Constitution,

LIFE EVENTS

1820
Susan Brownell Anthony is born in Adams, Massachusetts.

1868-1870
Anthony works as the editor of the feminist weekly, *Revolution.*

1869
Anthony and Elizabeth Cady Stanton found the National Woman Suffrage Association.

1872
Anthony illegally votes in the presidential election. She is arrested for civil disobedience, but the case is dropped.

1906
Anthony dies in Rochester, New York.

1920
U.S. women are granted the right to vote.

granting women the right to vote. Later that year, more than eight million women voted for the first time under what became known as the "Susan B. Anthony Amendment." In 1973, she was inducted into the National Women's Hall of Fame. In 1979, the U.S. Mint honored her by issuing the one-dollar Susan B. Anthony coin—the first U.S. currency with a woman's picture on it. ◇

Jane Austen
Novelist
(born 1775 • died 1817)

Jane Austen wrote about upper middle-class life in the English countryside during the 18th century. Her novels, including *Pride and Prejudice* and *Sense and Sensibility*, feature strong-willed female characters who try to stay true to themselves in a society that thinks little of women who do not have suitable husbands. Austen's tales have gained new popularity in recent years, as film and television versions of her stories delight wide audiences.

Youthful Years

Born December 16, 1775, in Steventon, Hampshire, England, Jane was the daughter of a minister, George Austen, and his wife, Cassandra. Jane had six brothers and one sister. She was very close to her older sister, also named Cassandra, and the two remained together throughout Jane's life.

Few details are known about Jane Austen's personal life because Cassandra burned many of Jane's

44

letters after her death. However, we do know that Jane received most of her education at home. She gained her love of literature from her mother and her love of learning from her father. Jane valued her family and remained with them. She never married.

Being the daughter of a minister, Jane learned Christian values that are often exhibited by the characters in her books.

Product of Her Era

During her childhood, Jane enjoyed performing plays with her family at home. Her mother was quick to make up tales and poems. The Austens lived comfortably, and Jane later used her knowledge of middle-class life in her novels. She also learned about life outside her world from friends and relatives, including her brothers, who attended college and served in the navy.

> "Let other pens dwell on guilt and misery."
> —Jane Austen

Jane Austen grew up in an era in which "proper women" did not work outside the home. Instead, they were expected to marry men from "respectable" families who had steady incomes or inherited fortunes. Such men could ably provide for them and any children they might have.

Many of Austen's novels deal with women hoping to find the right husbands. Although Austen herself never married, she was proposed to on at least one occasion. After saying yes to Harris Bigg-Wither, a man who had inherited his family's fortune, she supposedly changed her mind the next day. Some historians report that Austen fell in love with another man but never married because he died.

Writing About Love

Austen began writing around 1787, during her childhood. Some of her notebooks, which she wrote between the ages of about 11 and 18, have survived. Simply titled "Volume the First," "Volume the Second," and "Volume the Third," the notebooks included poetry, stories, and plays. She liked to write in the family's sitting room, but was very protective of her work. If someone other than a close family member entered the room unexpectedly, she would cover up her writing with whatever was handy.

At the age of 19 or 20, Austen began her first novel,

TOPICAL TIDBIT

Was Jane Austen Clueless?

Many of Jane Austen's novels have been made into movies in recent years. The movies are usually set in the 18th century, complete with fancy period costumes. However, in 1995, Austen's novel *Emma* was made into a movie that was set in modern Los Angeles. That version, called *Clueless*, starred Alicia Silverstone as Cher, the film's name for the Emma character.

Sense and Sensibility, which she originally named for the story's main characters, Elinor and Marianne. The book tells the story of two sisters who experience many ups and downs as their hearts and minds lead them one way, but social circumstances lead them another. Austen followed with *Pride and Prejudice* and *Northanger Abby*.

It took until 1811 for one of Austen's books to be published. When *Sense and Sensibility* finally came out, Austen's name was not on its cover. Instead, it was said to be "by a lady." At that time, it was uncommon for women to have books published under their own names.

Austen's book was a success. She continued writing and published *Mansfield Park, Persuasion*, and *Emma*. Her work was popular with readers, including England's Prince George. Austen's life

LIFE EVENTS

1775
Jane Austen is born in Steventon, Hampshire, England.

1803
Austen sells her novel *Northanger Abby* to a publisher, though it is not published until 14 years later.

1811
Sense and Sensibility is Austen's first published book.

1813
Pride and Prejudice is published.

1815
Emma is published.

1817
Austen dies in Winchester, Hampshire, England. *Northanger Abbey* and *Persuasion* are published the same year, after her death.

was cut short when she became sick. Historians believe that she had Addison's disease, an illness marked by weakness, weight loss, and stomach problems. She died on July 18, 1817, in Winchester, England. She was 41 years old. She is buried in Winchester Cathedral.

Compassion and Humor

Jane Austen's work was different from that of other writers of her day, and it influenced many writers who came after her. Austen's characters were average, middle-class people—not wealthy or famous or great adventurers. She treated them with compassion and gentle humor. Besides being entertaining to read, Austen's novels stand as a detailed record of what life was like in 18th-century England. They continue to be popular today. ◇

Lucille Ball
Television Star and Comedian
(born 1911 • died 1989)

Lucille Ball has delighted generations of television viewers with her off-beat humor. She used exaggerated facial expressions, witty words, and physical comedy to become a television legend. Her show *I Love Lucy* was a hit throughout the 1950s. The program has remained popular in reruns as new audiences discover that they, too, love Lucy.

Lucy Dreams of Being a Star

Lucille Désirée Ball was born on August 6, 1911, and grew up in Jamestown, New York. Her father died when she was very young. During her childhood, Lucy dreamed of becoming an entertainer, even though she was painfully shy. She left home at age 15 and attended drama school in New York, New York. She wanted to dance in Broadway musicals. However, competition for roles was fierce, so she had a hard time finding work.

Lucy turned to modeling, using the name Diane

Belmont. Soon, she got a break: She was offered a small role in the movie *Roman Scandals* (1933).

Throughout the 1930s and 1940s, Lucille Ball appeared in about 70 movies. Although many of those roles were minor, she eventually starred in such movies as *Stage Door* (1937) and *Room Service* (1938). On the set of *Too Many Girls* (1940), she met the man who would greatly influence her life and career—Desi Arnaz, a Cuban bandleader. The two married in 1940, but continued to pursue their separate careers—Ball as an actor in Hollywood and Arnaz as a bandleader, often on tour.

The Role of a Lifetime

In addition to film work, Ball was featured on the CBS radio show *My Favorite Husband* from 1947 to 1951. It was so popular that she was asked to create a version of it for television. She was eager to take on the project, but wanted Arnaz to play her husband. Network executives frowned at the idea. They thought that the American public would not like the couple because Ball was American and Arnaz was Cuban. But Ball and Arnaz convinced the network to let them try.

> "Knowing what you cannot do is more important than knowing what you can."
>
> —Lucille Ball

They created their own production company, Desilu Productions, for the show. The program was called *I Love Lucy,* and it followed the antics of homemaker Lucy Ricardo; her Cuban bandleader husband, Ricky Ricardo; and their friends and landlords, Fred and Ethel Mertz. Many of the episodes featured Lucy's wacky attempts to break into show business. Often, Lucy's antics were disastrous, but very funny to watch. *I Love Lucy* quickly became the number-one show in America and remained a popular hit during the 1950s.

Ball was a master of physical comedy. Her actions, movements, and facial expressions were just as funny as the things she said. In one episode, Lucy sees William Holden, a famous actor, in a restaurant. She tries to get a good look at him, but bumps into a waiter who drops a plate of food in Holden's face.

I Love Lucy also brought technical changes to the television industry. Most shows at that time were broadcast live from New York City, where they were shot with only one camera. Ball and Arnaz wanted to stay in Hollywood, so *I Love Lucy* was filmed and edited before it went on the air. This was easier to do

TOPICAL TIDBIT

"Lucy is Enceinte"

When Lucille Ball became pregnant during *I Love Lucy*, TV censors would not allow the cast to use the word *pregnant*. In those days, that was considered too adult for television. So the episode was entitled "Lucy Is Enceinte." The word *enceinte* (*on-SONT*) means "pregnant," but is hardly ever used anymore.

because they used three cameras instead of the usual one—a first for TV. Because *I Love Lucy* was put on film, it has survived. Other shows of that era are gone forever.

Lucy Goes Solo

The antics of the Ricardos and Mertzes ended in 1960, when Ball and Arnaz divorced in real life. After the breakup, Ball took over Desilu Productions. (At the time, she was the only woman to head a major Hollywood production company.) Desilu produced several popular TV series, such as *The Untouchables* and *Star Trek*.

Ball continued to act as well, starring in other television shows—as a guest star in other programs and in series of her own, including *The Lucy Show* (1962-1968) and *Here's Lucy* (1968-1974). In the late 1960s, she sold Desilu Productions for $17 million.

LIFE EVENTS

1911
Lucille Désirée Ball is born in Jamestown, New York.

1933
Ball appears in her first movie.

1940
Ball marries band-leader Desi Arnaz.

1951
The show *I Love Lucy* premieres on television on October 15.

1962-1974
After *I Love Lucy* ends, Ball stars in two TV shows of her own: *The Lucy Show* and *Here's Lucy*.

1968
Ball and her new husband, Gary Morton, begin Lucille Ball Productions.

1989
Lucille Ball dies.

In addition to her career, Ball raised two children: Lucy Arnaz and Desi Arnaz Jr. She died on April 26, 1989, following open-heart surgery. Arnaz had died of cancer three years earlier.

"The First Lady of Comedy"

Lucille Ball's style of comedy was so successful that many people have copied it. Ball received many awards, including several Emmys.

Ball's face is still familiar to countless people around the world: More than four decades after its original TV run came to an end, *I Love Lucy* is still being broadcast in reruns, becoming a favorite of generations of new viewers. When *Time* magazine selected the 100 most influential people of the 20th century, Lucille Ball—"the first lady of comedy"—was on the list. ◇

Clara Barton
Founder of the American Red Cross
(born 1821 • died 1912)

Clara Barton devoted her life to helping others—on battlefields and in hospitals. She started the American Association of the Red Cross (now the American Red Cross), a relief organization that continues to provide supplies, medicine, food, and funds to people who are victims of war, natural disasters, disease epidemics, and famines.

Independent Spirit

Born Clarissa Harlowe Barton on December 25, 1821, in Oxford, Massachusetts, Clara was taught at home by her brothers and sisters, who were much older. She gained nursing experience by caring for one of her brothers, who was ill. When Clara was 15, she became a teacher.

In 1852, Clara Barton started her own school in Bordentown, New Jersey. Under her leadership, the number of students at the school rose significantly.

However, town officials told Barton that the school had become too big to be managed by a woman—a man would have to run it. In that era, people had limited ideas about what a woman could and could not do. As a result, Barton resigned.

Before the Civil War began in 1861, Barton worked as a clerk in the U.S. Patent Office. It was unusual for "proper" women to work outside the home, but Barton got away with it because she was not married. When the Civil War broke out, Barton left the Patent Office to help wounded Union soldiers.

Relief Agent

Barton raised money to provide relief (food and medical supplies) for the soldiers on the battlefield, in camps, and in hospitals. She served as a nurse, assisting surgeons who had to remove bullets, stitch up wounds, or amputate soldiers' arms and legs. She worked endless hours to help the men, earning the nickname "Angel of the Battlefield."

After the war ended in 1865, Barton tried to locate soldiers who were missing in action. In 1869, she headed to Europe to rest.

> "I may be compelled to face danger, but never fear it, and while our soldiers can stand and fight, I can stand and feed and nurse them."
>
> —Clara Barton

While in Europe, she learned of the activities of the International Red Cross, an organization that had been formed in Switzerland in 1864.

Barton volunteered at the International Red Cross to help soldiers who were wounded in the Franco-Prussian War (1870-1871). However, the organization would not let her treat war victims because she was a woman. So Barton worked independently. She returned to the United States in 1873 and urged the country to begin its own branch of the Red Cross organization.

American Association of the Red Cross

Although the Red Cross provided many important services, the U.S. government was not interested in starting such an organization. Government officials wanted to stay out of Europe's wars and problems, and they considered the Red Cross to be a European organization. Barton worked long and hard to convince leaders to start the American Association of the Red Cross (now called the American Red Cross).

She finally succeeded in 1881 and began the American branch of the Red Cross. Barton thought that the Red Cross organizations should provide relief services to people during *all* times—in peace and war. So she urged the International Red Cross to adopt what is called the "American Amendment." It called for the organization to help victims of natural disasters and food shortages as well.

TOPICAL TIDBIT

The International Red Cross

The idea for the International Red Cross came from Henri Dunant, a Swiss humanitarian, who saw wounded soldiers left to die during the Battle of Solferino, in Italy, in 1859. In 1864, delegates from 16 countries attended a meeting in Switzerland, called the Geneva Convention, and founded the organization to help the wounded.

Serving as head of the American branch, Barton directed relief activities during the Spanish-American War, in 1898. She also oversaw assistance to victims of disasters, such as the 1889 flood in Johnstown, Pennsylvania, and the 1900 hurricane that nearly wiped out Galveston, Texas.

Despite her hard work, Barton had trouble directing others. She wanted to do things herself or in her own way. Barton was asked to resign in 1904. She died on April 12, 1912, in Glen Echo, Maryland.

Barton's Legacy

The American Red Cross has helped millions of people since 1881. It is a fitting tribute to its founder, who worked selflessly to relieve the suffering of the sick, wounded, and homeless. Her house and office in Glen Echo, Maryland, are now a National Historic Site. ◇

LIFE EVENTS

1821
Clarissa Harlowe Barton is born in Oxford, Massachusetts.

1862
Barton serves as a front-line nurse for the Army of the Potomac.

1864
Barton serves as superintendent of nurses for the Army of the James. The same year, in Europe, the International Red Cross is founded.

1869
Barton serves in Europe during the Franco-Prussian War.

1881
Barton founds the American Red Cross. She serves as its president until 1904.

1912
Barton dies in Glen Echo, Maryland.

Sarah Bernhardt
Actor
(born 1844 • died 1923)

Known as the "Golden Bell," Sarah Bernhardt was once regarded as the best actor in the world. She trekked to the battlefields of Europe during World War I (1914-1918), to entertain the soldiers. She even gave a command performance for Napoleon III, ruler of France. She suffered through hardship, yet remained devoted to the stage, becoming an inspiration to actors everywhere.

> "Life begets life. Energy creates energy. It is by spending oneself that one becomes rich."
> —Sarah Bernhardt

Studying for the Stage

Sarah Bernhardt was born Henriette-Rosine Bernard to Julie Bernard on October 22 or 23, 1844, in Paris, France. When Henriette-Rosine was a young girl, her mother could not take care of her, so the child

was sent to a convent to be raised by nuns.

At first, Henriette-Rosine wanted to become a nun. She was persuaded to become an actor by the Duke de Morny, a family friend. When she was 16, she began training at the Paris Conservatoire, one of the finest acting schools in France. She changed her name to Sarah Bernhardt when she set out to become an actor.

Two years later, with the help of the Duke, Bernhardt left school for the Comédie-Française, the national theater of France. She was kicked out the following year for slapping another female actor. For the next couple of years, Bernhardt worked in many acting troupes, gaining experience with each performance.

"The Divine Sarah"

In 1869, Bernhardt landed the role of a minstrel in François Coppée's *Le Passant* ("The Passerby") at the Odéon theater. The critics loved her fiery red curls and graceful movements. In particular, the critics thought she had a pleasant voice that displayed real emotions that the audience could understand. They called her the "Golden Bell," because her voice rang out loud and clear.

Bernhardt thrilled audiences with her portrayal of male and female heroes in plays by Victor Hugo, Alexandre Dumas, and William Shakespeare. It did not matter what role she was playing—audiences packed the theater wherever she performed.

During the 1880s, the "Divine Sarah," as she was called, formed her own theater troupe. At that time, Bernhardt met playwright Victorien Sardou. He began writing pieces designed to highlight her acting ability, using exotic sets and costumes.

In 1899, Bernhardt transformed the Théâtre des Nations into the Théâtre Sarah Bernhardt, producing plays there until her death in 1923.

Never Stop Performing

During her career, Bernhardt traveled throughout the world. She performed in the United States, Russia, Canada, Australia, and England. She ventured as far as South America to please her adoring fans. In 1905, while performing in Rio de Janeiro, Brazil, Bernhardt injured her right knee in an accident during a performance. The injury never healed, and gangrene—a serious infection—set in. By 1911, she could not walk without being helped and, four years later, her leg had to be amputated. This did not stop Bernhardt from acting, however. She chose parts that allowed her to sit in a chair while on stage.

TOPICAL TIDBIT

The Comédie Française

The Comédie Française is the national theater of France. Originally founded in 1405 as a religious theater, it holds the record for being the oldest national theater in the world. Today, the theater produces modern works as well as plays that were written centuries ago.

During Bernhardt's lifetime, France was in turmoil. In the 1870s, France went to war with Germany. Bernhardt opened the doors of the Odéon theater, organizing a hospital there to care for wounded soldiers.

Forty years later, during World War I (1914-1918), when she was in her 70s, Bernhardt traveled to the battlefields of Europe to perform for the soldiers. She believed that it was her patriotic duty to entertain the troops, even though her leg had been amputated and she was confined to a wheelchair. For her efforts, she was awarded the Legion of Honor from the French government.

Her Life in Writing

Later in life, Bernhardt wrote several books, including *L'Art du théâtre* ("The Art of the Theater"), *Ma Double Vie: Mémoires de Sarah Bernhardt*

LIFE EVENTS

1844
Sarah Bernhardt is born Henriette-Rosine Bernard in Paris, France.

1866-1872
Bernhardt is highly successful performing at the Odéon Theatre.

1880
Bernhardt leaves Paris to tour Europe and the United States.

1899
Bernhardt renames the Théâtre des Nations, calling it the Théâtre Sarah Bernhardt. She produces plays there until her death.

1909
Bernhardt writes and stars in *Un coeur d'homme* ("A Man's Heart").

1923
Bernhardt dies.

("My Double Life: Memoirs of Sarah Bernhardt"), and a novel—*Petite idole* ("Small Idol").

Sarah Bernhardt died on March 6, 1923, in Paris, France. She will always be remembered as one of the greatest stage performers of all time. Her golden voice and emotional portrayals thrilled audiences of the past and are an inspiration to actors today. ◇

Mary McLeod Bethune

Educator

(born 1875 • died 1955)

Mary McLeod Bethune devoted her life to the education and fair treatment of African Americans in the U.S. She believed that, through education, people could create better lives for themselves. Bethune worked tirelessly and rose through the ranks to become an adviser to President Franklin Roosevelt. She went on to become the first African American woman to head a federal agency.

Helping Those at Home

Mary Jane McLeod was born on July 10, 1875, on a farm near Mayesville, South Carolina. Mary's parents, Samuel and Patsy McLeod, had been slaves before gaining their freedom after the Civil War (1861-1865). Many of the McLeods' 17 children had been sold into slavery, but not Mary—she was born after her parents were free.

President Harry S. Truman with Mary McLeod Bethune, May 18, 1949.

As a young girl, Mary helped her parents on the farm, planting and harvesting rice and cotton. Mary's mother wanted her to learn how to read and write. So when Mary was eleven years old, she walked eight miles each day to attend classes offered to African American children by the Presbyterian Church.

Mary was a gifted student. She was chosen by her

teacher to attend Scotia Seminary in North Carolina. Because she had good grades, she then received a scholarship to the Moody Bible Institute in Chicago, Illinois. Mary trained to be a missionary in Africa. But instead of traveling overseas, she decided to help the needy in her own country. She returned to Mayesville and began teaching.

Education Is the Key

Mary McLeod taught at many schools during the next several years. In 1898, she married Albertus Bethune; the following year, she gave birth to a son, Albert. In October 1904, Mary McLeod Bethune opened her own school, called the Daytona Normal and Industrial School for Negro Girls, in Daytona Beach, Florida.

At first, Bethune's school was held in her home and had only five students. She taught the girls how to read and write, as well as how to cook and sew. The school was very

> "From the first, I made my learning, what little it was, useful every way I could."
>
> —Mary McLeod Bethune

successful, so Bethune started expanding. Soon the school had more than 400 pupils—both girls and boys—and was moved to 14 buildings on a 23-acre campus. In 1923, Bethune's school merged with the

Cookman Institute in Jacksonville, becoming Bethune-Cookman College.

During the 1920s, Bethune offered night classes to adults so that they could pass tests in order to vote in elections. This angered many white hate groups, whose members believed that blacks should not be allowed to vote. Bethune continued classes, even after being threatened and bullied. She became a champion of civil rights for African Americans across the U.S.

Influencing Presidents—and a Nation

Bethune fought for the rights of African Americans, becoming a leader and spokesperson for many groups,

TOPICAL TIDBIT

Women's Army Auxiliary Corps (WAAC)

In 1941, during World War II, Representative Edith Nourse Rogers of Massachusetts introduced a bill into Congress calling for a women's branch of the U.S. Army. On May 15, 1942, it became law and the Women's Army Auxiliary Corps—later known as the Women's Army Corps—was born. The many women who enlisted in the corps were known as WACs (pronounced *wax*). As adviser to the Secretary of War, Mary McLeod Bethune fought discrimination by ensuring that African American women were among those selected to become WAC officers.

including the National Association of Colored Women and the National Urban League. President Calvin Coolidge took notice of Bethune's work and appointed her to the Child Welfare Conference in 1928. In 1932, she was appointed to the White House Conference on Child Health by President Herbert Hoover. She then served as President Franklin D. Roosevelt's Special Adviser on Minority Affairs between 1936 and 1944. Roosevelt named her director of the National Youth Administration's Negro Affairs division, making Bethune the first African American woman to head a federal-level government agency.

Bethune used her influence with President Roosevelt to promote more blacks into leadership roles in the U.S. government. She formed a small group of leading African Americans that met often to discuss politics in Washington.

LIFE EVENTS

1875
Mary Jane McLeod is born near Mayesville South Carolina.

October 1904
Bethune opens a school in Daytona Beach, Florida.

1935-1949
Bethune founds and serves as president of the National Council of Negro Women (NCNW).

1936-1944
Bethune serves as Director of Negro Affairs under President Roosevelt.

1945
Bethune serves as a consultant on interracial understanding at a conference that leads to the establishment of the United Nations.

1955
Mary McLeod Bethune dies.

Bethune's group, which became the Federal Council on Negro Affairs, was often referred to as the "Black Cabinet." They met with top government officials to help create a better life for blacks in the U.S.

A Lifetime of Achievement

During her lifetime, Mary McLeod Bethune helped many people improve their lives through education. She received many awards and honors, including the Thomas Jefferson Award for leadership. In 1973, she was inducted into the National Women's Hall of Fame. After Bethune's death on May 18, 1955, her home in Washington, D.C., was turned into a National Historic Site. ◇

Shirley Temple Black
Actor and Ambassador
(born 1928)

During the Great Depression of the 1930s, America and its people were suffering. The economy was terrible, jobs were scarce, and many people struggled just to eat every day. However, there was a little girl who represented all that was good about America. Through song and dance, Shirley Temple gave hope to the American public.

"On the Good Ship *Lollipop*"

America's "little sweetheart," Shirley Jane Temple, was born on April 23, 1928, in Santa Monica, California. Discovered at a dancing school when she was just three years old, Shirley was featured in a series of short films called "Baby Burlesks." The films were comedies in which Shirley imitated well-known actors in some of their most famous roles.

In 1934 Shirley appeared in her first leading role in the movie *Little Miss Marker*. She made nine movies that year, including *Bright Eyes*, which featured the

Shirley Temple, dressed for her role in *Wee Willie Winkie* (1937).

famous song-and-dance number "On the Good Ship *Lollipop*." By the end of the year, she was one of America's favorite movie stars.

For her work, Shirley received a special Academy

Award for "outstanding contribution to screen entertainment during the year 1934." Four years later, she was at the top of Hollywood. As the number-one box-office star, Shirley Temple was one of the highest-paid actors—and she was only ten years old! People stood in long lines to see her latest films.

"Goodwill Ambassador"

Shirley's popularity grew. She sang and tap-danced with many of Hollywood's stars, including Buddy Ebsen (who later played Jed Clampett on the TV series *The Beverly Hillbillies*). Shirley was often paired with tap-dancing legend Bill "Bojangles" Robinson. In most of her films, Shirley played a poor little girl, usually an orphan, who rose above the poverty in her life by always looking on the bright side of things and

TOPICAL TIDBIT

"Mr. Bojangles"

Bill "Bojangles" Robinson (1878–1949), is considered one of the best tap-dancers the world has ever seen. He made movies and television shows, and performed on Broadway. Robinson was one of the first actors to break down racial prejudice in Hollywood. A statue in Richmond, Virginia, honors him.

making the best of her poor circumstances. In *Just Around the Corner* (1938), Shirley and Mr. Bojangles beat out poverty by dancing to raise money for the unemployed.

President Franklin D. Roosevelt called Shirley Temple a "goodwill ambassador" because her dimpled smile, golden curls, and high spirits brought her audiences a sense of happiness and hope during the despair of the Great Depression. For a few pennies, Americans could go to the movies and have their cares and sadness lifted for a few hours by little Shirley Temple. Roosevelt said, "As long as our country has Shirley Temple, we will be all right."

> "I stopped believing in Santa Claus when my mother took me to see him in a department store and he asked for my autograph."
>
> —Shirley Temple Black

When Shirley became a teenager, her career slowed down. She was no longer the cute little girl that audiences had loved, and there were few roles for teens in those days. She appeared in several films, including *The Bachelor and the Bobby-soxer* (1947) and the John Wayne classic, *Fort Apache* (1948). Slowly, however, her fans abandoned her. She retired from acting in 1950, when she married Charles A. Black, a television executive.

U.S. Ambassador

In the 1960s Shirley Temple Black tried her hand at politics and ran for Congress. She lost. But like the little girl in the movies, she did not give up. Black worked for the Republican Party and, in 1969, was appointed as U.S. representative to the United Nations' General Assembly. As representative, Shirley Temple Black worked with other delegates from around the world to discuss ways in which member nations could help preserve the environment and the world's natural resources.

Black continued her career in politics. She became a diplomat, serving as the U.S. ambassador to Ghana from 1974 to 1976. She was later assigned as ambassador to Czechoslovakia (now split into two countries, the Czech Republic and Slovakia). She served in that post for four years.

Black also served in the

LIFE EVENTS

1928
Shirley Jane Temple is born in Santa Monica, California.

1932-1949
At the height of her career, Shirley Temple makes 60 movies in 17 years.

1950
Temple marries Charles A. Black, a television executive.

1950
Shirley Temple Black makes an unsuccessful run for Congress.

1969-1970
Black is the U.S. representative to the United Nations.

1974-1976
Black is the U.S. ambassador to Ghana.

1989-1992
Black is U.S. ambassador to Czechoslovakia.

White House, as President Gerald R. Ford's chief of protocol, welcoming foreign officials into the United States. In 1981, she was a member of a U.S. delegation that took part in a special meeting on the problems of African refugees.

Representing America

Shirley Temple will always be remembered as the little curly-haired girl who danced and sang her way into the hearts of moviegoers, representing the American spirit in times of trouble. As an adult, Shirley Temple Black continued to represent the American way of life to people throughout the world—as a diplomat. ◇

Elizabeth Blackwell
First Female Doctor
(born 1821 • died 1910)

Elizabeth Blackwell was the first woman to earn a medical degree in the United States. Through her determination and hard work, she broke down barriers, inspiring and leading other women into the medical profession.

Becoming a Teacher

Elizabeth Blackwell was born on February 3, 1821, in Counterslip, England. When Elizabeth was 11 years old, her family moved to the United States. They lived for several years in the New York City area before moving to Cincinnati, Ohio. Elizabeth's father hired private tutors to teach his children.

In the late 1830s, Elizabeth and her sisters opened a private school. This was the beginning of long teaching careers for Elizabeth and her sister Emily. Elizabeth eventually left her family home to teach in Kentucky, North Carolina, and South Carolina. While she was in the Carolinas, Elizabeth Blackwell began learning about medicine from country doctors. She wanted to learn more.

Becoming a Doctor

In 1847, Blackwell applied to several medical schools, including Harvard and Yale, but was refused. At that time, women did not study medicine; it was considered a male profession. Blackwell believed that she could be a good doctor, even a surgeon, if given the chance. Finally, in 1848, she was accepted to Geneva Medical College (now Hobart and William Smith Colleges) in Geneva, New York.

Blackwell got into medical school on a fluke. The admission board thought that someone was pulling a prank by sending a woman's name to the medical school. Playing along, the board asked the students to vote whether or not they would like a woman among them. Not taking it very seriously, the students said yes. They were all surprised when Blackwell arrived.

> "If society will not admit of woman's free development, then society must be remodeled."
> —Elizabeth Blackwell

Many of Blackwell's classmates did not want a woman to become a doctor and they were mean to her. Her teachers would not let her participate in classroom activities. Later, however, when they saw

how seriously she took school, they supported her. Blackwell graduated from Geneva Medical College in 1849. She was the top-ranked student of the class.

Blackwell continued her studies in England and France. While in Paris, she got an eye infection, which left her blind in one eye. This dashed her hopes of becoming a surgeon.

In 1851, Blackwell returned to New York to practice medicine. No one would hire a female doctor, so she raised money and opened her own clinic in a poor section of New York City. At first, she had few patients. She wrote and lectured about the importance of cleanliness, and people began coming to her when they needed medical care. In 1857, together with her younger sister, Emily—who had also become a doctor—and Dr. Marie Zakrzewska, Blackwell opened the New York Infirmary of Women and Children.

Teaching Medicine to Women

For the next several years, Elizabeth Blackwell traveled through Europe and lectured on "Medicine as a Profession for Ladies." The lectures were based on a series of papers that she wrote and published in 1852, called *The Laws of Life, With Special Reference to the Physical Education of Girls*.

During the Civil War (1861-1865), Blackwell founded the Women's Central Association of Relief, which

TOPICAL TIDBIT

A Place to Study

The Women's Medical College of the New York Infirmary was one of the first medical schools in the U.S. geared to teaching women. Opened in 1868 by Elizabeth and Emily Blackwell, with the help of Florence Nightingale, the college remained in operation for more than 30 years.

trained nurses to care for wounded soldiers. In 1868, the Blackwell sisters opened the Women's Medical College of the New York Infirmary. Shortly afterward, Elizabeth Blackwell returned to England, leaving Emily in charge.

Between 1875 and 1907, Elizabeth Blackwell taught classes in women's health at the London School of Medicine for Women. She died on May 31, 1910 in Sussex, England, and was buried in Scotland.

Blazing the Way

Blackwell spread her influence by writing a number of books on medicine, as well as an autobiography. As the first woman to receive a medical degree in the U.S., she opened the doors of medicine to women throughout the world. A statue honoring her stands on the campus of Hobart and William Smith Colleges. ◇

LIFE EVENTS

1821
Elizabeth Blackwell is born in Counterslip, England.

1849
Blackwell graduates from Geneva Medical School in New York.

1853
Blackwell opens a private medical clinic in New York City.

1868
Elizabeth and Emily Blackwell open the Women's Medical College of the New York Infirmary.

1869
Blackwell moves back to England.

1895
Blackwell publishes her autobiography.

1910
Elizabeth Blackwell dies in Sussex, England.

Nellie Bly
(Elizabeth Cochrane Seaman)
Journalist
(born 1867? • died 1922)

Nellie Bly was a famous reporter who wrote about important social issues of her day—including the plight of the mentally ill, the poor, and working women. Casting light on the difficulties faced by her subjects, she wrote articles that brought about social reform (improvement) by government officials and private citizens. Bly worked to improve the role of women in society, daring to show that women could be independent and adventurous. Beginning in 1889, she traveled around the world in 72 days—alone.

Independent Spirit

Elizabeth Cochran was born in Cochran's Mills, Pennsylvania, on May 5—probably in 1867, though historians are not sure of the year. She was the daughter of Michael Cochran, a wealthy businessman, and his second wife. She was called Nellie by her family.

(She later added an *e* to Cochran because she thought it looked more sophisticated.) When Nellie was six, her father died, and the family fell on hard times.

As Nellie grew up, she wanted to pursue a career outside the home to help her mother. However, she lived in an era when "proper women" were supposed to be wives and mothers only, not career women. After she and her mother moved to the industrial city of Pittsburgh, Pennsylvania, Nellie learned a lot about the working classes, including female factory workers.

"Lonely Orphan Girl" Becomes Nellie Bly

In the mid-1880s, a *Pittsburgh Dispatch* columnist wrote a negative piece about women, called "What Girls Are Good For," stating that women were ill-suited for careers. Nellie sent an angry letter, signed "Lonely Orphan Girl," to the editor. The editor was impressed with her writing and hired her as a reporter.

Few women of the day used their real names when writing for publication, so the newspaper called her "Nellie Bly" after a famous song by Stephen Foster. Bly began writing about female factory workers and the poor. She even traveled to Mexico to report on poverty there. Bly's reporting on controversial topics angered powerful people, who put pressure on the newspaper. After that, she was assigned to "women's" subjects, such as fashion and cooking.

> "If we want good work from others or wish to accomplish anything ourselves, it will never do to harbor a doubt as to the result of an enterprise."
>
> —Nellie Bly

Unhappy with her situation in Pittsburgh, Nellie Bly headed to New York in search of a new job. An editor at the *New York World* gave her an assignment, daring her to go undercover at a home for mentally ill women. Bly had herself committed to the mental institution for 10 days, then wrote a detailed report of the conditions she experienced there, which included terrible health care, inedible food, unclean conditions, and cruel treatment. Her articles were later published as *Ten Days in a Mad House*. Bly's undercover reporting, among the first of its kind by any reporter, male or female, led to improvements at mental-health facilities.

Around the World in 72 Days

Bly continued to break new ground, reporting—from firsthand experience—on conditions in prison, a chorus line, and a sweatshop. Then she told her

TOPICAL TIDBIT

Father of Science Fiction

French author Jules Verne wrote the book *Around the World in 80 Days*. Many of his books tell futuristic tales with heroes using advanced technologies. Considered the father of science fiction, Verne wrote *Journey to the Center of the Earth* and *20,000 Leagues Under the Sea*, among others.

editors that she wanted to travel around the world, like the fictional hero Phileas Fogg in Jules Verne's popular novel, *Around the World in 80 Days*. The editors were against the idea, thinking that a man should make the trip. She finally convinced them to let her go, however, and Nellie Bly became the first person, male or female, to complete such a trek so quickly.

Bly's journey began on November 14, 1889. Her plan was to visit London, England; Singapore; Brindisi, Italy; and Hong Kong. She traveled by ship, train, carriage, and other means as she attempted to beat Fogg's fictional time of 80 days. In

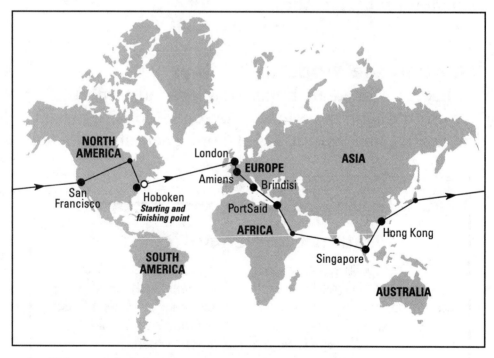

This map shows major stops on Bly's record-setting world trip.

the process, she met author Jules Verne himself. When she returned to New York, she was greeted by cheering fans. She had set a record: 72 days, 6 hours, 11 minutes, and 14 seconds. At age 25, she had become the most famous reporter in the country.

A Life Well Spent

In 1895, Bly retired from journalism and married millionaire Robert Seaman. He died 10 years later. Bly managed his business and created programs to help the workers improve their health and education. Later in life, she returned to reporting. She died on January 27, 1922.

Full of spirit and ambition, Nellie Bly broke many of the barriers that society put upon women in the late 19th century. She showed the world how courageous and determined a woman can be. ◇

LIFE EVENTS

1867?
Elizabeth Cochran is born in Cochran's Mills, Pennsylvania.

1885
Nellie Bly is hired as a reporter for the *Pittsburgh Dispatch.*

1889-1890
Bly makes her famous trip around the world in 72 days for Pulitzer's newspaper, the *World.*

1895
Bly marries Robert Seaman, a millionaire businessman.

1904
After her husband's death, Bly takes control of his factory and insists on providing equal pay for female workers.

1922
Bly dies in New York, New York.

Margaret Bourke-White
Photojournalist
(born 1906 • died 1971)

It is often said that "one picture paints a thousand words." Such is the case of photographs taken by Margaret Bourke-White. A pioneer in the field of photojournalism, she traveled throughout the world, with camera in hand, telling stories about people and places through her photographs.

Architecture and Industry

Margaret White was born on June 14, 1906, in New York, New York. She grew up in the small New Jersey town of Bound Brook. Margaret's father was an inventor who designed printing presses. Margaret traveled with him to factories where he set up his machines. Later, when Margaret began her career as a professional photographer, her first subjects were industrial machines.

After graduating from Cornell University in 1927,

Margaret began a career as a photographer. She wanted a professional sounding name—one that would be remembered easily. She chose to combine her mother's maiden name, Bourke, with her father's name, White.

In 1929, Henry Luce, the publisher of *Time* magazine, asked Margaret Bourke-White to join the staff of *Fortune*, his new magazine. She also worked with Luce as a photographer for *Life* magazine. The magazines featured photo-essays—groups of photographs that told a story without much text.

Bourke-White's first subjects were buildings and machinery, such as the Chrysler Building in New York, the Fort Peck dam in Montana, and the Krupp Iron Works in Germany. Pictures of industrial sites in the Soviet Union were the basis for her 1934 book, *U.S.S.R.: A Portfolio of*

Photographs. She also produced documentary films on the Soviet Union, entitled *Eyes on Russia* and *Red Republic*.

In 1935, Bourke-White met the author Erskine Caldwell, who was famous for his novels *Tobacco Road* and *God's Little Acre*. Bourke-White and Caldwell worked together on several projects—he wrote the text and she took the photographs. The most famous work they did together is called *You Have Seen Their Faces*. The book, published in 1937, shows what life was like in the Deep South during the Great Depression. Bourke-White and Caldwell were married in 1939, but divorced a few years later.

> "The beauty of the past belongs in the past."
>
> —Margaret Bourke-White, on modern photography

Bourke-White Goes to War

When World War II (1939-1945) broke out in Europe, Bourke-White wanted to be one of the first photographers on the scene. She boarded a ship for North Africa. The ship was struck by enemy torpedoes and sank, but Bourke-White survived unharmed and finished the trip. Through her photographs in *Life* magazine, she showed the American public events faced daily by the average soldier.

Bourke-White continued photographing the horrors of war as a correspondent. Working with U.S. military forces, she was chosen to travel with the troops of U.S. General George S. Patton into the Buchenwald death camp, which had been operated by the Nazis.

Inside the camp, Bourke-White was sickened by what she saw. She wrote, "I saw and photographed the piles of naked, lifeless bodies, the human skeletons in furnaces, the living skeletons who would die the next day because they had had to wait too long for deliverance." Her photographs were used to bring to justice the men who had committed crimes of war.

Later in Life

After the war's end, Bourke-White was given many new assignments for *Life*, including a two-year mission to interview and photograph Mohandas K.

TOPICAL TIDBIT

Life Magazine

Henry Luce, the owner of Time-Life Books, published several magazines, including *Time* and *Life*. After 36 years of publication, *Life* was laid to rest in 1972, due to high printing costs. Time-Life Books continued to issue special editions. In the 1990s, *Life* magazine was returned to monthly publication. That ended in 2000. It is still published occasionally, to document special events.

Gandhi, a leader of India's independence movement. During the Korean War (1950-1952), she served as a correspondent for the United Nations (UN).

In 1952, Bourke-White was diagnosed with Parkinson's disease, an illness that results in uncontrolled shaking. Her hands were no longer steady, so she could not hold a camera. She turned her talents to writing articles and books, taking photographs when she could. Bourke-White died on August 27, 1971, in Stamford, Connecticut.

The story of Margaret Bourke-White can be found in her autobiography, *Portrait of Myself*. Bourke-White's courage as one of the world's first photojournalists opened the door for others, especially women. Bourke-White's photographs are displayed in museums throughout the world. ◇

LIFE EVENTS

1906
Margaret White is born in New York, New York.

1927
White begins her career with industrial photography in Ohio.

1929
Bourke-White begins work as a photographer for *Fortune* magazine.

1936-1969
Bourke-White works as a photographer for *Life* magazine.

1963
Bourke-White publishes her autobiography, *Portrait of Myself*.

1971
Margaret Bourke-White dies in Stamford, Connecticut.

Charlotte Brontë and Emily Brontë
Novelists
(Charlotte Brontë: born 1816 • died 1855)
(Emily Brontë: born 1818 • died 1848)

At a time in history when women were discouraged from many of the pursuits of men, Charlotte and Emily Brontë paid no attention to the limits that society might put on them. As female writers, they took on the literary critics of the day and succeeded. Their novels are now standard reading material for students throughout the world.

> "It is vain to say human beings ought to be satisfied with tranquility: They must have action; and they will make it if they cannot find it."
>
> —Charlotte Brontë

Growing Up on the Moors

Charlotte and Emily Brontë were born in Thornton, England—Charlotte on April 21, 1816,

Charlotte
Brontë

and Emily on July 30, 1818. Their father was a minister. When the girls were very young, he took a post in Haworth, a small town on the Yorkshire moors.

The moors were a dreary place. Sharp rock formations dotted the marshy landscape, and the weather was cold and damp. The girls played inside most of the time. There were four other Brontë children—Maria, Elizabeth, Patrick Branwell (the only boy, who was known by his middle name), and Anne. The children had fun telling stories about imaginary worlds. They played with wooden dolls, turning them into the citizens of these worlds.

The oldest sisters, Maria and Elizabeth, attended the Clergy Daughters' School in Lancashire. After their mother died in the early 1820s, Charlotte and Emily were also sent to the school. Maria and Elizabeth became ill in 1825, and all four girls returned home. Soon afterward, both Maria and Elizabeth died.

Charlotte left home in 1831 to attend school at Roe Head. She came home a year later to take care of her younger brother and sisters, teaching them what she had learned. In 1835, she took a teaching position at Roe Head. Emily went with her. The two sisters dreamed of opening their own school, but they could not afford to do so.

Careers in Publishing

In 1846, Charlotte found some poems that Emily had written. Charlotte thought that they should be published. In the mid-19th century, women were discouraged from becoming authors, but the Brontë sisters did not care. They wanted to write.

Charlotte, Emily, and Anne decided to combine their writing talents by publishing a book of poetry and short stories. The sisters saved enough money to cover the

Emily Brontë

cost of printing. They did not think that a book written by women would sell, so they used pseudonyms (false names) and called the book *Poems by Currer, Ellis and Acton Bell*. They sold two copies.

The following year, the Brontës contacted a publisher in London who agreed to publish three books. Each of the sisters wrote a novel: Charlotte wrote *Jane Eyre*, Emily wrote *Wuthering Heights*, and Anne wrote *Agnes Grey*.

> "If I could I would always work in silence and obscurity, and let my efforts be known by their results."
>
> —Emily Brontë

Jane Eyre was an instant success. When writing the book, Charlotte remembered her lonely year at the Clergy Daughters' School. It had left a lasting impression on her. In the novel, Jane Eyre grows up as an orphan at the Lowood School. Life at Lowood is terrible: There is little to eat, the schoolmaster is very harsh with his young students, and Jane's best friend dies of tuberculosis.

Emily's novel, *Wuthering Heights*, features the stormy love affair between Cathy and Heathcliff, who live a harsh life on the moors. At the time, it was criticized as being too dark and wild. Today, however, it is considered one of the greatest novels ever written.

Anne's novel, *Agnes Grey*, told the story of a governess. It sold well but never gained critical acclaim.

The Tragedy of the Brontës

Shortly after publication, tragedy struck the Brontë family. Branwell died in 1848. Emily took ill at his funeral and died later that year, on December 19. Anne also became ill and died of tuberculosis on May 28, 1849.

Charlotte Brontë continued to write novels, including *Shirley*, *Villette*, and *The Professor*. She married Arthur Bell Nicholls in 1852. Three years later, on March 31, 1855, Charlotte died of tuberculosis.

Survived by Great Works

The Brontës were all laid to rest at the Church of St. Michael in Haworth, England. In 1928, the minister's house on the church's property was turned

TOPICAL TIDBIT

The Youngest Brontë

Anne Brontë, the youngest of the six Brontë children, was born in 1820 and died of tuberculosis at age 29. Like her older sisters, Anne taught for a time, as a governess, but returned home to live with her siblings. Anne wrote poetry and two novels, which were first published under her pseudonym, Acton Bell. Although both novels—*Agnes Grey* and *The Tenant of Wildfell Hall*—are still in publication, as are her poems, Anne Brontë is not considered as accomplished a writer as her two older sisters.

into a museum to honor the famous writing sisters.

Although they had a brief writing career, Charlotte and Emily Brontë made it acceptable for women to become authors during the 19th century. The qualities of the characters in their stories depicted the innermost thoughts and feelings of real people. Their works are now classics of English literature. ◇

LIFE EVENTS

1816
Charlotte Brontë is born in Thornton, England.

1818
Emily Brontë is born in Thornton, England.

1846
Charlotte, Emily, and their sister Anne publish a book of poems under the names Currer, Ellis, and Acton Bell.

1847
Charlotte Brontë publishes *Jane Eyre* and Emily publishes *Wuthering Heights*.

1848
Emily Brontë dies.

1855
Charlotte Brontë dies of tuberculosis.

Rachel Carson
Biologist and Environmentalist
(born 1907 • died 1964)

Rachel Carson grew up loving the natural world. As a biologist, she was one of the first people concerned about pollution and pesticides and their impact on Earth, animals, and humans. Her famous book *Silent Spring* warned people about the dangers of chemicals. Today she is considered the mother of modern environmentalism.

> "Those who dwell, as scientists or laymen, among the beauties and mysteries of the earth are never alone or weary of life."
> —Rachel Carson

Science or Writing?

Born May 27, 1907, in Springdale, Pennsylvania, Rachel Louise Carson loved to explore her family's land. Her mother encouraged her love of nature.

Rachel also had a natural talent for writing, and at 10 years old, she began sending her stories to children's magazines.

The Carsons had little money, but they had enough to send Rachel to the Pennsylvania College for

Women (now Chatham College). Rachel studied writing and literature, but was also required to take science courses. She loved science, and changed her major from writing to zoology (the study of animals). Her decision caused concern on campus, because many people at that time considered science to be a man's field. Rachel graduated in 1929.

Rachel Carson continued her studies at Johns Hopkins University, receiving a master's degree in zoology in 1932. Three years later, her father died, so Carson needed to earn enough money to support her mother. She found work at the U.S. Bureau of Fisheries (later the U.S. Fish and Wildlife Service) writing radio scripts. Her job combined her main interests—science and writing.

Writing About the Sea

In all, Carson worked for the Fisheries Bureau for about 15 years. During that time, her sister died and Carson began to raise her sister's two children. Carson never married.

She began researching oceans for her radio program. This research led to the publication of articles and several books, including *Under the Sea-Wind*, *The Sea Around Us*, and *The Edge of the Sea*. Carson's writing was popular with readers because she told the scientific story of nature in a way that most people could understand.

During World War II (1939-1945), shortages of food—particularly of beef and pork—were common. American women were looking for alternatives, and Carson provided just that. She prepared booklets that taught homemakers how to cook various fish dishes. By the early 1950s, Carson's books were bringing in enough money so that she could leave the Bureau and write full time. She and her mother settled in Maine, near the sea.

Warning of a "Silent Spring"

In 1958, Carson learned that birds were dying on a friend's property in Massachusetts. Carson thought it was caused by a chemical spray used to kill insects. Such sprays were used throughout the country to keep insects from destroying crops. Carson had heard about problems with chemical sprays while

TOPICAL TIDBIT

Chemical Sprays

Rachel Carson warned about the dangers of using chemical sprays, called pesticides. Pesticide sprays make it possible for farmers to send more crops to the market. They also help stop the spread of certain diseases. However, some sprays harm birds and animals. Some such chemicals eventually poison humans, too.

working with the Fisheries Bureau years earlier, so she decided to investigate further.

Carson discovered that while the chemicals did kill pesky insects, they also polluted the water and seeped into the food chain. Instead of killing only insects, the chemicals killed birds and other animals as well. Carson studied hundreds of reports and talked with many scientists about the chemicals. Then, in 1962, she compiled her research in a book called *Silent Spring*. It told of a day when no birds would be left to sing because they would have been killed off by chemicals.

Although Carson's facts were accurate, she received a lot of criticism, especially from chemical companies. They threatened her with lawsuits. Some people called her an "alarmist" and a "hysterical woman." Carson also had many supporters, too, including nature groups, such as the Audubon Society. President John F. Kennedy was another supporter. Influenced by *Silent Spring*, he appointed a special committee to study the uses and effects of pesticides. The debates between Carson's opponents and supporters caused more people to read her book and voice their concerns.

Her Work Made a Difference

Rachel Carson died of cancer on April 14, 1964, in Silver Spring, Maryland. She never knew the great impact that her book would have on the world. Because she had the courage to speak out, *ecology* and *environment* have become household words.

Rachel Carson is credited with inspiring the formation of the Environmental Protection Agency (EPA) and the creation of Earth Day. She was inducted into the National Women's Hall of Fame, and *Time* magazine named her one of the 100 most influential people of the 20th century. ◇

LIFE EVENTS

1907
Rachel Louise Carson is born in Springdale, Pennsylvania.

1936-1951
Carson works for the U.S. Fish and Wildlife Service.

1941
Carson publishes *Under the Sea-Wind.*

1951
Carson publishes *The Sea Around Us.*

1962
Silent Spring, which details the potential problems of pesticides, is published.

1963
Carson testifies before Congress, calling for new measures to be taken to protect the natural environment.

1964
Carson dies of cancer.

Mary Cassatt
Impressionist Painter
(born 1844 • died 1926)

Mary Cassatt is the only American artist to be considered one of the French Impressionists. Using her family and friends as models, she created more than 220 prints and paintings. Her works of art hang in galleries and museums throughout the world.

Learning to Paint

Mary Stevenson Cassatt was born in Allegheny (now Pittsburgh), Pennsylvania, on May 22, 1844. Her family was wealthy and Mary learned about art from a private tutor. When she was 17, Mary went to the Pennsylvania Academy of Fine Arts. When she graduated, she traveled abroad to study in the finest museums and art centers of Europe, including Belgium, Italy, and Spain. In the 1870s, she went to Paris, France, where she made her home.

> "I am independent! I can live alone, and I love to work."
>
> —Mary Cassatt

A portrait of Mary Cassatt, painted by her friend Edgar Degas.

Mary Cassatt was well versed in traditional painting methods and her early works follow that example.
In 1872, one of her pieces was selected for display at
the Paris Salon—the most important art show in

Paris. Juries made up of art critics selected which paintings were worthy of being exhibited at the Salon. Cassatt's paintings were chosen five years in a row, 1872 through 1876, which was quite an accomplishment. After that, however, the juries began to reject Cassatt's work, and she grew restless with the continuing criticism.

Paris in the 1800s

Paris in the late 1800s was the gathering place for artists with a new vision. One group of artists had developed a new style of painting called Impressionism. Impressionism steered away from paintings that focused on the emotions of the subject, or the hidden meanings of the painting. Impressionists preferred to capture moments in time. It was almost as if they were painting snapshots. The background of their paintings was just as important as the foreground. The Impressionists used the effect of sunlight on water or trees to show the time of day in their paintings. They used different tones of the same color (often pastels) to show light and dark.

The critics did not like this new type of art, and banned the Impressionists' work from the Paris Salon. The artists, however, held their own exhibition, which Cassatt attended. She marveled at the paintings, and was strongly influenced by them. She became friends with one of the best Impressionist painters of the time,

Edgar Degas. He taught her how to create the effects and encouraged her to experiment on her own. Cassatt loved it. She painted what she liked and felt free from the critical eyes of the juries.

Painting and Printing

Degas was impressed with Cassatt's work. He asked her to display her art at the Impressionists Show, which she did from 1879 to 1881, and again in 1886. After the last Impressionists Show in 1886, Cassatt sent many of her works to the Durand-Ruel gallery in New York. Her first solo show as an Impressionist was held there in 1893. Many shows in the United States and Europe soon followed.

At this time, Cassatt became interested in Japanese

TOPICAL TIDBIT

The Metropolitan Museum of Art

Mary Cassatt was influential in making Impressionism one of the foundations of modern art. Cassatt was friends with a wealthy industrialist named Henry Osborne Havemeyer (1847-1907) and his family, and she encouraged them to purchase Impressionist paintings. In 1929, Havemeyer's widow donated many of the paintings to the Metropolitan Museum of Art in New York, New York. The Havemeyer Collection is one of the largest Impressionist collections in the world.

prints, which she had seen at an exhibit. The works were simple, with clean lines and bright colors. She began making prints in that style as well. She focused on women and children in their natural settings, doing everyday things, such as brushing their hair, reading a book, or sipping tea.

Printing is different from painting. Cassatt would etch a design into a piece of metal, usually copper. Then she would apply colored ink to the metal and press the metal onto a piece of paper. She had to carefully clean and prepare the metal each time she changed colors. This process sometimes took days.

Worldwide Acclaim

As Cassatt got older, her eyesight began to fail. In 1910, she was forced to give up printmaking because she could no longer etch the metal

LIFE EVENTS

1844
Mary Stevenson Cassatt is born in Allegheny, Pennsylvania.

1861-1865
Cassatt studies at the Pennsylvania Academy of Fine Arts.

1870s
Cassatt settles in Paris, France, to paint.

1890
Cassatt attends an exhibition of Japanese prints that influence her later works.

1898
Cassatt paints *Mother Feeding a Child*, one of her best-known paintings.

1926
Cassatt dies near Paris, France.

plates. She continued to paint until she could no longer see the canvas. She died on June 14, 1926, at the Chateau de Beaufresne, near Paris, France.

Mary Cassatt is considered one of the greatest American painters, but admiration for her work knows no boundaries. She was awarded the French Legion of Honor for her work. She also was inducted into the National Women's Hall of Fame. Her work, especially portraits of mothers and their children, is displayed in museums around the world. ◇

Catherine the Great
Empress of Russia
(born 1729 • died 1796)

Catherine II, also known as Catherine the Great, began educational and cultural programs in Russia during her reign as empress. Responsible for creating schools and hospitals, Catherine also expanded interest in the fields of literature, architecture, and art.

A Royal Marriage

Sophie Friederike Auguste von Anhalt-Zerbst was born on May 2, 1729, in Stettin, Prussia (now Szczecin, Poland). She was the daughter of a German prince.

At the age of 15, Sophie left Prussia to become the young bride of her cousin Karl Ulrich, who was a duke and heir to the Russian throne. (He later became known as Emperor Peter III of Russia.)

The couple married in 1745 in St. Petersburg, one of two capital cities of the Russian Empire. The other capital city, Moscow, was located in western Russia. Once married, Sophie became a Grand Duchess. She

took the name Yekaterina Alekseyevna; *Yekaterina* is Russian for "Catherine."

The marriage was not a happy one. Catherine was very strong-willed and eager to succeed. She liked to read philosophy and literature. Many historians believe that Peter possessed a weak character and often behaved unreasonably.

Empress of All Russia

In February 1762, Peter III became emperor. Peter's policies greatly differed from traditional Russian values. He proved himself a poor leader. So in July 1762, with the help of the Imperial Guard, Catherine overthrew her husband. A few days later, Peter was killed. Historians believe that Catherine did not take part in the murder of her husband.

Although not a native Russian, Catherine had no problem winning the support of the Russian people. The military and upper classes of society respected and admired her. In September 1762, she became Empress of All Russia.

The Reign of Catherine the Great

Catherine reigned for 34 years—a period that is considered one of the most successful in Russian his-

TOPICAL TIDBIT

Crown Jewels of the Romanovs

The Romanovs were a famous ruling family in Russia during the 18th and early 19th centuries. Catherine the Great's husband, Peter, was a Romanov. To show the wealth of the nation, the Romanovs had the best craftspeople create exquisite jewelry containing gold, diamonds, rubies, sapphires, and other precious stones and metals. The Romanov's treasures are famous around the world.

tory. Catherine wanted to "civilize" Russia by expanding cultural and educational programs in Russia. First, she called for the building of hospitals and other health-care centers, encouraging Russian health-care workers to develop equipment and medicines to fight disease.

Catherine also created schools, including the Russian Academy of Letters, which trained teachers, and the Smolny Institute for Girls. She passed laws that created publishing houses and journalism programs.

> "I praise loudly, I blame softly."
>
> —Catherine II of Russia

She founded art programs, which brought attention to the work of local craftspeople. Catherine moved into the summer palace, called the Tsarskoye Selo (Tsar's Village or Emperor's Village). She hired architects to remodel many areas of the palace and gardens. She collected art treasures from around the world and displayed them in a new wing of the palace, which she called the Ermitage. Now known as the State Hermitage Museum, it contains one of the most remarkable art collections in the world.

During Catherine's reign, Russia waged war against the Ottoman Empire in Turkey. After several years of fighting, the Russian army took control of the Crimea, extending the Russian border by an additional 200,000 square miles.

A Great Place in History

Catherine died of a stroke on November 17, 1796, at Tsarskoye Selo (now the Pushkin Palace), near St. Petersburg, Russia.

Under her leadership, the Russian empire had thrived. Her educational and cultural programs are still practiced in Russia today. She is considered one of the greatest rulers of the Russian Empire, and is fondly remembered as Catherine the Great. ◇

LIFE EVENTS

1729
Sophie Friederike Auguste von Anhalt-Zerbst is born in Stettin, Prussia.

1745
Sophie marries Karl Ulrich. They become Peter III and Catherine II of Russia.

1754
Catherine's first son, Paul, is born. (He became emperor after her death.)

1762
Catherine overthrows her husband and becomes Empress of Russia.

1762-1796
Catherine II rules Russia, focusing attention on health care, education, and art.

1796
Catherine the Great dies of a stroke.

Cleopatra VII
Queen of Egypt
(born 69 B.C. • died 30 B.C.)

As Queen of Egypt, Cleopatra influenced Roman officials to protect Egypt from invaders, as well as add to the cultural life of its citizens. Cleopatra built many temples and statues. She also compiled the world's largest library, in Alexandria, which contains thousands of written works. When Cleopatra died, the Roman Empire took control of Egypt for several centuries.

Queen of the Nile

Cleopatra was born in 69 B.C. Her ancestors were from Macedonia, a region in northern Greece. They had ruled Egypt since the 4th century B.C. Many historians believe that Cleopatra did not look like an Egyptian, but like a Greek, with light hair and green eyes.

Cleopatra was the daughter of Ptolemy XII (*TAHL-uh-mee*), king of Egypt. She lived in the royal palace in Egypt's capital city, Alexandria. The palace stood beside the *mouseion* (*MOO-say-yon*), meaning

A bust of Cleopatra.

"museum" or "place of learning." Cleopatra was schooled at the *mouseion*. She learned to speak many languages and became a gifted politician.

In 51 B.C., when she was 17, Cleopatra assumed the throne with her younger brother, Ptolemy XIII. They ruled Egypt as husband and wife until 48 B.C., when Ptolemy seized power and banished Cleopatra from Egypt. She fled to Syria, a nation northeast of Egypt.

Cleopatra and the Romans

Cleopatra did not want to give up her claim to the Egyptian throne. She raised an army with the hopes of overthrowing her brother. She enlisted the help of Julius Caesar, emperor of the Roman Empire. Both Cleopatra and Caesar were very clever. Caesar thought that if he helped Cleopatra, she would be loyal to him, and so would the people of Egypt. Cleopatra wanted to use Caesar's power to her advantage. She thought that she could remain in control of her empire.

Together, Cleopatra and Caesar took control of Egypt. In 47 B.C., Caesar made Cleopatra queen, and she gave birth to a son, Caesarion. In 44 B.C., Caesar was murdered, and his nephew, Augustus Caesar, became emperor of Rome.

Augustus Caesar put a section of the empire under the control of his trusted general, Marc Antony. Cleopatra traveled to Asia to meet Antony. Legend has it that she traveled there on a barge made of gold. Marc Antony fell in love with Cleopatra. He

> "For her actual beauty, it is said, was not in itself so remarkable . . . but the contract of her presence, if you lived with her, was irresistible; the attraction of her person . . . and the character that attended all she said or did, was something bewitching."
>
> —Plutarch

eventually abandoned his duties in Asia to marry Cleopatra and stay in Egypt, where they had three children. Antony's neglect of Asia led to major conflicts between Egypt and Augustus Caesar.

The Death of a Queen

In 32 B.C., Augustus Caesar declared war against Egypt. Cleopatra and Antony met Augustus Caesar's forces, but were defeated. Then Antony received word that Cleopatra was dead. The loss of his wife was too much to bear, and he committed suicide.

Cleopatra, however, was not dead. When she heard that Marc Antony had killed himself, she was devastated. Fearing that Augustus Caesar was coming for her, Cleopatra committed suicide in Alexandria on August 30, 30 B.C. Historians are unsure if she took poison or, as the legends say, let

TOPICAL TIDBIT

It's Not All About Looks

Cleopatra was known for her incredible influence over men. Through the years, it has been assumed that this was because she was quite beautiful. Historians today, however, believe that Cleopatra's charm lay not in her looks, but in her engaging personality and ability to manipulate people.

a poisonous snake bite her. According to Plutarch, a Greek historian, the guards found Cleopatra "stone dead, lying upon a bed of gold."

A Queen for the Ages

The life of Cleopatra has fascinated people for centuries. Many plays, movies, and books have been produced about the Egyptian queen, including William Shakespeare's famous play *Antony and Cleopatra*. The great queen also lives on in depictions carved into the walls of temples in Egypt, in statues in museums, and in coins featuring her image. ◇

LIFE EVENTS

69 B.C.
Cleopatra is born in Egypt.

51 B.C.
Cleopatra and her brother, Ptolemy XII, begin to rule Egypt.

47 B.C.
Cleopatra overthrows her brother with the help of Julius Caesar. Her son, Caesarion, is born. (Caesarion later ruled Egypt as Ptolemy XV Caesar.)

44 B.C.
Julius Caesar is murdered. Marc Antony takes control of the Egyptian section of the Roman Empire.

36 B.C.
Cleopatra and Marc Antony marry.

30 B.C.
Cleopatra dies in Alexandria, Egypt.

Hillary Rodham Clinton
First Lady and Senator
(born 1947)

Hillary Rodham Clinton is more than just a former First Lady. She has been active in politics most of her life and has worked hard on children's issues, such as health care, adoption, and education. Her husband led the Clinton-Gore team that was elected in 1992 and reelected in 1996; she, herself, was elected to the U.S. Senate in 2000.

> "[We] all have an obligation to give something of ourselves to our community."
> —Hillary Rodham Clinton

Early Years in Politics

Hillary Diane Rodham was born on October 26, 1947, in Chicago, Illinois, to Dorothy and Hugh Rodham. She and her two younger brothers grew up

in Park Ridge, a suburb of Chicago. She loved to swim, dance, skate, and play tennis and volleyball. Her father owned a fabric store, and her mother was a homemaker. Hillary's belief in family and community began as a young girl. Active in the Girl Scouts, she organized food drives for local charities and was involved in student government. She was always interested in the fair treatment of people, regardless of their gender, race, or religion.

Hillary studied political science at Wellesley College in Massachusetts, and went on to receive a law degree from Yale University. She joined the Democratic Party in the late 1960s, hoping to make the world a better place in which to live. She was particularly interested in helping children.

While at Yale, Hillary met William Jefferson Clinton, known as Bill. They got married in 1975, and moved to Little Rock, Arkansas, a year later. Both Hillary and Bill taught at the University of Arkansas.

The Road to the White House

In 1978, Bill Clinton was elected governor of Arkansas. He appointed Hillary as chairperson of the Rural Health Advisory Committee. The committee created programs to promote health care in rural

TOPICAL TIDBIT

Girl Scouts of America

As First Lady, Hillary Rodham Clinton was named honorary president of the Girl Scouts of America. First established by Juliette Gordon Low in 1912 in Savannah, Georgia, the Girl Scouts of America is the largest national organization for girls. It has more than 2.5 million members nationwide.

(noncity) areas of Arkansas. All the while, Hillary held a job practicing law. In 1981, she gave birth to a daughter, Chelsea.

In 1984, Hillary was named Arkansas Woman of the Year, and was listed twice by the National Law Review as one of America's most influential lawyers.

In 1992, Bill Clinton was elected president of the United States and Hillary became First Lady. Bill appointed her to head the Task Force on National Health Care Reform, resulting in a proposal for a national health-care system. Despite Hillary's hard work, the U.S. Senate voted down the health-care plan.

As First Lady, Hillary sponsored many conferences at the White House regarding child care and early childhood development. Hillary continued to work toward providing medical care for pre-school children and boosting health care for all children. She promoted adoption and was the leader of the Adoption and Safe Family Act, which became law in 1997.

Senator Clinton

While her husband was finishing his second term as president, Hillary Rodham Clinton ran for office. She wanted to represent the state of New York in the U.S. Senate. Clinton began a "listening tour"—traveling around the state, talking with the citizens of New York and listening to their concerns and needs. The tour paid off, and she was elected.

On January 3, 2001, she was sworn in as a senator, becoming the first First Lady to hold elected office. She immediately joined several committees, including the Environment and Public Works Committee. As a member of the Labor, Health, Education, and Pensions Committee, she continues to support health-care and education programs for children.

Author as Well as Activist

In 1996, Hillary Rodham Clinton's best-selling book, *It Takes a Village, and Other Lessons Children Teach Us*, was published. She believes that by working together and volunteering time and resources, people can bring about change, making the world a better place in which to live. Clinton continues to be a role model for promising lawyers and women seeking a career in politics. ◇

LIFE EVENTS

1947
Hillary Diane Rodham is born in Park Ridge, Illinois.

1973
Rodham graduates from Yale Law School.

1975
Hillary Rodham marries Bill Clinton.

1991
The *National Law Journal* names Hillary Rodham Clinton one of the 100 most powerful lawyers in America.

1996
Clinton publishes her book, *It Takes a Village, and Other Lessons Children Teach Us.*

2001
Hillary Rodham Clinton is sworn in as a U.S. senator from New York.

Nadia Comaneci
Olympic Gymnast
(born 1961)

Nadia Comaneci (*NAHD-yah KOH-mahn-EECH*) will always be remembered as she was in 1976: a 14-year-old gymnast who charmed the world with her performance at the Olympic Games. Her drive and determination have influenced thousands of athletes, all striving for what she achieved—a perfect score.

Becoming a Gymnast

Nadia Elena Comaneci was born on November 12, 1961, in Onesti, Romania. She started school when she was three. When she was six years old, Nadia began training as a gymnast, under the direction of Bela and Marta Karolyi. They saw in her a natural ability to perform gymnastic routines—skills on the balance beam, uneven parallel bars, vault, and floor exercises. In 1969 Nadia was chosen to attend a school geared to training gymnastic athletes.

During her first year of training, Nadia entered a gymnastics competition and placed 13th. The follow-

ing year, Nadia won the Romanian national title. She competed in many contests over the next several years. Then, in 1976, she went to the Olympics.

A Perfect Score

The 1976 Summer Olympics were held in Montreal, Quebec, Canada. Nadia was part of the Romanian team and first to compete for her country. On July 18, she stepped up to the uneven parallel bars. Not quite 5 feet tall and weighing only 86 pounds, Nadia began her routine. Swinging from bar to bar and performing the required movements, Nadia thrilled the judges with her ability and skill. She received a perfect score of 10 for her performance—the first perfect 10 ever awarded at an Olympic Games.

Nadia received three gold medals for her performances in the Olympic games that year—for the uneven parallel bars, the balance beam, and all-

TOPICAL TIDBIT

Fate at the Olympics

Nadia Comaneci first met American gymnast Bart Conner at the 1976 Olympics, where Conner, then 17, had also competed. They met again in 1990, when Nadia was still new to the U.S. They became fast friends, then fell in love. They were married in a traditional Romanian ceremony on April 26, 1996. Conner is the only American gymnast to win gold medals at every level of national and international competition. At the 1984 Olympic Games, he won two gold medals (one individual and one team).

around. When she returned home to Romania, she was given a hero's welcome and was honored with one of the government's highest awards—Hero of the Socialist Party. In front of the world, Nadia Comaneci had achieved what no one else had ever done before—a perfect score.

Retiring at 22

Over the next several years, Comaneci won more competitions and earned more medals and awards. At the 1980 Olympic Games held in Moscow, she won two gold medals, but lost the all-around competition to Soviet gymnast Yelena Davydova. The judges debated for nearly 30 minutes about who should receive the gold.

> "Hard work has made it easy. That is my secret. That is why I win."
> —Nadia Comaneci

In 1981, Comaneci's coaches, the Karolyis, refused to return to Romania after a competition in the United States. At that time, Romanian citizens could not leave Romania without the government's permission. The Karolyis did not have permission to stay in the U.S., but they stayed anyway. They were branded as traitors. Thinking that Comaneci might try to join them, the Romanian government limited her travel and kept a close watch on her. This was a tough time for Comaneci, who felt like a prisoner in her own country.

In 1984, at the age of 22, Comaneci retired from competition and began coaching the Romanian national gymnastics team. She also judged several competitions.

By the late 1980s, the Communist governments that ruled Romania and the neighboring Soviet Union were undergoing big political changes. In 1989, Comaneci saw the chance to escape and she did. Leaving her family behind, she fled to Hungary, then to the American Embassy in Vienna, Austria. She arrived in New York on December 1, 1989.

Comaneci Today

Today, Comaneci lives in Norman, Oklahoma, with her husband Bart Conner, who was also an Olympic gymnast. Conner and Comaneci operate

LIFE EVENTS

1961
Nadia Elena Comaneci is born in Onesti, Romania.

1969
Comaneci begins Gymnastics High School in Romania.

1971
Comaneci wins the all-around in her first international competition, in Yugoslavia.

1976
At the Olympics in Montreal, Canada, Comaneci earns the first-ever perfect score and wins three gold medals.

1980
Comaneci wins two gold medals at the Olympics in Moscow, Russia.

1996
Comaneci is inducted into the Gymnastics Hall of Fame.

the Bart Conner Gymnastics Academy, offering classes to children. They give motivational talks and host cable-television shows. Each February, the academy sponsors the Nadia Comaneci Invitational, a gymnastics competition for children.

Nadia Comaneci continues to make history. In 1996, she was inducted into the Gymnastics Hall of Fame as one of the "most influential Olympians." Also, in 1999, ABC-TV and the *Ladies' Home Journal* listed Comaneci among the 100 most important women of the 20th century. In November 1999, she was honored with the title of Best Woman Athlete by the World Sports Awards of the Century, hosted in Vienna, Austria. ◇

Marie Curie
Scientist, Teacher, Humanitarian
(born 1867 • died 1934)

The international Nobel Prize is awarded to a few extraordinary people each year for their contributions to physics, chemistry, medicine, literature, economics, and peace. Marie Curie is the only woman in history to have received this honor twice, and in two different categories. As a scientist, Curie discovered radioactivity in minerals, leading to a whole new science—nuclear physics. She was the first female professor at the Sorbonne University in Paris, and the first woman in Europe to receive her doctorate degree. She will forever remain an inspiration to women and scientists alike.

A Scientist's Beginnings

Manya Sklodowska was born on November 7, 1867, in Warsaw, Poland. She was the youngest of five children. (Later, she used *Marie*, the French

spelling of her name.) Her parents were teachers who believed that both boys and girls should receive a full education. Marie loved to play with alphabet blocks, and surprised her family by learning to read when she was only three.

Marie's mother died when she was young, and Marie became very close to her father. She was curious about the glass tubes, scales, rocks, and minerals that he used to conduct physics experiments. She studied physics and math to be like her father. Marie was a very good student and graduated from high school at the top of her class when she was 15.

Radium and Polonium

In 1891, after working as a teacher, Marie Sklodowska left Poland to attend the Sorbonne University in Paris, France. She devoted her time to studying chemistry, math, and physics. She worked very hard at her studies—so hard, in fact, that on several occasions, she became ill because she didn't eat or sleep. In 1893, she received her degree, again at the top of her class. She continued her schooling and eventually received her doctorate in physics.

TOPICAL TIDBIT

What's in a Name?

Marie and Pierre Curie were allowed to name the two elements they discovered. *Radium* comes from the Latin word *radius*, meaning "ray" or "beam," because it gives off rays or beams of energy—it glows in the dark. *Polonium* is named for Poland, Marie Curie's native country.

In 1895, Marie Sklodowska married Pierre Curie, a fellow scientist and professor at the University of Paris. They eventually had two daughters. The Curies worked side by side, conducting experiments on what Marie called "radioactivity"—the way certain types of minerals give off energy. They set up a laboratory in a shed near Pierre's classroom. They sifted through sacks of minerals, hoping to find some that were radioactive.

Finally, they found one. The Curies experimented with pitchblende, a mineral filled with uranium. They tested pitchblende in many ways—by burning it, crushing it, and mixing it with different chemicals—to see if they could separate out the radioactive elements. In 1898, after several years of research, the Curies discovered two new elements that gave off radiation—radium and polonium.

> "You cannot hope to build a better world without improving the individuals. To that end, each of us must work for our own improvement and, at the same time, share a general responsibility for all humanity, our particular duty being to aid those to whom we think we can be most useful."
> —Marie Curie

The Nobel Prize

In 1903, Marie and Pierre Curie—along with Henri Becquerel, another scientist studying radio-activity—shared the Nobel Prize for physics for their discoveries. A year later, the French government created a new science department at the Sorbonne, and Pierre was named as the director. Before he could begin, however, he was hit by a horse-drawn wagon and killed.

Marie Curie was asked to take his place at the Sorbonne. In 1906, she became the first female professor at the university. In 1911, she became the first person ever to receive a second Nobel Prize. This time, she was honored for her work in chemistry—for removing radium from radioactive minerals to be used in cancer medicines.

Other Work

During World War I (1914-1918), Marie Curie and her daughter Irène developed x-radiography (the use of X rays), using radium-coated film in special cameras. The x-rays helped doctors pinpoint bullets and pieces of metal inside the bodies of wounded soldiers, so that the fragments could be removed. Marie and Irène trained 150 female nurses how to operate the X-ray machines, pioneering a new branch of medical research. (Irène Curie and her husband, Jean-Frédéric Joliot, later shared the

1935 Nobel Prize for chemistry for their own research, which also involved radioactivity.)

Throughout the rest of her life, Marie Curie remained a scientist and professor. She died of leukemia (a type of blood cancer) on July 4, 1934, in a hospital near Sallanches, France. It was later discovered that her illness had been caused by exposure to radiation.

A Pioneer in Science

Marie Curie is considered one of the greatest scientists of the 20th century. She opened the doors of science to women throughout the world.

In 1914, the Radium Institute opened at the University of Paris. Now called the Curie Foundation, it is an international center for the study of nuclear physics. ◇

LIFE EVENTS

1867
Manya Sklodowska is born in Warsaw, Poland.

1895
Sklodowska marries scientist Pierre Curie.

1898
The Curies discover the radioactive elements radium and polonium.

1903
The Curies receive the Nobel Prize in physics.

1904
Pierre Curie dies. Marie Curie continues their research and takes Pierre's place at the Sorbonne.

1911
Marie Curie receives a Nobel Prize for chemistry.

1934
Marie Curie dies.

Diana
Princess of Wales
(born 1961 • died 1997)

When Diana Spencer married Great Britain's Prince Charles, millions of people worldwide watched the wedding on television. People were fascinated by the shy, beautiful woman who was now a princess. Diana was popular with the British people and known for her beauty, grace, and compassion. Diana's life, however, was far from a fairy tale. She struggled with depression, an eating disorder, the end of her marriage, and the intrusion of the media.

A Friend of the Royals

Born July 1, 1961, in Sandringham, England, Diana Frances Spencer was the daughter of wealthy parents. The family lived on an estate that her father rented from the royal family. Diana, one of four Spencer children, knew the queen's family during her childhood, as they were neighbors.

When Diana was six years old, her parents separated. It was a tough and lonely time for the little

girl. Her mother left the family, and Diana and her siblings remained with their father. Diana was sent to boarding schools in England and Switzerland.

Upon her return to England, she found work as a nanny and, later, as a kindergarten teacher. Diana

Spencer loved working with children, and her great skill with them continued throughout her life.

She soon began to date Prince Charles, who was 12 years older. The couple announced their engagement on February 24, 1981. At that time, Diana was very timid around the press—so much so that she was often referred to as "Shy Di." She was not accustomed to living a public life and having her every move photographed. Much of the press loved her, however. Charmed by her beauty, shyness, and grace, they continued to pursue and photograph her.

Wedding of the Century

When Charles and Diana got married on July 29, 1981, 700 million people worldwide watched them

TOPICAL TIDBIT

In Line for the Throne

Diana's sons, Prince William of Wales and Prince Harry, are almost as popular with the press as their mother was. Both are still somewhat more protected from the media than their mother was. However, William is especially fascinating to many people, partly because he looks very much like his mother. (His handsome face often graces teen magazine covers as a "heartthrob.") He also draws so much attention because if anything should happen to his grandmother the queen and his father the prince, young William would be crowned king of Great Britain.

exchange vows on television. Viewers were enchanted by the royal wedding and watching Diana become a princess. At first, the couple seemed very happy, especially following the birth of their son, Prince William, a year later. Their second son, Prince Henry (known as Harry), was born in 1984. Prince William is second in line— after his father—to become king of England upon the death of Charles's mother, Queen Elizabeth II.

As Her Royal Highness, the Princess of Wales, Diana attended many public functions with her husband. She accompanied him on trips to foreign countries and became involved in many charities. At one time, she was said to be president of more than 100 organizations. Diana enjoyed reaching out to others, but royal life was demanding and she had little or no privacy.

Over time, Charles and Diana became distant from each other, and they legally separated in 1992. Diana later told the press that she had loved Charles, but that he had never really loved her the same way. She also confessed that she had suffered from depression,

> "I've always thought that people need to feel good about themselves, and I see my role as offering support to them, to provide some light along the way."
>
> —Diana,
> Princess of Wales

an eating disorder, loneliness, and low self-esteem. This surprised many people, who had thought of her as living a happy life as a glamorous and famous princess—a celebrity. In 1996, the couple were divorced.

Life After Divorce

Diana lost the title of Her Royal Highness, but continued to be a member of the royal family because she was the mother of two princes. Devoting much of her time to her sons, she wanted to step out of the spotlight and asked the press to give her some space. She cut back on her charity work for a while.

In time, Diana resumed her charity work with the homeless, sufferers of AIDS, victims of land mines, and organizations devoted to helping children around the world. She shocked many people by touching, holding, and hugging children with AIDS. By doing so, she showed the world that they did not have to be afraid of people with AIDS, and she demonstrated how to have compassion for people with serious diseases.

"The People's Princess"

The press had never given up pursuing Diana to photograph her and report on her activities. On August 31, 1997, Diana and her friend Dodi al-Fayed were in Paris, France. The car they were in, which was speeding to escape from photographers, crashed. Diana, Fayed, and their driver were killed. News of Diana's death, at age 36, shocked and saddened millions of people around the world.

Princess Diana lent youth and style to Britain's royal family, which was often considered conservative and stuffy. She was more than glitter and glamour, however. Despite her personal problems, Diana devoted her life to others—including her sons and the various charities she supported. Called "England's Rose" and "the people's princess," she was, and still is, mourned and missed by many people throughout the world. ◇

LIFE EVENTS

1961
Diana Frances Spencer is born in Sandringham, England.

1981
Lady Diana Spencer and Prince Charles are married at St. Paul's Cathedral in London.

1982
Charles and Diana's first son, Prince William, is born.

1984
Prince Henry (known as Harry) is born.

1980s-1990s
Diana dedicates much of her time to charities.

1996
Diana and Charles are divorced.

1997
Diana dies in a car accident in Paris, France.

Emily Dickinson
Poet
(born 1830 • died 1886)

Emily Dickinson was one of America's finest poets. Her nontraditional verse was unlike other poetry of the day. Dickinson had her own style that was ahead of its time. Her writing, which became popular only after her death, has inspired many poets who came after her, including poets writing today.

Fighting Tradition

Emily Elizabeth Dickinson was born on December 10, 1830, in Amherst, Massachusetts. Her parents, Edward and Emily Dickinson, had three children. Emily, the middle child, was close to her older brother, Austin, and her younger sister, Lavinia. Her father, a lawyer, became the treasurer of Amherst College. Emily attended a local school, the Amherst Academy, from 1840 to 1847.

Emily lived at a time when people set strict limits on what women could do. She was sent to Mount Holyoke Female Seminary for a year. While at the

school from 1847 to 1848, Emily refused to blindly accept Christianity. She had many questions about religion. Her unwillingness to follow traditional practices later surfaced in her poetry.

Returning home, Emily took up gardening and attended social gatherings with Lavinia. Encouraged to write verse by one of her father's law clerks, Emily started to write poetry.

After Edward Dickinson was elected to Congress in the mid-1850s, his daughters visited him in Washington, D.C. During the trip, Emily met the

Reverend Charles Wadsworth. They exchanged letters for many years, and often discussed religious matters.

Farewell to the Outside World

Eventually, Emily Dickinson stopped attending social gatherings. She preferred to entertain at home, and she continued to live at her parents' house. Her brother, Austin, and his wife, Susan, lived in the house next door.

Emily and Lavinia had male friends, but neither ever married. In those days, "proper" unmarried women were not supposed to move out and live on their own, nor were they supposed to work outside the home, so Emily and Lavinia continued their lives in Amherst.

> "The soul should always stand ajar. Ready to welcome the ecstatic experience."
> —Emily Dickinson

In addition to poetry and gardening, Emily spent time preparing baskets of flowers or fruit to send to the sick and her friends and family. She loved to write letters and corresponded with many men and women.

As the years passed, Dickinson slowly withdrew completely from the outside world. Despite this reclusive existence, she led a happy life. Her poems are full of emotion and passion. For someone who had only once traveled away from Amherst, Dickinson wrote vividly about many experiences, including love, death, nature and religion.

A Style All Her Own

Dickinson compiled her poetry into little booklets, which she kept in a drawer. She sent many poems to friends and relatives. Some people recognized her talent, and seven poems were published. However, most people thought that her work was too different.

Most poets at the time wrote in a traditional style. They observed certain standards for punctuation, rhyming, and meter (the number of syllables in each line of poetry). Dickinson broke from tradition by experimenting with these and other elements of poetry. For instance, she would use dashes instead of words to emphasize ideas. She rhymed words that

TOPICAL TIDBIT

Emily's Editor

Emily Dickinson discussed her poems with Thomas Wentworth Higginson, an American minister and literary man. Higginson was an unusual man, and, like Dickinson, was ahead of his time. He opposed slavery, supported women's rights, and commanded the first black regiment formed during the Civil War. He later edited Dickinson's first book, *Poems by Emily Dickinson*.

were not exact rhymes, so the reader has to exaggerate the pronunciation. Dickinson was not writing to be published, so she wrote freely and openly. Although it may not seem so now, Dickinson's writing was controversial in its day.

A Place in History

Emily Dickinson died of kidney failure on May 15, 1886, in Amherst. After her death, Lavinia found more than 1,000 poems in her room, and worked to get them published. Some of the verse was heavily edited for publication in *Poems by Emily Dickinson* in 1890. Since then, however, Dickinson's poems have been published in their original form. She is one of the most popular American poets ever. Fans visit her home in Amherst, which is now a National Historic Landmark. ◇

LIFE EVENTS

1830
Emily Elizabeth Dickinson is born in Amherst, Massachusetts.

1847
Dickinson graduates from Amherst Academy.

1852
Dickinson's first poem is published anonymously, without her permission.

1858-1886
Dickinson writes more than 1,100 poems.

1862
Dickinson meets literary critic Thomas Wentworth Higginson, who becomes her friend and editor.

1886
Dickinson dies of kidney failure.

Isadora Duncan
Founder of Interpretive Dance
(born 1877 • died 1927)

Isadora Duncan floated across the stages of Europe as a free spirit, dancing naturally to the sounds of music. Her new style of dance—known as interpretive dance—expressed poetry, music, and nature through the graceful movements of a Greek goddess.

Teaching Dance

Dora Angela Duncan was born in San Francisco, California. According to church records, she was born on May 26, 1877. Other sources list her birth date as May 27, 1878. She later changed her name to Isadora.

Isadora's mother was a music teacher who taught her four children to sing and dance, appreciate classical music, and recite poetry. When Isadora was five years old, she announced to her family that she was

now a dancer, and began giving lessons to her friends and classmates. Like her mother, Isadora was a natural-born teacher. By the 1890s, the Duncans had created a "theater" in their backyard so that Isadora and her pupils could perform.

Gliding Across the Stage

In 1896, Isadora Duncan joined Augustin Daly's theater troupe in New York and began performing on the stage professionally. When she was 21, she left for Europe. With little money, she boarded a cattle boat bound for England. While in London, Duncan spent time at the

> "What one has never experienced, one will never understand."
> —Isadora Duncan

British Museum studying ancient Greek works of art—marble sculptures and painted vases. The Greek figures in the paintings and sculptures seemed to be suspended in air and time, with their tunics (gowns) flowing in the breeze. This is how Duncan wanted to dance, like a free spirit gliding through time and space.

Duncan, who had learned classical ballet as a child, followed the traditional steps. But she also wanted to move to the music that flowed in her heart. She wanted to move freely, to express the feelings that she had while listening to music. To create the effect of the ancient Greeks in her dances, Duncan wore tunics made of lightweight fabrics. She danced barefoot, with her hair falling loose and free, and her silk scarves blowing in the breeze.

Duncan danced like a Greek goddess at private parties for London's high-society ladies. Soon she made it to the stage, thrilling audiences as she glided to airy music. She traveled throughout Europe, performing her dance numbers to packed theaters. She gave lectures and demonstrations of how nature, poetry, and music could be combined into what she called "the dance of the future."

Rough Roads to Travel

Although musicians, writers, and artists loved her light and airy dancing, many people thought that Duncan was too free-spirited in her personal life. They criticized her as being a supporter of "free love"—a controversial movement during the late 19th century and early 20th century of people who did not believe in marriage.

She was also criticized as being revolutionary in

TOPICAL TIDBIT

The "Isadorables"

After Isadora Duncan's children died in 1913, she gave the name "Duncan" to six of her best dancing students, hoping that they would carry on her name. They did, but not by the name of Duncan. Members of the press called them "Isadorables."

her political views. Duncan believed that people should not be tied down by government and society, but should have the individual freedom to live as they desired.

Duncan had several stormy romances—first with stage designer Gordon Craig, and later with Paris Singer of sewing machine fame. She had two children, Deirdre and Patrick. In 1913, tragedy struck when the children and their governess drowned after their car slid into the Seine River in France.

In 1922, Duncan married a Russian writer who died three years later. Then she moved to Nice on the French Riviera, where she spent the next two years. She died on September 14, 1927, in Nice, in a freak accident: As she rode in a speeding sports car, her trademark flowing scarf got caught in the wheels and broke her neck.

LIFE EVENTS

1877 or 1878
Dora Angela Duncan is born in San Francisco, California.

1901
Duncan studies painting and Greek statue art in London.

1904
Duncan opens her first dance school, in Germany.

1921
Duncan opens the Soviet School of Dance in Moscow.

1927
Duncan gives the last performance of her life in Paris, France.

1927
Duncan dies in Nice, France.

Isadora Duncan never stayed in one place very long. Throughout her life, she lived in the United States, Greece, France, England, Russia, and South America. She opened dance schools in Russia, Germany, and the United States. Her legacy lives on in the world of interpretive dance. ◇

Amelia Earhart
Pioneering Pilot
(born 1897 • died 1937?)

As one of the world's first female airplane pilots, Amelia Earhart showed that women were just as capable as men of flying airplanes. She became famous in an era when aviation was still new. At that time, most people had never flown in planes, nor did they think about traveling to foreign countries by air. Not only did Earhart fly planes, but she made several  long distance flights across continents and oceans, with companions and alone.

Becoming a Pilot

Amelia Mary Earhart was born on July 24, 1897, in Atchison, Kansas. She saw her first airplane when she was 10 years old. It did not make much of an impression on her then, even though there were few aircraft in those days.

> "As soon as we left the ground, I knew I myself had to fly!"
>
> —Amelia Earhart (on her first time in a plane)

Amelia's parents separated in 1914, and Amelia and her sister, Muriel, went to live in Chicago with their mother. Around 1917, during World War I, Amelia headed to Canada to serve as a nurse at a Red Cross hospital.

Amelia left Canada to begin medical classes at Columbia University in New York City. However, she moved to California in 1920 to be with her parents, who had reunited. While there, she went to an air show with her father and went up in a plane. She loved it immediately and began to take lessons with Anita "Neta" Snook. After a few months, Amelia Earhart bought her first plane.

Flying Solo

Earhart competed in various air shows and set speed and altitude records. Because there were few air shows then, Earhart needed to find another job. She traveled to Boston in 1925 to work as a social worker. A year later, she was asked if she wanted to fly across the Atlantic Ocean—becoming the first woman to do so. She was eager to make the trip, which occurred on June 18, 1928. Earhart was only a passenger on this trip; the plane was piloted by Wilmer Stultz and Louis Gordon. However, when the flight was successful, Earhart became a celebrity, and she published her account of the trip in the book *20 Hours, 40 Minutes*.

During this time, Earhart met and married publisher George Putnam. She still wanted to fly into the record books herself. On May 20-21, 1932, Earhart flew across the Atlantic Ocean alone. She was the first woman to make the flight and had the fastest time.

Between her historic flights, Earhart took a job at Transcontinental Air Transport. It was her job to show

TOPICAL TIDBIT

Earning Her Wings

Amelia Earhart was not the only pilot making records in the early days of aviation. Jacqueline Cochran was another woman who broke records and worked as a test pilot. Cochran, who believed that women should help out in World War II (1939-1945), established the Women Air Force Service Pilots (WASPs).

other women that it was fun and comfortable to travel by plane. In January 1935 Earhart made another "first" flight—she flew across the Pacific Ocean from Hawaii to California. She was not only the first woman to make the flight successfully, but the first person. All previous attempts had ended in disaster.

Mysterious Disappearance

In 1937, Earhart attempted to fly around the world. She took Fred Noonan along as her navigator.

Earhart waves good-bye as she leaves for her around-the-world flight.

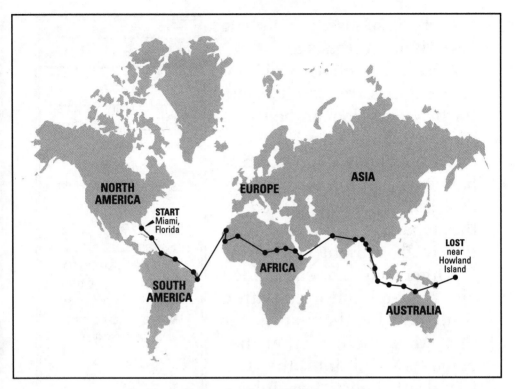

Earhart's flight plan included these stops.

Along the way, she wrote articles about her experiences and sent them off when they stopped to refuel. The articles were later published as *Last Flight*.

By July 2, Earhart and Noonan had completed 22,000 miles out of 29,000. They were heading to Howland Island in the Pacific Ocean on the last, most difficult leg of the trip. A U.S. Coast Guard cutter was near the island keeping track of Earhart and Noonan through radio contact. Earhart sent several messages, but did not seem able to hear the Coast

Guard's response. The plane never reached the island.

When the plane did not arrive, a massive search began. Earhart and Noonan had vanished without a trace.

No one knows what really happened. Some people say that Earhart was captured by the Japanese, who were getting ready to fight World War II. Others say that she landed on an island and lived with a fisherman for the rest of her life. Most believe that her plane crashed into the sea. Her death is listed as July 2, 1937, the day she and Noonan disappeared.

Earhart's Legacy

Amelia Earhart inspired other women to be adventurous and try flying. She made historic flights in a time when aviation was new. She was often the first person—male or female—to do so. ◇

LIFE EVENTS

1897
Amelia Mary Earhart is born in Atchison, Kansas.

1920
Earhart takes her first airplane ride.

1932
Earthart becomes the first woman to fly solo across the Atlantic, and she sets a time record while doing so.

1935
Earhart becomes the first pilot ever to survive a cross-Pacific flight from Hawaii to California.

1937
Earhart departs on a round-the-world-flight.

1937
Earhart and her navigator disappear over the Pacific Ocean and are presumed dead.

Elizabeth I
Queen of England
(born 1533 • died 1603)

Queen Elizabeth I of England shattered the myth that a woman could not be an effective ruler. During her 45-year reign, she fought threats to the throne and to her kingdom from warring nations. A clever politician, she consulted with parliament and advisory boards when creating policies, earning the respect and cooperation of the men in those governmental groups. She was one of the most popular and successful rulers in history.

Another Daughter!

Born September 7, 1533, in Greenwich, England, Elizabeth was the daughter of King Henry VIII and his second wife, Anne Boleyn. Elizabeth grew up in an era of great change and instability in England. Much of the tension came from Henry's desire to have a son to succeed him as king of England. At that time, women were regarded as weak, impractical, and ineffectual. Many people, including Henry,

believed that women could not be good rulers. He was desperate for a son.

Henry's first wife, Katherine, gave birth to a daughter, Mary. When Katherine could not produce a son, he wanted to divorce her and marry Anne

Boleyn. But all of England was Catholic, a religion that did not allow divorce. So Henry changed the national religion to Protestantism, which did allow divorce. This change outraged many people and caused religious tension throughout the country. Catholics were even murdered.

After Henry's divorce, he married Anne, who gave birth to Elizabeth. Henry was disappointed that Elizabeth was not a boy. When Anne could not produce a son, Henry had her beheaded so that he could remarry again. With his third wife, Jane Seymour, Henry finally had a son, Edward. The boy proved to be a frail child, so Henry kept trying. In all, he married six times, but never had another son.

Henry planned to leave the throne to Edward. That left Elizabeth third in line to inherit the throne—after her half-brother Edward, and half-sister, Mary.

Rival Sisters

Although Henry had executed Anne, Elizabeth felt loved by Henry and his sixth wife, Catherine Parr. Elizabeth was educated by tutors, one of whom made sure that she learned the same subjects as boys, including literature, Greek, and Latin. This helped Elizabeth when she became queen.

After Henry died in 1547, Edward VI became king. A sickly man, he died in 1553, and Mary became queen. Mary tried to return England to the Catholic faith. She had many Protestants killed in the process, earning the nickname "Bloody Mary." In an effort to maintain peaceful relations with the Spanish Empire, she married Philip II of Spain, a Catholic. Mary always saw Elizabeth, who had been raised Protestant, as a threat. In fact, Mary ordered Elizabeth jailed, then later confined to her room, because she was afraid that Elizabeth might try to take the throne.

Mary died in 1558 and 25-year-old Elizabeth became queen. She returned England to Protestantism.

Knowing that people thought of women as weak, she worked with the men of Parliament and established advisory councils. She listened to their ideas, accepting some and rejecting others. Her strategy proved effective as she gained their trust and respect. Slowly, Elizabeth proved that women were anything but weak.

> "I myself will be your general, judge, and rewarder of every one of your virtues in the field."
>
> —Elizabeth I to her army on the eve of the Spanish Armada, 1588

"The Virgin Queen"

As the new queen of England, Elizabeth had many proposals of marriage, including one from her late sister's husband, Philip. But if she got married, her husband would become king, and Elizabeth did not want to share power with any man. In fact, she later went to war against Philip when, in 1588, he sent a massive fleet of Spanish ships—called the Spanish Armada—to invade England. The English navy soundly defeated the Spanish in one of the most impressive sea victories ever.

Elizabeth completed her reign unmarried and childless. Instead of marriage and family, she focused on ruling the country. During her reign—called the Elizabethan Era—England's economy prospered. So did the arts, through the work of such writers as Christopher Marlowe and William Shakespeare. Called "the Virgin Queen" and "Good Queen Bess," Elizabeth remained popular with her subjects until her death on March 24, 1603, in Richmond, England.

TOPICAL TIDBIT

Elizabeth's Other Mary

Elizabeth had a cousin, Mary Stuart—known as Mary, Queen of Scots (1542-1587). Many Scots feared that Mary would lead an army against England's queen. Mary, a Catholic, fled from Scotland to avoid trouble. When she arrived in England, Elizabeth put her in jail. When Elizabeth learned that Mary was plotting to take the throne, Elizabeth had her cousin beheaded.

Good Queen Bess

Elizabeth I proved that women could be powerful, fair, and brilliant leaders. She brought religious stability to England and was a fierce leader in times of war. Under her rule, politics, art, and business thrived. She was well-loved by the English people. ◇

LIFE EVENTS

1533
Elizabeth is born to Henry VIII and Anne Boleyn.

1558
After Queen Mary's death, her half-sister Elizabeth ascends to the throne.

1559
Elizabeth reestablishes the Protestant Church of England.

1588
Elizabeth successfully leads England's army against the attack of the Spanish Armada.

1563-1601
Elizabeth enacts the Poor Laws to help remedy poverty in England.

1603
Elizabeth dies in Richmond, England.

Ella Fitzgerald
Jazz Singer
(born 1917 • died 1996)

"Is it live or is it Memorex?" was a popular slogan used by the Memorex Corporation to promote their audiotapes during the 1970s and 1980s. The ads showed jazz singer Ella Fitzgerald shattering a glass with her voice. Considered one of the most influential singers of the 20th century, Fitzgerald recorded more than 2,000 songs during her 60-year career.

The Rising Star

Ella Fitzgerald was born on April 25, 1917, in Newport News, Virginia. When Ella was young, her family moved to Yonkers, a suburb of New York City. She loved to dance, and dreamed that someday she would become a famous dancer.

When Ella was 15, her mother died. Ella moved in with her aunt, who lived in Harlem—a section of New York where many African Americans lived, and where jazz music was thriving. Two years later, Ella entered a talent contest at Harlem's famous Apollo

Ella Fitzgerald sings at the Savoy Ballroom in New York City, in 1941. Bill Beason plays drums, and Dick Vance and Irving Randolph play trumpet.

Theater. Ella had planned to dance, but she was so nervous that her legs were shaking. So she sang "The Object of My Affection" instead. She won over the crowd and took first prize.

"A-Tisket, A-Tasket"

In 1935, Ella Fitzgerald met Chick Webb a band-leader and famous drummer, who hired her as a singer. They played to packed crowds at the Savoy Ballroom. They also recorded songs, such as "Love and Kisses." In 1937, Fitzgerald was voted Most Popular Girl Vocalist by the readers of *Down Beat*—a jazz magazine. A year later, Fitzgerald thrilled crowds with her top hit, "A-Tisket, A-Tasket," based on a children's nursery rhyme.

Audiences loved the cheerfulness of Fitzgerald's voice. Many people thought that it sounded full of sunshine and happiness. In 1942, Fitzgerald left the band to begin a solo career. In 1948, she embarked on a world tour.

First Lady of Song

Fitzgerald's voice had a range of three octaves, which meant that she could sing pretty much anything, high or low. Fitzgerald was also great at scat singing. "Scat" is when a singer uses syllables instead of words to sing a song. For instance, Fitzgerald would imitate the sound of a trumpet by singing "Scooby-do-wop-bop-

> "Just don't give up trying to do what you want to do. Where there is love and inspiration, I don't think you can go wrong."
>
> —Ella Fitzgerald

bop!" Audiences loved it, and gave Fitzgerald the nickname, "First Lady of Song." Over the course of her career, Fitzgerald sold more than 40 million albums.

Among Fitzgerald's many albums, 19 were called "songbooks." Each songbook featured a different composer or songwriter, such as George and Ira Gershwin, Irving Berlin, Cole Porter, and Duke Ellington.

Fitzgerald often performed on stage and made television appearances with other jazz musicians such as Dizzy Gillespie, Benny Goodman, and Duke Ellington. On average, she performed 45 weeks per year. In addition to touring and recording, Fitzgerald appeared in several movies, including *Pete Kelly's Blues* and *Ride 'Em Cowboy*.

Fitzgerald suffered from diabetes, which affected her eyesight and made it difficult for her to stand for long periods of time. As a result, starting in 1971, her concerts were often canceled or postponed. Fitzgerald also suffered from heart problems. In 1986, she was hospitalized and had surgery. In the early

TOPICAL TIDBIT

Scat!

The first scat singers imitated the sounds made by trumpeter Louis Armstrong. Ella Fitzgerald was one of the best scat singers—male or female—ever. Other scat singers include Bessie Smith, Scatman Crothers, and Cab Calloway.

1990s, both of Fitzgerald's legs were amputated because of diabetes. She died on June 15, 1996, in California.

An Extraordinary Singer

Throughout her life, Ella Fitzgerald received many awards, including the National Medal of Arts and the Lincoln Center Medallion, which, until that time, was given only to classical musicians. Fitzgerald also received more than a dozen Grammy Awards, including the Lifetime Achievement Award. Fitzgerald was inducted into the Down Beat Hall of Fame, which honors jazz musicians. In 1995, she was inducted into the National Women's Hall of Fame. In 1998, the Smithsonian Institution in Washington, D.C., opened an exhibit featuring her work in the music industry. ◇

LIFE EVENTS

1917
Ella Fitzgerald is born in Newport News, Virginia.

1935
Fitzgerald makes her first recording, "Love and Kisses."

1938
"A-Tisket, A-Tasket" becomes Fitzgerald's first hit recording.

1942
Fitzgerald begins her career as a solo artist.

1967
Fitzgerald receives the lifetime achievement award at the Grammys.

1974
Fitzgerald performs in New York with Frank Sinatra and Count Basie.

1996
Ella Fitzgerald dies in Beverly Hills, California.

Margot Fonteyn
Prima Ballerina
(born 1919 • died 1991)

The title *prima ballerina assoluta* is not awarded very often. It is only given to the most extraordinary ballerinas. Margot Fonteyn *(fahn-TAYN)* was honored with the title in 1979. She received the title from the Royal Ballet of London for her contributions to the field of dance. She is considered one of the greatest ballerinas of the 20th century.

Studying Ballet

Margot Fonteyn was born Margaret Hookham, on May 18, 1919, in Reigate, England. Her family called her Peggy. Later, she changed her name to Margot Fonteyn.

Margot began taking ballet lessons at age four, while her family lived in Hong Kong. She spent many hours learning the dance steps and graceful movements that later became her trademark on the stage as a prima ballerina.

In 1934, when she was 14, Margot and her family

Margot Fonteyn and Rudolph Nureyev rehearse for a
performance of *Le Corsiare*, in 1962.

returned to England. There, Margot studied under
Sarafima Astafieva, a well-known ballet dancer of
the time. Each day, Margot practiced for hours,
repeating the same steps and movements over and

over again until her teacher thought that she was ready to dance in front of an audience. Margot auditioned for a spot in the Vic-Wells ballet troupe (later known as the Royal Ballet). The audition landed her the role of a snowflake in *The Nutcracker*.

Leaping to the Top

That same year, Margot Fonteyn made her first solo performance in *The Haunted Ballroom*. Audiences loved her. Fonteyn's exquisite skill, grace, and sensitivity to the music made her dancing remarkable. Then, in 1935, the lead ballerina left the Vic-Wells troupe. Fonteyn was chosen to take her place as lead ballerina.

During the next 20 years, Fonteyn danced across the stages of Europe and the U.S. She teamed up with ballet producer Frederick Ashton, who choreographed new ballets especially for her. She also danced the lead roles in *Ondine*, *Romeo and Juliet*, and *Swan Lake*. Fonteyn's most famous role was in *The Sleeping Beauty*, which she first danced in 1939. Her performance as Aurora is widely considered the best ballet performance to date.

By 1954, Fonteyn was one of the most sought-after

> "Great artists are people who find the way to be themselves in their art."
> —Margot Fonteyn

ballerinas in the world. She became the president of the Royal Academy of Dancing in London, England. The following year, she married Roberto Emilio Arias, Panama's ambassador to Great Britain.

Margot Fonteyn's Comeback

Just when she was about to retire from dancing, Fonteyn was introduced to a newcomer to the European stage—Rudolph Nureyev. Nureyev had been a dancer with the Kirov Ballet in Leningrad, Soviet Union (now St. Petersburg, Russia). He joined London's Royal Ballet in 1962 and he became Fonteyn's partner. For nearly 15 years, they danced together for packed theaters. Thousands of fans held their breath, watching the graceful couple glide and leap across the stage.

TOPICAL TIDBIT

Dynamic Duo

Margot Fonteyn and Rudolph Nureyev were perhaps the most famous ballet pair in history. They respected one another's talent, but were very different people. Nureyev was 20 years younger than Fonteyn, and the two had drastically different personalities. Many people think that it was their differences that created the energy that audiences saw on stage.

After retiring from the stage in the 1970s, Fonteyn moved to Panama to be with her husband. She sponsored many ballets that were aired on television. She also wrote several books, including *The Magic of Dance* and *A Dancer's World*. Fonteyn died of cancer on February 21, 1991, in Panama City, Panama.

Prima Ballerina

Many people believe that Margot Fonteyn was one of the finest ballerinas of all time. In 1956, Fonteyn was given the honorary title of Dame of the Order of the British Empire, the highest award given by the British government. ◇

LIFE EVENTS

1919
Margot Fonteyn is born Margaret Hookham in Reigate, England.

1934
Fonteyn's family returns to England and Margot studies with Sarafima Astafieva.

1935
Fonteyn becomes the prima ballerina of the Vic-Wells Ballet.

1962
Well into her career, Fonteyn begins a partnership with Russian dancer Rudolf Nureyev.

1979
Fonteyn is awarded the title *prima ballerina assoluta* by the Royal Ballet of London.

1991
Fonteyn dies in Panama City, Panama.

Dian Fossey
Zoologist
(born 1932 • died 1985)

Most of what is known today about mountain gorillas comes from research conducted by Dian *(DEE-ahn)* Fossey. For more than 18 years, she lived with mountain gorillas in East Africa. She befriended them and ate with them. They became part of her family and they accepted Fossey as one of their own.

> "Immediately I was struck by the physical magnificence of the huge, jet-black bodies blended against the green."
>
> —Dian Fossey, on seeing mountain gorillas for the first time

Going to Africa

Dian Fossey was born on January 16, 1932, in San Francisco, California. She loved animals all her life. While in college, she studied veterinary science and occupational therapy. (Occupational therapy helps disabled people do everyday tasks.)

Dian Fossey holds a photo of one of the gorillas she studied,
September 24, 1970.

Fossey had always longed to visit Africa. In 1963, she made the trip. While in eastern Africa, she met anthropologists Louis and Mary Leakey, who were searching for early human fossils. They discussed with Fossey how important it was to study apes in order to learn more about the evolution of humans.

Dian took particular interest in one type of ape, the endangered mountain gorilla.

When Fossey got back to the U.S., all she could think about was returning to Africa. In 1967, with the help of the Leakeys, she established the Karisoke Research Centre in Rwanda's Virunga Mountains. There, she studied gorillas in their natural environment.

Gorillas in the Mist

The Virunga Mountains border three African nations—Rwanda, Uganda, and Congo (formerly Zaire). Along the slopes of these mountains is a dense rain forest. The area is usually topped with a cold mist. Everything that Fossey needed for her research laboratory had to be carried up the mountain. She employed local men to help haul the equipment and

TOPICAL TIDBIT

Mountain Gorillas

Mountain gorillas are an endangered species, with only about 5,000 to 15,000 left in existence. They live in the rain forests of eastern, central Africa. The average male gorilla stands between five and six feet tall and weighs between 300 and 600 pounds. Females are much smaller. Gorillas walk on all four limbs, often leaning on their fists.

to work as cooks, guards, and trackers (to follow the tracks made by the gorillas).

At first, Fossey watched the gorillas from a distance. When they saw her, they were frightened. They would scream to warn the other gorillas, then run away. To get a closer look, Fossey used binoculars and spied on them from behind trees. Soon the gorillas got used to her presence and stopped running away. They ignored her as they ate thistles, celery, and blackberry leaves growing in the forest.

The Karisoke Research Center is in
northwestern Rwanda.

Fossey watched the gorillas very closely, recording their habits in a notebook that she kept with her at all times. She could identify each gorilla by its markings and coloring, as well as its personal habits. She gave the gorillas names, such as Uncle Bert, Peanuts, and Digit. Uncle Bert was an older gorilla, with a lot of silver fur. Peanuts was a show-off, always beating his chest. He was the first gorilla to make personal contact with Fossey by touching her hand. Digit, however, was her favorite. He was very playful as a youngster and loved it when she tickled him. For nearly 18 years, Fossey watched Digit grow into an adult.

The Fight Against Poaching

On several occasions, Fossey returned to the U.S. She gave lectures about her work and was featured in *National Geographic* magazine. In the late 1970s, she became very outspoken about a terrible problem facing the mountain gorillas—poaching, which is the illegal killing of wild or endangered animals. Poachers were killing gorillas and cutting off the hands and feet to sell as ashtrays. Fossey became even more involved when her beloved Digit was killed by a poacher.

Fossey worked with Rwandan government officials to stop the poaching. She devoted much of her time and resources to patrolling the area surrounding the Karisoke Research Center to keep it free from poachers. On several occasions, Fossey caught poachers and scared them by pretending that she was a witch. The poachers hated her. On December 26, 1985, Fossey was found murdered in her cabin. Although her murderers were never found, many people believe that she was killed by poachers.

An Important Legacy

Dian Fossey's story was told in the 1988 film *Gorillas in the Mist*, based on her book of the same name.

She wrote in her diary, "I had a deep wish to see and live with wild animals in a world that hadn't yet been completely changed by humans." She got her wish, and in the process, advanced the understanding of one of man's closest living relatives. Fossey is buried in Rwanda, alongside Digit. ◇

LIFE EVENTS

1932
Dian Fossey is born in San Francisco, California.

1963
Fossey takes a seven-week safari, her first trip to Africa.

1967
Fossey establishes the Karisoke Research Center in Rwanda.

1970-1974
Fossey completes her doctorate in zoology at Cambridge University in England.

1983
Fossey publishes her research for a general audience in *Gorillas in the Mist*.

1985
Dian Fossey is found dead in her hut in Rwanda.

Anne Frank
Diarist and Holocaust Victim
(born 1929 • died 1945)

If Anne Frank had never kept a diary, few people would know that she lived during World War II and died in a Nazi concentration camp. She would be just another of the millions of Nazi victims whose stories died with them. However, Anne's story lives on through the diary that she kept while in hiding from the Nazis. A brave teenager, Anne Frank left a record for the world to remember.

Escape to the Netherlands

Annelies Marie Frank, known as Anne, was born on June 12, 1929, in Frankfurt, Germany. She was the second daughter of Otto and Edith Frank; her older sister was named Margot. The Franks were Jews whose families had lived in Germany for many generations.

As Anne's childhood began, the political situation in Germany was changing. The country was experiencing hard times. Germans were facing mass unemployment, food shortages, and money problems.

Adolf Hitler and the Nazi Party promised change. Many people voted for Adolf Hitler to come to power; those who didn't support him were bullied and threatened by the Nazis to vote for him, anyway.

Hitler became a dictator. He unjustly blamed the Jews for all of Germany's problems. Many Germans disagreed with him, but were afraid to stand up to the Nazis. The Franks escaped from Nazi Germany in the early 1930s by moving to Amsterdam, the Netherlands. Thinking that the family was out of Hitler's reach, Otto Frank set up a business.

In Amsterdam, Anne began to have a normal childhood. However, the Nazi threat was never far away. In 1939 the Nazis began World War II by invading Poland. The Franks thought that they were safe in the Netherlands. They did not know that Hitler planned to conquer all of Europe and kill all the people that he thought were inferior, including blacks, socialists, the mentally ill, and, especially, Jews.

> "We all live with the objective of being happy; our lives are all different and yet the same."
>
> —Anne Frank

The Nazis Invade

By 1941, the Nazis controlled much of Europe, including the Netherlands. The Nazis took away the Jews' rights. Anne and other Jews could not attend school with non-Jews, own bicycles, ride in cars, or go to movies or parks. Each Jew was forced to wear a yellow star on his or her clothing so the Nazis could identify them quickly.

The Franks knew that Jews were being rounded up and sent to work camps. They had heard rumors that Jews were being slaughtered at the camps. Otto Frank prepared several rooms in his office building so that he and his family could hide there. A bookcase blocked a secret stairway leading to their hideout. A few co-workers and friends helped the Franks.

Years in Hiding

The Franks moved to the hideout on July 6, 1942, when Anne was 13. Anne hung up postcards and pictures of movie stars in her room. She took her diary, which she called "Kitty," with her and began keeping a detailed record of life in hiding.

In addition to the Frank family, four other Jews shared the hideout: Hermann and Auguste van Pels, and their son Peter, and Fritz Pfeffer. As the war

TOPICAL TIDBIT

The Quiet Helper

Mies Giep helped the Franks while they were in hiding. She struggled to find enough food to feed the eight people. She brought the group news, becoming their only link to the outside world. It was Mies who found Anne's diary and kept it safe, hoping Anne would return.

raged on, Anne wrote about the group. She explained what it was like to be trapped, unable to go outside. Because people worked in the building where they were hiding, they had to be silent and still during the day, so nobody would hear them. Anne wrote about her fears, the future, and the possibility of love. She described the friends who secretly brought them food and news. Anne recorded the events as she learned of them.

Meanwhile, the Nazis continued to round up Jews and send them to camps, where most of them were starved or worked to death, shot, or poisoned with gas. On August 4, 1944, after more than two years in hiding, someone reported the hideout to the Nazis. The group was arrested and sent to the camps where everyone but Otto died. Anne and Margot died of typhus—a disease common in unclean areas—in the spring of 1945. Just a few weeks later, Germany lost the war and camp prisoners were set free.

LIFE EVENTS

1929
Annelies Marie Frank is born in Frankfurt, Germany.

1930s
Anne's family moves to the Netherlands to avoid the Nazis.

1942
The Frank family moves into a hideout in Otto Frank's office building.

1944
The Franks' hideout is discovered and reported to the Nazis.

1945
Anne dies of typhus in a concentration camp.

A Message of Hope

After the war, Otto returned home and found that Anne's diary had survived. He had "Kitty" published in 1947; today it is available worldwide, in more than 50 languages.

Anne's powerful story describes only a few of the millions of people persecuted and murdered by the Nazis. It also carries a message of hope. Even after two years in hiding, Anne wrote, "I still believe, in spite of everything, that people are still truly good at heart."

Time magazine put Anne Frank on its list of the 100 most influential people of the 20th century. Her family's hideout in Amsterdam is now a museum. ◇

"So much has happened it's as if the whole world had suddenly turned upside down."

—Anne Frank, diary entry for June 8, 1942

Betty Friedan
Founder of the Feminist Movement
(born 1921)

Betty Friedan has directly influenced the way women are treated in this country. Her best-selling 1963 book, *The Feminine Mystique*, has been translated into many languages. Betty's work with the National Organization for Women (NOW) has inspired other women's rights groups to fight for an end to the inferior status that women receive throughout the world.

> "A girl should not expect special privileges because of her sex, but neither should she adjust to prejudice and discrimination."
>
> —Betty Friedan

Becoming a Feminist

Betty Naomi Goldstein was born in Peoria, Illinois, on February 4, 1921. She graduated from Smith College in 1942, with a degree in psychology.

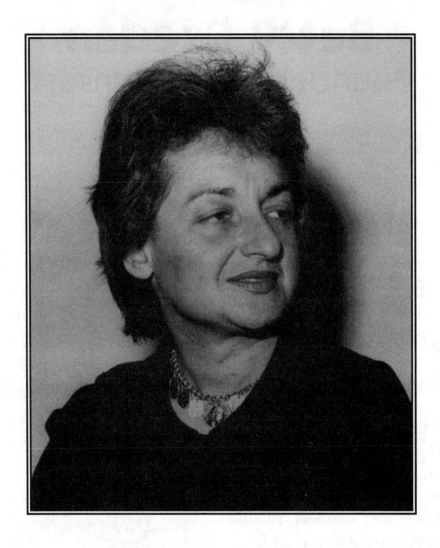

Betty moved to New York City, where she met, and later married, Carl Friedan. The couple had three children, and Betty was a devoted wife and mother.

During the 1950s, however, Betty Friedan was not satisfied with being just a homemaker. She wanted to do more, but had always been taught that she should be content to be a wife and mother. All her life, women had been told that they should be happy at home. Women should not seek personal satisfaction through their own accomplishments, but be happy with the accomplishments of their husbands and children.

In 1957, Friedan used her knowledge of psychology to create a questionnaire that asked women if they were personally fulfilled with being homemakers. She asked her classmates from Smith College to complete the questionnaire. The results of the survey were revealing—Friedan was not alone. Many other women were dissatisfied with their limited role in society.

The Feminine Mystique

In 1963, Friedan compiled the results of her surveys and wrote *The Feminine Mystique*. In the book, she discussed "the problem that has no name"—the dissatisfaction of women who were forced to live out their dreams through their husbands and children, rather than through accomplishments of their own. According to the book, women were strongly discouraged from pursuing other avenues, such as careers, because their role in society was that of wife and mother.

Friedan also noted that women were discriminated against by men and by society as a whole. For instance, women were paid lower salaries than men, even if they did the same work. If a woman chose to focus on her career instead of getting married and having children, she was considered too independent. If a woman was married with children and chose to work, she was thought to be a bad mother. Society did not believe that a woman could do both.

Friedan thought that women deserved better, and that women needed to break these unfair stereotypes. *The Feminine Mystique* was an overnight success, causing many women to reevaluate their lives.

Making Policy, Not Coffee

In 1966, Friedan founded the National Organization for Women (NOW). The group's mission was to gain rights for women equal to those given to men, especially in the workplace. Under

TOPICAL TIDBIT

Women's Rights Throughout the World

In the United States and Europe, women's rights issues mostly relate to employment practices. In other parts of the world, however, a woman must fight for more basic rights, such as the right to expose her face in public, the right to prosecute a man who beats her, the right to get an education, and the right to hold a job.

Friedan's leadership, the group worked to remove from job applications qualifications that were based on gender. NOW also fought to get women elected to government office, to create day-care facilities for working mothers, to set up family-planning centers, to gain pregnancy leave from employers, and to get pensions for women. Today, the group has more than 250,000 members, both women and men.

Friedan also played an active role in the formation of the National Women's Political Caucus in 1971. She believed that women should be more active in the political arena—"to make policy, not coffee." One of the major achievements of the Caucus was to create the Equal Rights Amendment (ERA) to the U.S. Constitution, which demanded equal pay for equal work. Despite a tough fight, the ERA

LIFE EVENTS

1921
Betty Naomi Goldstein is born in Peoria, Illinois.

1942
Friedan graduates from Smith College with a degree in psychology.

1963
Friedan publishes *The Feminine Mystique.*

1966
Friedan founds the National Organization for Women (NOW).

1971
Friedan helps found the National Women's Political Caucus.

1996
Friedan publishes *The Fountain of Age,* which calls for fair treatment of the elderly.

failed to pass in 1982. However, since that time, 30 states have ratified it as part of their state constitution.

Still Active

By establishing NOW and the National Women's Political Caucus, Betty Friedan has influenced the treatment of women around the world. She remains a role model for women and girls everywhere. Today, Friedan lectures about women's issues. She has written three other books, all regarding civil rights. ◇

Indira Gandhi
Prime Minister of India
(born 1917 • died 1984)

Indira Gandhi had politics in her blood. She followed in the footsteps of her father, Jawaharlal Nehru, who was the first prime minister of India after it gained its independence from Britain in 1947. Indira later became India's highest official, serving as prime minister for four terms, beginning in 1966. Her life was cut short in 1984, when she was assassinated by religious extremists.

The Struggle for Independence

Indira Priyadarshini Nehru was born during World War I, on November 19, 1917, in Allahabad, India. At that time, India was a British colony and subject to British law. Many people in India, like Indira's father, Jawaharlal Nehru, wanted to see India gain its independence from Great Britain.

Indira's father was a member of the Indian National Congress—a political group that supported the ideas of Mohandas K. Gandhi, also called

Indira Gandhi and her father, Jawaharlal Nehru, visit President and Mrs. Kennedy at the White House, November 7, 1961.

Mahatma Gandhi. (*Mahatma* means "Great Soul.") The Mahatma believed in nonviolent protest against British rule. Indira's father worked closely with the Mahatma and became a powerful Indian leader as well.

On several occasions, Indira's father was jailed for defying the British. Indira grew up in this atmosphere of struggle, watching her father and others pay the price for their belief in independence. But she also saw the struggle end in victory after the end of World War II (1939-1945) when the British granted independence to India.

Following in Her Father's Footsteps

Indira attended school at Visva-Bharati University in Bengal and at Oxford University in England. She also became involved in politics with her father. In 1942, she married Feroze Gandhi (no relation to Mahatma Gandhi). They eventually had two sons, Rajiv and Sanjay.

In 1947, Jawaharlal Nehru became the first prime minister of independent India. Gandhi worked closely with her father and became an important member of the Congress party. She became the party's president in 1959. Within a few years, Gandhi suffered two great losses—her husband died in 1960 and her father passed away in 1964.

> "You cannot shake hands with a clenched fist."
> —Indira Gandhi

After Nehru's death, Lal Bahadur Shastri became prime minister of India. He appointed Indira Gandhi minister of information and broadcasting. After Shastri's death in 1966, Gandhi became the third prime minister of independent India. In all, she held the post for about 15 years.

Leading a Nation

When Indira Gandhi took office, India was full of religious tension and civil unrest. Gandhi was often challenged by members of her own party. At first, members of her party thought that they could control her, but they soon learned otherwise. Gandhi had an independent spirit and her own ideas.

In India at that time, overpopulation was a problem that led to high unemployment and food and housing shortages. During her years as prime minister, Gandhi took many steps to address the situation.

TOPICAL TIDBIT

India's Spiritual Leader: Mahatma Gandhi

Mohandas K. Gandhi (1869-1948) was a man who believed strongly in peace. He did not want India to have a violent war against Great Britain to gain independence. Instead, he protested against British rule in peaceful ways, including hunger strikes. After India gained its independence, the nonviolent Gandhi was shot to death during a prayer meeting.

She worked with other nations to acquire food and loans to help her people. In later years, she was harshly criticized for a law she passed. It required men with two or more children to undergo an operation that would make them unable to father any more children.

Gandhi also helped other nations in times of struggle. She sent Indian troops to help East Bengal become the independent nation of Bangladesh, in 1971. That same year, she was re-elected prime minister. However, she was accused and convicted of breaking election laws. Ordered to resign in 1975, she instead declared a state of emergency and jailed her political opponents.

LIFE EVENTS

1917
Indira Priyadarshini Nehru is born in Allahabad, India.

1942
Indira marries Feroze Gandhi.

1947-1964
Indira Gandhi serves as aide to her father, Prime Minister Jawaharlal Nehru.

1964-1966
Indira Gandhi serves as minister of information.

1966
Gandhi becomes prime minister of India.

1984
Indira Gandhi is assassinated in India.

Her Later Years

Indians found themselves under more government-imposed restrictions, and Gandhi's popularity declined. When she called for new elections in 1977, she lost. However, she rallied in 1980 and was elected prime minister again. Indira Gandhi was assassinated on October 31, 1984, by her own bodyguards, who were religious extremists.

Indira Gandhi had led her nation through difficult years after its independence. Although she was sometimes criticized for restricting her people's freedom, she worked to improve conditions in India. Gandhi had groomed her son Sanjay to take over for her, but he died in an airplane crash in 1980. She then encouraged her other son, Rajiv, to seek office. He was elected prime minister several days after his mother's death. He, too, was assassinated while in office. He died on May 21, 1991. ◇

Judy Garland
Actor, Singer, Dancer
(born 1922 • died 1969)

At age two, Judy Garland began entertaining audiences. By 17, she was not only known for her singing, but for her dancing and acting as well. Judy became a superstar in her teens, and quickly learned that fame has a high price, as she struggled to stay at the top of her profession. Her cheerful screen image masked the emotional and physical problems that she had in her off-screen life.

The Gumm Sisters

Judy Garland was born Frances Ethel Gumm on June 10, 1922, in Grand Rapids, Minnesota. She was named for her parents Frank and Ethel Gumm. Frances was the youngest of three sisters, so everyone called her "Baby."

Baby's parents were former vaudeville performers. As soon as their daughters could walk, they involved the girls in a vaudeville act. When Baby was two years old, she sang before a theater audience for the

Judy Garland as Dorothy in *The Wizard of Oz.*
1939.

first time. At four, she joined her sisters' singing act, and they performed as "The Gumm Sisters."

The Gumm Sisters performed on the radio and on stage. Their mother served as their manager. During a trip to sing at the World's Fair in Chicago in 1934, a comedian suggested that they change their name because audiences snickered when they heard it. They chose Garland— and "Baby" changed her name to Judy.

A Star Is Born

When the Gumm Sisters broke up in the mid-1930s, Judy Garland signed on with Metro-Goldwyn-Mayer (MGM) studios and had small roles in a few movies, including *Every Sunday*. Soon, however, she was landing larger roles, which featured her as

> "Movies are my life's blood. . . I love to work, I love to sing, I love to act."
>
> —Judy Garland

both an actor and a singer. She teamed up with comic actor Mickey Rooney in several of his "Andy Hardy" movies, bringing her into the spotlight as one of America's fastest-rising young stars.

It was her performance in *The Wizard of Oz* (1939) that movie lovers most remember. As Dorothy, the farm girl who gets swept away to the land of Oz by a tornado, 17-year-old Garland captured the hearts of the American people. Garland had beaten child megastar Shirley Temple in auditions for the part.

Audiences loved Garland in *The Wizard of Oz*, especially her singing of "Somewhere Over the Rainbow." She was awarded a special Academy

Award for best juvenile performance. She was one of Hollywood's biggest stars.

The Other Side of the Rainbow

Garland followed *The Wizard of Oz* with other movies, including *Meet Me in St. Louis*, *The Harvey Girls*, *Easter Parade*, and *In the Good Old Summertime*. Garland was a "triple threat"—she could act, sing, *and* dance.

Despite her promising career, Garland suffered from emotional and physical problems, often due to stress. Biographers believe that she had bouts of depression. She took diet pills to stay thin and sleeping pills to relax. She also started drinking. Garland's problems affected her ability to perform and her career suffered. In 1949, she was fired from MGM. She made a small comeback with 1954's *A Star Is Born* and 1960's *Judgment at Nuremberg*.

TOPICAL TIDBIT

Liza with a *Z*

Judy's daughter Liza Minnelli is also an award-winning singer and actor. Her stage performances have won her three Tony awards and millions of fans. Minnelli has also made a number of movies. She won an Academy Award in 1972 for her performance in the film *Cabaret*.

Garland also had difficulty in her relationships She was married five times. Her second husband was film director Vincente Minnelli. The couple had a daughter, Liza, in 1946. Judy later married Sid Luft and had two more children, Lorna and Joey.

The Show Goes On

Despite the problems in her personal life, Judy Garland always had a smile and a song for her audiences. After her film career, she continued to perform in nightclubs and concert halls. She won a Grammy Award in 1961 and appeared in TV specials. From 1963 until 1964, she hosted *The Judy Garland Show*, a variety series on CBS. Garland died of an accidental drug overdose on June 22, 1969, in London, England. Today she is a film legend loved by audiences the world over. ◇

LIFE EVENTS

1922
Frances Ethel Gumm is born in Grand Rapids, Minnesota.

1935
Judy Garland signs a contract and begins working for MGM studios.

1939
Garland stars in *The Wizard of Oz*, making her the most popular young actress in Hollywood.

1962
Garland's record, *Judy at Carnegie Hall*, receives five Grammy Awards.

1963-1964
Garland stars in her own TV program, *The Judy Garland Show*.

1969
Judy Garland dies in London, England.

Althea Gibson
Tennis Champion
(born 1927 • died 2003)

Until the mid-20th century, African-American athletes were not allowed to participate in many amateur and professional sporting competitions in the United States. The major teams and tournaments in the country were open only to white players. However, in the late 1940s and early 1950s, black players, such as baseball's Jackie Robinson and tennis's Althea Gibson, crossed the color line. Finally, athletes of color were allowed to compete with other top players from around the world. On the tennis court, Althea Gibson proved that she was an exceptional athlete.

A Welcomed Escape

Althea Gibson was born on August 25, 1927, in Silver, South Carolina. Her family, which was poor, moved to New York City in 1930. In New York, Althea had trouble in school. She did not like going to classes and often skipped school. She always got in trouble for it when she got home.

Sports provided Althea with an escape from her troubles. She enjoyed table tennis (Ping-Pong), and got some instruction through public programs at local parks. Then a friend gave her a tennis racket. Althea discovered a natural talent and love for tennis.

In those days, however, tennis was considered a sport for wealthy white people. There were separate clubs, sports facilities, and matches for black players and white players. No matter how good an African American athlete played the game, he or she was not allowed to compete with whites.

> "No matter what accomplishments you make, someone helped you."
> —Althea Gibson

Althea did not care about the race issues. She loved the game. In 1941, she began taking lessons at the Harlem Cosmopolitan Tennis Club, an organization for African American players.

Rising Star

Althea Gibson quickly showed her skill in tennis. In 1942, she won the all-black American Tennis Association (ATA) tournament. Eventually Gibson dropped out of school. In 1946, however, Dr. Hubert Eaton became interested in 19-year-old Gibson's tennis career. He took her to North Carolina to live, study, and take tennis lessons. A year later, Gibson again became the ATA National Champion—a title that she held for 10 years. Still, she was denied the right to compete in major international competitions.

In the late 1940s, doors began to open for African Americans. In 1947, Jackie Robinson became the first black player to join a major-league baseball team. Gibson was not far behind. A white tennis player named Alice Marble complained to readers of *American Lawn Tennis* magazine that discrimination was keeping talented athletes like Gibson from competing against the finest players in the world. The tennis community took notice, and Gibson was invited to enter the tennis competition at Forest Hills in New York in 1950. She became the first African American to compete in that contest.

From that point on, Gibson was given more invitations to compete, and she took advantage of the offers. In 1951, she became the first African American to compete at Wimbledon, in England. In 1956, she became the first black player to win the French Open. That same year, she participated in a

TOPICAL TIDBIT

The Williams Sisters

Althea Gibson paved the way for two of tennis's current superstars: Venus and Serena Williams. Each sister plays singles tennis and mixed doubles; together, they make up one of the most formidable doubles teams around. In 2000, they posted a 15-0 record for doubles and became the first sister team to win an Olympic gold medal for doubles tennis.

goodwill tour of Southeast Asia, sponsored by the U.S. State Department. In 1957, she rose to the top of her profession by winning major championships at Wimbledon and the U.S. Open. When she returned to New York, a ticker-tape parade was held in her honor.

Other Pursuits

In 1953, Gibson graduated from Florida A&M University. In 1957, she showcased her singing talents at a dinner during that year's Wimbledon tournament. Two years later, she recorded an album called *Althea Gibson Sings*.

Gibson was a well-rounded athlete. Soon after she retired from tennis competition, in 1958, she took up golf. She was so good that she joined the Ladies Professional Golf Association (LPGA) in 1964, and competed

LIFE EVENTS

1927
Althea Gibson is born in Silver, South Carolina.

1942-1952
Gibson is the American Tennis Association's National Champion.

1950
Gibson is invited to compete at a competition with white players in Forest Hills, New York.

1951
Gibson is the first African American to compete at Wimbledon.

1957
Gibson wins at Wimbledon and the U.S. Open.

1964
Gibson joins the Ladies Professional Golf Association (LPGA).

2003
Gibson dies.

in golf tournaments. Gibson married Will Darben in 1965. Ten years later, she took a job with the New Jersey Department of Recreation.

Inducted into many sports halls of fame, Gibson also worked with the Althea Gibson Foundation, an organization that helps city children learn more about golf and tennis. After ailing for some time, Gibson died on September 28, 2003. Althea Gibson will be long remembered for breaking the color barrier in tennis, clearing the path for other African American athletes. ◇

Jane Goodall
Ethologist
(born 1934)

Jane Goodall lived in the jungles of Africa to study chimpanzees in their natural habitat. When she first began to study the chimps' behavior, she hid behind trees and lay on the ground so as not to frighten them. Eventually, she won their trust and observed them more closely than any human had before. For more than 40 years, she has devoted her career to studying chimpanzees. Her books, reports, and TV specials have changed the way the world looks at these incredible animals.

Early Love of Animals

Jane was born on April 3, 1934, in London, England. As a child, she loved animals and was curious to learn more about how they lived, what they ate, and how they behaved.

At the age of four, Jane wanted to discover how hens laid eggs. So she sat in a chicken coop for hours, as still as could be, until she finally saw a

214

Jane Goodall gives Tess a kiss. Tess is an orphaned chimpanzee who was cared for at the Sweetwaters Chimpanzee Sanctuary in Kenya.

hen lay an egg. Jane's patience and persistence would pay off again and again in her life.

When Jane was five, World War II began when the Nazis tried to take over Europe. The German air force frequently bombed England, endangering the lives of British citizens. It was a very frightening time. Little Jane often escaped thoughts of war by reading stories like *Dr. Doolittle*, about a scientist who could talk to animals. She dreamed that someday she, too, would be able to talk to animals.

Pursuing Her Dream in Africa

By the time Jane Goodall was in her early 20s, she had saved up enough money to travel to Kenya to visit a friend. While there in 1957, she heard about scientists Louis and Mary Leakey, who were nearby studying fossils of early humans. Goodall made an appointment to see them and immediately impressed Louis Leakey. He hired her as an assitant, and Goodall's stay in Africa continued.

Goodall enjoyed working with the Leakeys, but she was less interested in studying animals that were long dead. She was eager to study the present, the living. When Louis had the idea to study chimpanzees near Lake Tanganyika in the country now known as Tanzania, Goodall jumped at the chance.

> "Every individual matters. Every individual has a role to play. Every individual makes a difference."
>
> —Jane Goodall

Goodall was excited about the project but needed someone to accompany her. Authorities in Kenya did not want a young woman to head into the wild alone. The camp where the study would be set up was remote and rustic. When Goodall's mother, Vanne, volunteered to accompany her, Goodall was given a green light. They set out for Gombe Stream Game Reserve (now Gombe National Park) in 1960.

Becoming a Chimp Expert

Jane Goodall's stay in Tanzania was supposed to last only three months. But it lasted much longer. Her first months there were spent watching the chimps through binoculars. If she got too close, the chimps would run away. Slowly, however, they got used to her presence and allowed her access to their private lives.

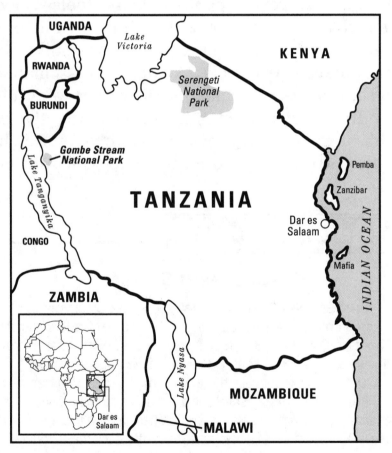

Jane Goodall has spent many years in Tanzania—at Gombe Stream National Park and in the capital, Dar es Salaam.

By getting so close, Goodall saw things that no human had ever seen before. She learned, firsthand, that many ideas people had about chimpanzees were false. For example, she watched chimps hunt other animals for food. Until then, people thought that chimps were vegetarians.

Goodall also saw chimps make tools out of sticks and use them. Previously, experts had believed that only humans were capable of using tools. Goodall watched as chimps put the sticks into termite or ant nests for the insects to crawl onto, then pull out the sticks and eat the insects. Goodall was fascinated.

In some ways, Goodall approached her work differently from other scientists. For instance, she gave each chimp a name, such as Gremlin or Galahad. Most scientists assigned numbers to their subjects.

TOPICAL TIDBIT

Roots and Shoots

Jane has always wanted to get young people involved in research and conservation. In 1991, Jane started Roots and Shoots in Dar es Salaam, Tanzania. Jane met with students from local schools and discussed the negative impact of poaching and hunting on animals, the environment, and even people. These students then established the same kind of discussion groups in their schools and communities. Today, there are more than 1,000 Roots and Shoots groups in fifty countries worldwide.

Goodall published her findings in books and articles. In 1964, she married Hugo van Lawick, a Dutch wildlife photographer. Together they produced several books and films. They later divorced. Goodall married Derek Bryceson in 1975. Bryceson died in 1980.

Goodall has become a world-renowned expert on chimps. She also earned her doctorate in ethology (the study of animals in their natural habitat) and raised a son.

Educating the World

Jane Goodall continues to work with chimpanzees. Her work has been the subject of many articles and National Geographic television specials. She founded the Jane Goodall Institute for Wildlife Research, Education, and Conservation in 1977, and continues to educate the world about chimps. ◇

LIFE EVENTS

1934
Jane Goodall is born in London, England.

1960
Goodall begins studying chimpanzees in Tanzania.

1965
Goodall earns her Ph.D. in ethology at Cambridge University.

1971
Goodall publishes her first book about her work with chimpanzees, titled *In the Shadow of Man.*

1977
Goodall founds the Jane Goodall Institute for Wildlife Research, Education, and Conservation.

1988
Goodall earns the National Geographic Society Centennial Award.

Martha Graham
Founder of Modern Dance
(born 1894 • died 1991)

Martha Graham took the American dance scene by storm, developing a new style and technique that was bold and innovative. Graham's stark choreography brought out the innermost emotions of the characters dancing on the stage and was a major influence on American dance of the 20th century. Some even call her the mother of modern American dance.

Martha Wants to Dance

Martha Graham was born in Allegheny (now Pittsburgh), Pennsylvania, on May 11, 1894. When she was a young girl, she wanted to dance. Her father forbid her to go to dance school, but dancing was in her blood.

When she turned 22, Graham enrolled in the Denishawn School of Dancing in Los Angeles, California. The school taught modern dance, using a combination of ballet movements and folk dancing from countries around the world. The Denishawn

Martha Graham rehearses with her partner and husband,
Erick Hawkins, in New York City, 1950.

dance company wore exotic costumes to create a feeling of other-worldliness for the audience.

Graham toured with the Denishawn troupe for seven years. In 1923, she moved to New York City—the hub of dance in America. Then she took a teaching post at the Eastman School of Music in Rochester, New York, and, after two years, was named director of the dance department. All the while, Graham kept dancing. She appeared in the Greenwich Village Follies from 1923 to 1925.

Her Own Dance Company

While living in New York, Graham decided that it was time to start her own dance company. To raise money, Graham modeled clothing, danced at the opening of the Radio City Music Hall in New York, and taught actors—including Gregory Peck and Bette Davis—how to move on the big screen.

> "Dance is the hidden language of the soul for the body."
>
> —Martha Graham

Graham started her own dance company for women in 1929. Graham's technique was new. Her dances included stark, angular movements, that showed the emotions of the characters. It was harsh and dramatic, and different from anything anyone had seen before. Critics did not like it, but audiences loved it.

Although Graham loved to dance, she eventually turned to choreography (composing dances). Graham used costumes, music, stage designs, and lighting to set the scene for the dance. She taught the women in her troupe dance steps, arm movements, and facial expressions that brought their characters to life.

Most of the time, Graham wrote the story line for the

dance herself. Many of the dances highlighted famous women throughout history, including Joan of Arc, Emily Dickinson, Charlotte and Emily Brontë, and women from Greek mythology.

To add to the overall experience for the audience, Graham hired famous composers Louis Horst and Aaron Copland to write the music for several of her productions. She also commissioned Isamu Noguchi, a well-known sculptor and designer, to create sets for the stage—something that had never been done before.

No Stopping Martha

Graham never stopped dancing. In all, she choreographed nearly 150 dance productions, appearing as the lead dancer in most of them. She gave her final

---

TOPICAL TIDBIT

Aaron Copland

Composer Aaron Copland worked with Martha Graham on the Broadway musical *Appalachian Spring* in 1944. Copland composed many musical scores that reflect the American frontier. He is most noted for *Fanfare for the Common Man* and for *Rodeo*, which includes the foot-tapping "Hoedown"—a compilation of American folk ballads.

stage performance in 1968 at the age of 74.

When she was 90 years old, Graham choreographed a dance to the musical piece *Rite of Spring*. *Rite of Spring*, composed in 1913 by the Russian-American composer Igor Stravinsky, is one of the first pieces of modern music. In 1984, the National Endowment for the Arts funded an effort to put Graham's teachings on film.

Dancing Queen

Martha Graham died on April 1, 1991. Her unique choreography changed the course of American dance. Through sharp movements, creative stage designs, and modern music, she transformed traditional dance productions into emotional representations of the stories being told. Her efforts were rewarded in 1976, when she received the Presidential Medal of Freedom, the highest honor given in the U.S. ◇

LIFE EVENTS

1894
Martha Graham is born in Allegheny (now Pittsburgh), Pennsylvania.

1916
Graham enters the Denishawn School of Dancing.

1923
Graham moves to New York and later begins teaching.

1929
Graham begins her own dance company.

1944
Graham choreographs and performs in *Appalachian Spring*.

1991
Martha Graham dies.

Ella Grasso
First Female Governor in the United States
(born 1919 • died 1981)

Ella Grasso devoted her life to the people of Connecticut. She believed in working-class people and they believed in her. They elected her the first female governor of that state. As Grasso advanced up the political ladder, she never lost an election. She served the people of Connecticut for 28 years and is an inspiration to all women in politics.

> "It is not enough to profess faith in the democratic process; we must do something about it."
>
> —Ella Grasso

Patriotic Beginnings

Ella Rose Tambussi was born on May 10, 1919, in Windsor Locks, Connecticut. Her parents were working-class people who had recently moved to the

U.S. from Italy. Ella was a good student. After grad-uating from high school, she attended Mount Holyoke College in Massachusetts, and earned her bachelor's degree in 1940. She received a master's degree in 1942. Later that year, Ella married school principal Thomas Grasso. They had two children.

In 1941, the U.S. entered World War II (1939-1945). Thousands of American men and women served in the military in Europe and the Pacific. Although Ella Grasso did not enlist in the armed forces, she worked within the United States to better equip U.S. soldiers overseas. Grasso took a job with the War Manpower Commission as the assistant director of research in Connecticut. The Commission hired and trained civilians (nonmilitary staff) to work in jobs that were important to the war effort, such as making airplanes and weapons, or shipping food to U.S. troops.

In many instances, the Commission helped business owners turn their factories into war production facilities. Often, women were recruited to perform jobs normally held by men, such as welding and assembly-line work. Grasso's department conducted research on where new factories should be built and the number of workers needed.

A Career in Politics

In 1943, Grasso got her first taste of politics when she joined the League of Women Voters and became a speechwriter for the Democratic Party. By 1952, Grasso was writing speeches for her own campaigns, and she was elected to the Connecticut House of Representatives. After serving two two-year terms, she became the Secretary of State in Connecticut in 1958, a position that she held for the next 12 years.

In 1970, Grasso was elected to the U.S. Congress, serving in the House of Representatives. After serving two terms, Grasso set her sights on becoming governor of Connecticut.

Governor of Connecticut

Grasso started campaigning in early 1974 to become governor of Connecticut. In November of that year, she was elected—the first time in U.S. history that a woman was elected as a governor. Before then, several women had served as governors, but none had been elected in their own right. In all those instances, women had served after their governor husbands died in office. Such governorships were considered "inherited." Grasso, however, was elected by the people.

Connecticut citizens voted for Grasso because she believed in the rights of working-class people. She supported women's issues and helped bring the state out of an economic slump. She delivered on her promise to listen to the needs of the people of Connecticut. During an economic crisis, she gave her $7,000 raise back to the state treasury.

Grasso also was known as the champion of minorities, women, young people, and senior citizens. She

TOPICAL TIDBIT

Nellie Tayloe Ross

Nellie Tayloe Ross was the first female governor in the United States. She was elected governor of Wyoming in 1924 after her husband—incumbent governor William Bradford Ross—died. She sought reelection in 1926 but lost. In 1933, Ross was appointed director of the U.S. Mint, becoming the first woman to hold such a high federal position.

gained the trust and support of many citizens in Connecticut. She was re-elected in 1978 to serve a second term as governor. In 1980, however, she became ill, and on New Year's Eve 1980, Grasso resigned. She died on February 5, 1981, in Hartford, Connecticut.

A Place in History

Ella Grasso served the people of Connecticut for 28 years. She was trusted by the people of her home state—she never lost an election. In 1993, Grasso was inducted into the National Women's Hall of Fame. A technical school has been named in her memory. ◇

LIFE EVENTS

1919
Ella Rose Tambussi is born in Windsor Locks, Connecticut.

1941
Tambussi works for the War Manpower Commission during World War II.

1942
Ella Tambussi marries Thomas Grasso.

1958-1970
Ella Grasso serves as secretary of state in Connecticut.

1971-1975
Grasso serves as a member of the House of Representatives.

1975-1980
Grasso serves as governor of the state of Connecticut.

1981
Ella Grasso dies in Hartford, Connecticut.

Florence Griffith Joyner
Track Star
(born 1959 • died 1998)

In 1988, Florence Griffith Joyner earned the title "World's Fastest Woman." That year, she won three gold medals at the Olympic Games in Seoul, Korea. Griffith Joyner dazzled the sports world with her speed and unique running suits. During her track career, she set several women's speed records and served on the President's Council on Physical Fitness and Sports.

A Good Student

Delorez Florence Griffith was born on December 21, 1959, in Los Angeles, California. She was the seventh of eleven children in a poor family. The Griffiths lived in a low-income housing project in the Watts district of L.A. Despite her humble beginnings, Florence excelled in sports and school.

Florence's family taught her to be confident and

Flo-Jo wins the semi-finals of the 200-meter race in Seoul, Korea, 1988. Flo-Jo went on to take the gold in the finals.

independent. Florence also liked to be different. She sometimes went to school with her hair in braids, one sticking up over her head. She also liked to take her pet snake to public places, such as the mall.

Florence started running when she was seven. She was fast and usually beat out the boys. When she was 14, she competed in the Jesse Owens National Youth Games and took first place. After graduation, she trained with a coach, Bob Kersee, at California State Univesity at Northridge. She then followed Kersee to the University of California at Los Angeles (UCLA), where she earned a bachelor of arts degree in psychology in 1983.

Star Runner

In 1984, Griffith made the U.S. Olympic team. She won a silver medal in the 200-meter dash at the Olympic Games, held in her hometown of Los Angeles. After the games, Griffith announced that she was retiring. For a time, she worked as a bank teller. Then, in April of 1987, Griffith decided

TOPICAL TIDBIT

Talented Family

Florence's sister-in-law, Jackie Joyner-Kersee, is often considered the greatest female athlete who ever lived. In 1988 Jackie won an Olympic gold medal in the heptathlon, scoring a record 7,291 points. The heptathlon includes seven events—high jump, broad jump, hurdles, javelin throw, shot put, and two running races.

to get back into shape. She wanted to try out for the 1988 Olympic Games.

In October 1987, she married Al Joyner, a fellow Olympian who won a gold medal for the triple jump at the 1984 Games. Al's sister was Jackie Joyner-Kersee, the wife of coach Bob Kersee and an exceptional athlete in her own right.

> "When anyone tells me I can't do something, I'm just not listening anymore."
>
> —Florence Griffith Joyner

With the help of Bob Kersee and husband Al Joyner, Florence Griffith Joyner stuck to a strict training program that included weight lifting. She worked hard to get into shape, and her efforts paid off at the Olympic trials in Indianapolis, Indiana. She broke the women's speed record in the 100-meter sprint. Her best time was 10.49 seconds, 0.27 seconds faster than the previous record-holder.

Going for the Gold

Griffith Joyner caught the media's attention at the Olympic trials, and not just by breaking records. She had her own sense of style, and ran her races in brightly colored one-legged body suits.

This media attention continued at the Olympic Games in Seoul, South Korea, where a reporter dubbed her "Flo-Jo." The nickname stuck. Not only were Flo-Jo's outfits outrageous, so were her long, brightly painted nails. She had painted one red, another white, one blue, and a fourth gold to represent her country and the gold medals she planned to win.

Flo-Jo did not disappoint her fans as she took home three gold medals—for the 100-meter sprint, 200-meter sprint, and 4-x-100-meter relay. She was also part of the team that won a silver medal in the 4-x-400-meter relay.

Because Flo-Jo was so fast and muscular, some people accused her of using steroids (special illegal drugs) to build up her body. She denied the charges, noting the weight-lifting training she had done, and she passed every drug test they gave her. Such rumors could not stop Flo-Jo, who had become the World's Fastest Woman.

LIFE EVENTS

1959
Delorez Florence Griffith is born in Los Angeles, California.

1973
Griffith wins first place in the Jesse Owens National Youth Games.

1984
Griffith wins a silver medal at the Olympics in Los Angeles.

1988
Griffith Joyner wins three gold medals at the Olympics in Seoul, South Korea.

1998
Griffith Joyner is named the Associated Press Female Athlete of the Year.

1998
Florence Griffith Joyner dies of heart failure in California.

In 1989, Flo-Jo retired from competition again. In late 1990, she and Al became parents—their daughter, Mary Ruth, was born in November. Along with motherhood, Flo-Jo turned her attention to new projects, which included setting up a foundation to help children from low-income families and serving on President Bill Clinton's Council on Physical Fitness and Sports. She also wrote a book called *Running for Dummies* and created an exercise video entitled *Flo-Jo Workout: The Mind, Body and Spirit*.

An Unexpected End

On September 21, 1998, the world was shocked to learn that Flo-Jo had died in Mission Viejo, California, of a heart seizure. She was only 38. Many people believed that she had been planning to try out for the 2000 Olympics.

During her short career, Florence Griffith Joyner won many awards, including U.S. Olympic Committee Sportswoman of the Year (1988). She was inducted into the U.S. Track and Field Hall of Fame in 1995. ◇

Fannie Lou Hamer
Civil-rights Activist
(born 1917 • died 1977)

During the 1960s and 1970s, Fannie Lou Hamer fought to end political and social discrimination faced by black Americans in the South. When Hamer spoke, people listened, including President Lyndon B. Johnson. Hamer was one of the leading civil-rights activists in the United States.

Picking Cotton

Fannie Lou Townsend was born on October 6, 1917, in Ruleville, Mississippi. She was the youngest of 20 children. When she was six, Fannie Lou joined the rest of the family picking cotton in the fields of a wealthy plantation owner. The Townsends were sharecroppers, which meant that they worked in the fields planting and harvesting crops for the owner of the plantation.

In return for their work, the Townsends were given a percentage of the profits. Although this may seem like a fair arrangement, it was not. The owner

Fannie Lou Hamer speaks to supporters of the Mississippi Freedom Democratic Party in Washington, D.C., September 17, 1965.

charged the family for the seeds they planted and billed them for using tractors and tools. The owner charged whatever price he wanted, and the Townsends had to pay it. Many sharecroppers never got out of debt, no matter how hard they worked.

Fannie Lou went to school, but dropped out in the sixth grade so she could work full time. In 1944, she married a sharecropper named Perry "Pap" Hamer, and the two began working the land, also as share-croppers at the Marlow plantation near Ruleville.

Registering to Vote

In 1962, Fannie Lou Hamer had had enough of sharecropping and wanted to gain some control over her life. She went to a meeting of the Student Nonviolent Coordinating Committee (SNCC) to register to vote. SNCC was an organization of young people who held peaceful protests in support of equal rights for blacks. At that time, citizens of southern states had to pass a test to register to vote. The voter-registration tests were designed to keep poor, uneducated people—especially African Americans—from voting.

Hamer took the test. She failed but was deter-

TOPICAL TIDBIT

Murder in Mississippi

In the summer of 1964, civil rights groups sent college students throughout the south to register African Americans to vote. Many students were bullied and beaten. Near Philadelphia, Mississippi, three students—two white and one black—were murdered, bringing about a federal investigation of the Ku Klux Klan, a white hate group.

mined to vote. She studied and took the test again the following month, but failed again. Hamer told the clerk, "You'll see me every 30 days till I pass." In 1963 she passed the test on her third attempt and became a registered voter.

> "I'm sick and tired of being sick and tired."
> —Fannie Lou Hamer

Getting registered to vote was just the first challenge. Blacks who got that far faced more obstacles, such as threats or even attacks by racist whites. News of Hamer's victory reached the Marlow plantation, and the owner fired her.

Hamer began working with SNCC to help other African Americans pass the voting test. When word got out that an African American woman was helping other blacks register to vote, they arrested Hamer and put her in jail. While there, Hamer was beaten so badly that she could not get up. She sustained permanent damage from that beating.

Challenging the Democrats

Hamer became a freedom fighter, seeking civil rights for all African Americans. In 1964, she helped establish the Mississippi Freedom Democratic Party (MFDP). The MFDP wanted to represent Mississippi's Democrats at the 1964 Democratic National Convention in Atlantic City, New Jersey. The MFDP's members believed that they represented Mississippi better than the all-white delegation from the Democratic Party. Still, the MFDP was not allowed to participate in the presidential nomination process.

An MFDP delegation—64 blacks and 4 whites—went to Atlantic City anyway. When they arrived, they demanded that their members be allowed to replace the official, all-white delegation. They were offered two spots out of the eight given to Mississippi delegates. The MFDP declined, saying that, according to the people of Mississippi, they should have all of the spots.

In a nationally televised speech, Hamer described the unfair treatment of blacks in the south. She talked about voter testing and the brutal beating she had received because she was a black who had registered to vote. Hamer's moving speech got

LIFE EVENTS

1917
Fannie Lou Townsend is born in Ruleville, Mississippi.

1944
Fannie Lou Townsend marries Perry "Pap" Hamer.

1963
After much effort, Fannie Lou Hamer gains her right to vote.

1964
Hamer helps establish the MFDP. She and other delegates travel to Atlantic City, New Jersey, for the Democratic National Convention.

1971
Hamer helps to found the National Women's Political Caucus.

1977
Fannie Lou Hamer dies.

the attention of the American people and of President Johnson. One of the first things Johnson did after the election was to help pass the Voting Rights Act of 1965, and sign it into law. It made it illegal to require voter-registration tests and to deny Americans the right to vote based on the color of their skin.

A Freedom Fighter to the End

Fannie Lou Hamer continued to fight for civil rights until her death on March 14, 1977. In Mississippi she created organizations to help poor African Americans become business owners, land owners, and farmers. She helped establish low-income housing programs, day-care programs, and fought to desegregate schools. She also continued the political fight for blacks and for women, helping establish the National Women's Political Caucus. Fannie Lou Hamer made a huge impact on people—white and black—around the nation. ◇

Dorothy Hamill
Figure Skater
(born 1956)

Dorothy Hamill combined grace and athletic skill in her figure skating routines throughout her career. Crowds first fell in love with her at the winter Olympic Games in 1976. That year, Hamill received the gold medal for women's figure skating. She became America's sweetheart and an American skating legend.

Beginnings of a Legend

Dorothy Stuart Hamill was born on July 26, 1956, in Chicago, Illinois. Her family soon moved to Riverside, Connecticut, where Dorothy grew up.

When she was eight years old, Dorothy went skating with her sister and a neighbor on a nearby frozen pond. She wore her brother's skates, which were too big, so she shoved socks into the toe. She watched other children skate backward and wanted to learn how to do it. So she asked her parents for skating lessons.

Dorothy Hamill leaps during rehearsal.

Dorothy showed a natural talent and love for ice skating. As she improved, her practice schedule got much more demanding. She practiced before school and after school, on weekends, and during vacations. She even lived away from home to train with the best teachers and coaches. Soon, Dorothy was ready to compete.

Winning the Gold

Dorothy Hamill's hard work paid off. She performed well in competitions, including the World Championships in 1974. She won a silver medal at that competition, and another one in 1975.

When Hamill headed to the Olympic Games in Innsbrook, Austria, in 1976, nobody thought that she would win. However, Hamill stunned the audience and judges with her performance and won a gold medal.

When Hamill participated at the Olympics, part of the competition was free-skating, where a skater performed a routine on the ice, like skaters do today. The other part of the competition was called the "compulsory figures." Compulsories required skaters to cut shapes into the ice with the blades of their skates. The more accurate the shapes, the higher the compulsory score. Today's skaters no

TOPICAL TIDBIT

Standing Apart

Because the compulsories are no longer part of ice-skating competition, skaters are finding new ways to get the extra edge they need to win in competition. Often, they invent new moves, or establish a specific style that they can call their own. Dorothy Hamill was known for her beautiful camel spin. She was so good at that spin, in fact, that commentators dubbed it the "Hamill Camel."

longer have to do this. They focus on free-skating. Those who can jump higher and spin faster get the highest scores.

Instant and Lasting Popularity

After the Olympics, Hamill competed in the 1976 World Championships in Götenborg, Sweden. There, she won her second gold medal. Her skating success and her kind, honest personality earned her the name "America's Sweetheart" and made her an instant celebrity. She appeared on television shows and commercials, and girls throughout the country wanted to get their hair cut short in the "wedge" style, just like Hamill's.

> "Every time you go out on the ice, there are slight flaws. You can always think of something you should have done better. These are the things you work on."
> —Dorothy Hamill

Hamill continued skating in various ice-skating shows, such as the Ice Capades and Champions on Ice. In fact, she has continued to participate in such shows into her 40s. For a time, she even owned the Ice Capades and served as its artistic director.

In addition to skating, Hamill spends a lot of time working with charity organizations, such as the

March of Dimes, the American Cancer Society, and the International Special Olympics. Her favorite pastime is hanging out with her daughter, Alexandra.

Talent and Compassion

Dorothy Hamill is a talented athlete and a caring person. She will forever hold a place in the hearts of ice skating fans around the world. Her skill as a figure skater has earned her induction into the Olympic Hall of Fame and the U.S. Figure Skating Hall of Fame. ◇

LIFE EVENTS

1956
Dorothy Stuart Hamill is born in Chicago, Illinois.

1969
Hamill wins the national novice title at the U.S. Figure Skating Championships.

1974 and 1975
Hamill wins the silver medal both years at the World Championships.

1976
Hamill wins the gold medal at the Olympics in Innsbrook, Austria, and the World Championships in Götenborg, Sweden.

1993
Hamill buys the Ice Capades and becomes its artistic director and star.

Lillian Hellman
Playwright and Author
(born 1905 • died 1984)

Lillian Hellman is one of the foremost play-wrights of the 20th century. In her plays, Hellman focused on social injustice and people's complicated relationships with one another. She showed that the selfishness of one person could cause the downfall of many others. Many of Hellman's plays have been made into movies. There have also been plays and movies made about Hellman's life and career. Most recently was *Dash and Lily*, a made-for-cable movie that detailed the 30-year romance between Hellman and famous detective writer Dashiell Hammett.

Becoming a Playwright

Lillian Hellman was born on June 20, 1905, in New Orleans, Louisiana, to Julia and Max Hellman. When she was five years old, Lillian and her family moved to New York City. While she was growing up, Lillian spent half of each year in New

York, and half the year at her aunts' boarding house in Louisiana.

When Hellman was a young woman, she attended college at New York University and Columbia University, but never earned a degree. Instead, she began working as a book reviewer for *The New York*

Herald Tribune in 1925. That same year, she married press agent Arthur Kober. In 1930, Hellman and Kober moved to Hollywood, where Hellman accepted a job reading movie scripts for MGM Studios. While in Hollywood, Hellman started to write plays. It was at this time that Hellman first met novelist and screenwriter Dashiell Hammett. In 1932, Hellman and Kober divorced, and Hellman and Hammett became companions and remained so for the next 30 years.

Success on the Stage and Screen

Hellman's first successful play, *The Children's Hour*, hit the stage in 1934. It is the story of how a troublesome student causes problems for her teachers

---

TOPICAL TIDBIT

Dashiell Hammett's Detectives

During the 1930s, Dashiell Hammett wrote many detective stories. His character Sam Spade was immortalized by Humphrey Bogart in the movie version of *The Maltese Falcon*. Hammett also wrote *The Thin Man*, which chronicled the adventures of husband-and-wife detective team Nick and Nora Charles. *The Thin Man* novel was made into several movies as well as a television series.

by spreading rumors. The play ran for nearly 700 performances. Hellman followed with several other plays—12 in all—including *Toys in the Attic* and *The Little Foxes*.

When Hellman wrote, she used a technique called the "well-made play." A well-made play has a very complex plot, building up suspense until the very end, when everything is wrapped up neatly. The audience was never left

> **"I cannot and will not cut my conscience to fit this year's fashions."**
> —Lillian Hellman

hanging or wondering what had happened. Always thought-provoking, her plays usually dealt with such evils as selfishness and injustice.

Most of the plays that Hellman wrote were made into feature-length films. In addition, Hellman adapted many literary works by other authors into plays for the stage and screen. She also wrote scripts for many movies, including *Dead End* and *Dark Angel*.

Trouble in Hollywood

During the 1950s, some officials in the U.S. government believed that many Americans were turning away from democracy in favor of communism. Some government officials thought that Hollywood was influencing the American people through movies. Many producers, actors, and screenwriters were called to testify before the House Un-American Activities Committee (HUAC) of the U.S. Congress. Hellman was questioned because the government suspected her of being a Communist. Hellman was asked to report the names of any people she knew with ties to the Communist Party, so that the HUAC could question them. Hellman refused to give out names. As a result, she was blacklisted. Her name was put on a list of people who the government wanted to punish by preventing them from getting work. Hellman's plays were not published or performed.

Hellman turned her talents to writing books. She recorded her personal experiences in a multivolume autobiography called *An Unfinished Woman*. She wrote about her years as a

LIFE EVENTS

1905
Lillian Hellman is born in New Orleans, Louisiana.

1934
Hellman's play *The Children's Hour* is first performed.

1941
Hellman wins her first New York Drama Critics' Circle Award for *The Watch on the Rhine*.

1952
Hellman is called before the House Un-American Activities Committee on suspicion of involvement in communist activities.

1969
Hellman publishes *An Unfinished Woman*, an autobiography.

1984
Lillian Hellman dies in Martha's Vineyard, Massachusetts.

child and young adult in New Orleans, New York, and Hollywood. *Pentimento* told the story of her stormy 30-year relationship with Dashiell Hammett; *Scoundrel Time* detailed her experiences with the HUAC and how it felt to be blacklisted.

Critical Acclaim

Lillian Hellman died on June 30, 1984 in Martha's Vineyard, Massachusetts, when she was 79 years old. Over the years, Hellman had received many awards for her work, including the New York Drama Critics' Circle Award for *The Watch on the Rhine* (1941) and again for *Toys in the Attic* (1960). She also received the Gold Medal for drama from the National Institute of Arts and Letters. Many of her works are still performed today. ◇

Audrey Hepburn
Actor and Humanitarian
(born 1929 • died 1993)

A symbol of glamour and grace, Audrey Hepburn dazzled moviegoers with her beautiful clothes, natural grace, and unending charm. She starred in romantic comedies and dramas opposite Hollywood's favorite leading men, including Humphrey Bogart, William Holden, and Gregory Peck. Hepburn also had a heart of gold: She spent many years helping starving children as a goodwill ambassador for UNICEF.

Resisting the Nazis

Edda Kathleen van Heemstra Hepburn-Ruston was born on May 4, 1929, in Brussels, Belgium. She was called Audrey. Her father was an English banker and her mother was a Dutch baroness. Audrey spent her early years in London, England. In 1935, her father left the family.

When World War II broke out in 1939, Audrey's mother thought that the Netherlands would be

Audrey Hepburn poses with her 1953 Oscar for Best Actress in *Roman Holiday*.

safer than England, so she and Audrey moved there. Unfortunately, the Nazis invaded the Netherlands in 1940. Audrey and her mother were not allowed to leave the country, so they made the best of the situation—Audrey attended school and studied ballet.

Life during the war was horrifying. Audrey's uncle and cousins were shipped off to work camps by the Nazis. Audrey wanted to do what she could to help force the Nazis out of the Netherlands. So she raised money for the Dutch Resistance (Dutch citizens fighting the Nazis) by giving secret dance performances. She also delivered messages between members of the Resistance and people in hiding. She tucked the messages into her shoes, so that the Nazis would not find them. As the war raged on, food was in short supply; Audrey ate tulip bulbs to keep from starving. Malnourishment caused her to grow up very thin. In later years, many people believed that Audrey stayed so thin on purpose, but it was a result of her having been starved during the war.

A Star Is Born

When the Nazis were defeated, Audrey Hepburn and her mother returned to England. Hepburn continued to study ballet in the hopes of becoming a dancer. She also took modeling jobs to earn extra money. That led to small acting parts. In 1951, Hepburn appeared in *The Lavender Hill Mob*, a British movie about bungling bank robbers. Later that year, Colette, a famous French playwright, asked Hepburn to take the lead in her new play, *Gigi*, when it opened on Broadway. Hepburn jumped at the chance.

Next came Hepburn's first starring role, in *Roman Holiday*, for which she won the 1953 Academy Award for Best Actress. Without meaning to, Hepburn's character started a fashion trend. In the film, she portrayed a princess who runs away from her royal duties for a day, cuts her hair short, and is seen wearing an oversized man's shirt with the sleeves rolled up. Soon after the movie premiered, women all over the United States cropped their hair and began wearing men's shirts.

> "For attractive lips, speak words of kindness. For lovely eyes, seek out the good in people. . . . For poise, walk with the knowledge that you'll never walk alone."
>
> —Audrey Hepburn

Hepburn continued to act throughout the 1950s and 1960s in such features as *Sabrina*, *My Fair Lady*, and *Breakfast at Tiffany's*. She also appeared in the film version of Lillian Hellman's *The Children's Hour*.

Hepburn was married twice, first to actor Jose Ferrer, then to psychiatrist Andrea Dotti. She had one child from each marriage: Sean Ferrer and Luca Dotti.

Feeding the World's Children

Beginning in the 1970s, Hepburn took on a different role—one she considered the most important of her life. Remembering her difficult childhood during the war, Hepburn devoted much of her time raising money to feed hungry children throughout the world.

In 1988, she became a "goodwill ambassador" for the United Nations Children's Fund (UNICEF), a group that raises money to help feed and clothe children in less developed countries, as well as provide them with medical care and education. Hepburn traveled all over the world promoting this cause. She spent the last several years of her life helping to feed starving children in South America and Africa. Hepburn died of colon cancer on January 20, 1993, in Tolochenaz, Switzerland.

TOPICAL TIDBIT

UNICEF

The United Nations International Children's Emergency Fund, commonly called UNICEF, was established in 1946 to help homeless children in the aftermath of World War II (1939-1945). In 1953, its official name changed to the United Nation's Children's Fund. Today, UNICEF supplies food, clothing, education, and health care to children in more than 130 countries. Donations are accepted from private citizens as well as governments.

Quiet Generosity

Audrey Hepburn's work in films and with UNICEF earned her one Academy Award (for *Roman Holiday*), four other Oscar nominations (for *Sabrina*, 1954; *The Nun's Story*, 1959; *The Children's Hour*, 1961; and *Breakfast at Tiffany's*, 1961) and the Jean Hersholt Humanitarian Award from the Academy of Motion Picture Arts and Sciences. Her kindness, elegance, and style had an impact on American culture 30 years ago, and still do today. ◇

LIFE EVENTS

1929
Audrey Hepburn is born in Brussels, Belgium.

1951
Hepburn plays the lead in the Broadway production of *Gigi*.

1953
Hepburn wins the Academy Award for Best Actress for her starring role in *Roman Holiday*.

1961
Hepburn stars in the highly successful film *Breakfast at Tiffany's*.

1988
Hepburn becomes a goodwill ambassador for UNICEF.

1993
Audrey Hepburn dies of colon cancer in Switzerland.

Billie Holiday
Jazz Singer
(born 1915 • died 1959)

During the 1930s and 1940s, a jazz singer made the world stop and listen to her sing, "I'm feeling so bad, I wish you'd make the music dreamy and sad." The words of the song tell the story of that singer—Billie Holiday—and her music.

Troubled Beginnings

Billie Holiday was born Eleanora Fagan on April 7, 1915, in Baltimore, Maryland. Her parents were Sadie Fagan and Clarence Holiday. Eleanor's father, a guitar player, abandoned Sadie and Eleanora, leaving them in poverty. When Eleanora was six years old, she went to work cleaning floors to help pay the bills. As she scrubbed, she heard recordings of jazz trumpeter Louis Armstrong fill the air. She felt a connection to the music.

When Eleanora was a young girl, she changed her name to Billie Holiday. She and her mother moved to New York. They lived in Harlem—the section where most African Americans in the city lived. In Harlem, a new generation of jazz musicians was on the rise.

Lady Sings the Blues

Billie Holiday wanted to make her career in Harlem as a singer and dancer. One day, when she was a teenager, she was cold, hungry, and sad. She walked up and down 7th Avenue in New York looking for work. Holiday entered the Log Cabin Club and asked for a job as a dancer. The owner, Jerry Preston, told her to dance. She tried a couple of steps, but Preston told her that she was not very good. Holiday then asked for a job as a singer. Preston told her to sing, and

> "She could express more emotion in one chorus than most actresses can in three acts."
>
> —actress Jeanne Moreau on Billie Holiday

Holiday went to the back of the bar where a piano player was practicing. As Holiday sang, her airy voice was so filled with emotion that the people in the bar were moved to tears. Preston gave her a job—as a singer rather than a dancer.

Holiday sang at clubs and bars for the next few years, making a name for herself as a jazz singer. In the early 1930s, she signed a contract with Columbia

Records, which teamed her with Benny Goodman and his orchestra. She also toured with other well-known bandleaders, including Count Basie and Artie Shaw. When she recorded with Lester Young, a famous jazz saxophonist, he gave her the nickname "Lady Day."

For more than a decade, Holiday was at the top of the jazz world. Her hits were sad love songs, including "One for My Baby (and One More for the Road)," "Lover Man," "God Bless the Child," "Say It Isn't So," and "The Man I Love."

A Tragic End

Holiday's personal life became troubled in the 1940s, when she started using drugs and alcohol. In 1947, she was arrested for heroin possession. Although her music was still popular, Holiday was not allowed to perform in New York City because of her police record. She held concerts outside the city limits and continued to record her music.

Over the next 10 years, Holiday was arrested several more times. The reports of Holiday's tragic life only made her music more popular. Her fans believed that they gained insight into her through her sad songs.

TOPICAL TIDBIT

From the Muddy Mississippi

Jazz music got its start along the banks of the Mississippi River—especially in New Orleans, Louisiana—at the turn of the 20th century. Its roots lie in spiritual music sung by slaves in the southern U.S. in the mid-1800s. It is considered to be the truest form of American music.

As Holiday's drug abuse continued, her voice began to fail, making her soft vocals turn low and husky. In 1959, she collapsed and was taken to a hospital in New York. Holiday died of liver failure on July 17, 1959, at the age of 44.

Her Music Lives On

At the height of Billie Holiday's singing career, her soulful jazz could move her audience to tears. Her gift of voice remains popular with many new fans who have discovered her recordings. In 1999, Holiday was inducted into the Rock and Roll Hall of Fame as one of the most influential singers of the 20th century. A statue honoring her memory stands in Baltimore, Maryland. ◇

LIFE EVENTS

1915
Billie Holiday is born Eleanora Fagan in Baltimore, Maryland.

1928
Holiday begins singing in nightclubs in Harlem, New York.

1933
Holiday signs a contract with Columbia Records and records with Benny Goodman and his band.

1944-1950
Holiday's popularity increases and she records her biggest hit, ""Lover Man."

1956
Holiday publishes her autobiography, *Lady Sings the Blues*.

1959
Billie Holiday dies.

Mae Jemison
Doctor, Engineer, Astronaut
(born 1956)

When she was young, Mae Jemison knew that she wanted to go into space. She studied hard and became a doctor, then an engineer. Then, in her 30s, Jemison joined NASA and headed into space, proving to the world that dreams can come true.

Becoming a Scientist

Mae Carol Jemison was born on October 17, 1956, in Decatur, Alabama. She was the youngest of three children and moved to Chicago with her family when she was three years old. During her childhood, she was interested in science, including the study of people (anthropology), the study of civilizations (archaeology), and the study of space (astronomy). Such subjects were often more appealing to boys than girls. But Mae liked science and decided to make it her career.

When Mae was just 16, she began attending Stanford University, studying African American his-

Mae Jemison, at parachute survival school, trained
hard to become NASA's first black, female astronaut.

tory and chemical engineering. After graduation in
1977, she went to medical school at Cornell
University. While studying to become a doctor, Mae
visited several developing nations, including

Thailand and Kenya, offering her medical services to the people who lived there.

Mae Jemison's experiences overseas helped her learn about the different health problems that affect people in developing nations, and what types of medical care are needed. After graduation, Jemison worked as a doctor in Los Angeles, California.

Joining the Peace Corps

Jemison enjoyed being in L.A., but she wanted to do more. In 1983, she joined the Peace Corps and traveled to Africa. The Peace Corps sends volunteers to developing nations to help local communities construct buildings and bridges, and plant and harvest crops. Some Peace Corps volunteers provide medical assistance and teaching services. Others train local residents in various technologies, so that the citizens can improve their living conditions and learn new skills. In turn, the local residents train others and the community helps itself.

> "I believe at the heart of science are the words *I think, I wonder, and I understand.*"
> —Mae Jemison

Jemison worked with the Peace Corps in Sierra Leone and Liberia in western Africa. Serving as a medical officer, she provided health-care services to local people. She also created manuals to help residents learn how to treat common medical problems.

In 1985, she returned to Los Angeles and again worked as a doctor. Her dream to go to space had not died, so Jemison found time to study engineering.

Flying Into Space

In the mid-1980s, Jemison applied to the NASA space program, but her first application was rejected. Although she was discouraged, she did not give up. She applied again and was later selected for the program. Jemison was one of 15 people selected from a pool of 2,000 applicants. When Jemison joined the space program in 1987, she became the first female black astronaut at NASA.

Training for the astronaut program is demanding,

TOPICAL TIDBIT

Stressing Science

Mae Jemison encourages young people, especially girls and African Americans, to take an interest in the sciences. In previous generations, science was considered a boys' subject, and girls were discouraged from studying math, chemistry, physics, biology, and the like. Mae Jemison has shown that females can make significant contributions in the world of science.

and Jemison rose to the challenge. At NASA, she combined her knowledge of medicine and engineering. In September 1992, Jemison again made NASA history when she became the first African American woman to rocket into space. Her dream had come true. Aboard the space shuttle *Endeavor,* Jemison studied gravity's effects on animals and people.

Jemison left NASA in 1993, to pursue other opportunities. She began her own company, called the Jemison Group, which works with new and advanced technologies. It also sponsors the Earth We Share science camp for students.

Jemison also began teaching at Dartmouth College, in Hanover, New Hampshire, and oversees the Jemison Institute there. The Institute assists developing nations with new and advanced technologies. Jemison has appeared on tele-

LIFE EVENTS

1956
Mae Carol Jemison is born in Decatur, Alabama.

1977
Jemison graduates from Stanford University and goes on to study medicine at Cornell University.

1983
Jemison joins the Peace Corps.

1987
Jemison is selected to join the NASA space program.

1992
On the shuttle *Endeavor,* Jemison becomes the first African American woman to travel in space.

1993
Jemison founds the Jemison Group, Inc., a technology company.

vision, in the *World of Wonder* on the Discovery Channel and on an espisode of *Star Trek: The Next Generation*.

Helping Others Fulfill Their Dreams

Jemison charted new territory by becoming the first black woman in space. She continues to share her knowledge with others, and she serves as a role model to women of all races. ◇

Joan of Arc
Military Hero, Martyr, Saint
(born about 1412 • died 1431)

Joan of Arc was a young Catholic woman in 15th-century France who changed the course of history. She claimed to hear voices that told her to lead French soldiers against the invading English army. Joan led her troops to important victories for France and inspired her fellow citizens to rise up against the English. Later, she was murdered for her convictions. Today, she is recognized as a Catholic saint.

Growing up in 15th-century France

Joan was born around 1412 in Domrémy, France. The daughter of peasant farmers, she could neither read nor write. At that time, England and France were Catholic nations. Although each nation had its own king, both looked to the Pope (leader of the Catholic church) to learn God's will. People who disagreed with Catholic practices or had different ideas were called heretics. Heretics were punished, tortured, and killed.

As Joan was growing up, France was at war with England. France's King Charles VI died in 1422, and his eldest son, the Dauphin, wanted to become king. However, England's king, Henry VI, wanted to take the French throne. Some French citizens supported France, others supported England. The war raged on.

271

Heavenly Voices

Joan was a very religious girl. When she was 13 years old, she began hearing voices. Sometimes she saw a great beam of light when they spoke to her. Joan believed that the voices were those of Catholic saints giving her messages from God. When Joan was 16, the voices told her that God wanted her to help the Dauphin become the new king of France.

> "Je suis cy envoyée de par Dieu, le roi du ciel." ("I am sent here by God, the King of Heaven.")
>
> —Joan of Arc, in her first letter to the English, March 22, 1429

Joan wanted to see the Dauphin, but was stopped by his guards. They could not imagine why a young girl thought that she could help the future king. Many people doubted that Joan was being sent by God. Some thought that she was a witch. In 1429, Joan was finally granted access to the Dauphin. She convinced him that she was, indeed, sent by God. He believed her and sent her into battle as the leader of her own soldiers.

Leading her troops into battle in Orléans, France, Joan wore a suit of armor, used a sword, and fought alongside her men. In an astonishing victory, the French drove the English out of the area. Joan became known as the Maid of Orléans. She continued to fight, and win, in other regions of France. Her energy, spirit, and impressive victories helped revive the French cause. No longer did the French feel defeated; they were eager to take back their nation. Joan helped the Dauphin become King Charles VII on July 17, 1429.

Heretic or Saint

Before she knew it, Joan had become a national hero. The English did not like this at all. They were outraged that she was a woman who wore mens' clothes and claimed to be sent by God. The English accused her of practicing witchcraft.

In May 1430, Joan was captured and sold to the English. She was later tried for heresy. Her crime was that she claimed to receive direct communication from God, when Catholics believed that God only communicated directly through the Pope. Joan did not have a lawyer to defend her and was repeatedly

TOPICAL TIDBIT

Condemned for Her Clothes

During Joan's trial, much was made of her wearing men's clothing. In fact, officials even added that to her list of crimes. They said that for a woman to insist on wearing men's clothing was an "act against God."

questioned and threatened with torture. She was found guilty and burned at the stake on May 30, 1431, in Rouen, France, at age 19. Charles VII did not come to her aid.

Saint Joan

About 20 years after Joan's death, Charles VII looked into her case. Several years later, under direction from the Pope, the case was reviewed and Joan was found innocent of all charges. Recognizing that Joan of Arc had died for her beliefs and had never turned her back on her religious convictions, the Catholic church proclaimed her a saint in 1920, nearly 500 years after her death. Joan of Arc is one of history's most famous female martyrs. ◇

LIFE EVENTS

About 1412
Joan is born in Domrémy, France.

1429
Joan meets with the Dauphin of France, who grants her an army. She wins key battles against the English. Following Joan's efforts, the Dauphin becomes Charles VII, king of France.

1430
Joan is captured and sold to the English.

1431
Joan is convicted of being a witch. She is burned at the stake in England.

Mother Jones
(Mary Harris Jones)
Labor Leader
(born 1830 • died 1930)

Mother Jones was a driving force behind the American labor movement. During the late 1800s and early 1900s, there were no laws to protect U.S. workers from unfair and unsafe working conditions. Mother Jones and other leaders of labor-reform movements forced big businesses to treat workers fairly.

> "I abide where there is a fight against wrong."
>
> —Mother Jones

Learning about Unions

Mary Harris was born near Cork, Ireland, on May 1, 1830. When Mary was a young girl, her family moved to Toronto, Canada. Mary went to school and studied to be a teacher.

In 1861, Mary married George Jones. They had four children and lived in Memphis, Tennessee. George was an iron molder who worked in a factory. He worked long hours and received little pay in

return. Also, his work was dangerous and there were no safety guidelines. Sometimes, the owners bullied workers by holding back pay. George and many other workers were unhappy with these conditions. George became a trade-union organizer.

A trade union is a group of people who work in a trade—such as iron molding—and join together to demand certain rights from their bosses. Trade unions talk with business owners on behalf of all the employees, for such benefits as fair pay and a safe work environment.

Along with trade unions were labor reformers.

Labor reformers worked to make conditions in all industries better. Reformers wanted to set the maximum number of hours a person could work in a week, set age requirements for child workers, and establish government-sponsored safety boards.

Mary Jones learned a lot by watching George organize his fellow iron molders. It was a dangerous job: Sometimes workers who talked about forming a union were beaten.

Death and Fire

When Mary was 37, tragedy struck her family. George and their four children died during a yellow fever outbreak in 1867. Not knowing what to do, Mary Jones moved to Chicago, Illinois, and opened a dressmaking shop.

Four years later, tragedy stuck again. On October 8, 1871, fire swept through the streets of Chicago. For three days, the city was ablaze; Chicago's business district and many residential areas burned to the ground. More than 250 people died and 90,000 were left homeless. Jones survived, but she lost her home and business.

"Join the Union, Boys!"

After losing everything in the fire, Jones joined the Knights of Labor, a group dedicated to improving working conditions. Known as "Mother Jones," She became a union organizer, following in her husband's footsteps. Her motto was, "Join the union, boys!"

Mother Jones was bold and determined. She helped organize clothing workers, streetcar workers, steel workers, and the United Mine Workers of America (UMWA).

Sometimes, to get business owners to listen to the needs of the workers, the unions would call for a strike. A strike is when workers stop working in protest. Sometimes the factories would close down. Striking workers often gathered outside the factories to raise awareness about why they were striking. Mother Jones would always join them.

Mother Jones led labor reforms as well. She was one of the founders of the International Workers of the World (IWW). Known as the Wobblies, the IWW had members all over the world. Unions in dozens of countries met with business owners to work out better

TOPICAL TIDBIT

March of the Mill Children

In July 1903, Mother Jones marched with a group of children from Philadelphia, Pennsylvania, to President Teddy Roosevelt's home in Oyster Bay, New York. She organized the march to protest unfair child labor practices. Her efforts brought the issue to the attention of President Roosevelt and the entire nation.

wages and working conditions while workers were on strike.

Sometimes, however, emotions flared during a strike and things got violent. The police would come in and arrest the union organizers, striking workers, and business owners for disturbing the peace. When Mother Jones was 89 years old, she was thrown in jail after she joined striking steel-mill workers.

An Inspiration to All

Mother Jones died on November 30, 1930, in Silver Spring, Maryland, at the age of 100. She had helped improve working conditions around the country. In 1984, she was inducted into the National Women's Hall of Fame. *Mother Jones* magazine, dedicated to promoting social change in the world, was named in her honor. ◇

LIFE EVENTS

1830
Mary Harris is born near Cork, Ireland.

1867
Mary Harris Jones loses her husband and four children to yellow fever.

1898
Jones helps found the Social Democratic Party.

1905
Jones helps found the Industrial Workers of the World to promote labor reforms.

1925
Jones publishes her autobiography.

1930
Mother Jones dies in Silver Spring, Maryland.

Frida Kahlo
Mexican Painter
(born 1907 • died 1954)

Filled with physical pain, Frida Kahlo turned to art to ease her suffering. Although she had critics who thought that her art was too graphic and morbid, she also had many supporters. Kahlo is one of the most famous Mexican painters to date. She continues to be an inspiration to artists, women, and the disabled.

A Life of Pain

According to her birth certificate, Magdalena Carmen Frida Kahlo y Calderón was born in Coyoacán, Mexico, on July 6, 1907. Frida, as she was called, was a mestizo—a mixture of European and Mexican heritages. She spent most of her life in her childhood home, called Casa Azul (Blue House).

Kahlo's life was filled with pain. When she was young, she contracted polio (a disease of the spine), which crippled her right leg. Then, in 1925, she was involved in a serious accident. Kahlo and a friend were riding on a bus that crashed into a streetcar.

Frida Kahlo painted this self portrait in 1929.

Splintered pieces of metal flew everywhere. Parts of an iron handrail pierced Kahlo's stomach, exiting through her hip. Her spine was cut in three places. She also broke several ribs, her collarbone, and one of her legs.

Kahlo had to undergo more than 30 operations to

fix the damage. She was placed in plaster casts from head to toe. The pain that she felt was unbearable. She spent month after month in bed, recovering from the operations and waiting for her crushed bones to heal. The doctors thought that she would never walk again.

Kahlo Turns to Art

While lying in bed, Kahlo began to paint. She taught herself different styles and techniques. She created unusual paintings, showing the pain and suffering she felt. Many of her paintings were self-portraits that showed parts of her internal organs. Other paintings were of women with dead children, women with deformed bodies, and women in emotional turmoil.

> "They thought I was a Surrealist but I wasn't. I never painted dreams. I painted my own reality."
>
> —Frida Kahlo

Some critics did not like the bright colors and subject matter of Kahlo's paintings. They referred to her images as "shocking." They called her a "Surrealist" painter—someone who paints unrealistic, strange dreams. Kahlo disagreed, saying that she just painted what she saw and what she knew from her own experiences.

Life With Diego

In the late 1920s, Kahlo asked Diego Rivera, a well-known artist, to review her work. Rivera found her work striking—full of emotion and feeling. The two became close friends. In 1929, Kahlo and Rivera were married.

Together, they lived in Kahlo's childhood home, Casa Azul. They entertained many famous people, including communist leader Leon Trotsky, composer George Gershwin, and financial wizard Nelson Rockefeller. As the couple's artwork gained success, Kahlo began wearing traditional Mexican clothing, including long flowing skirts and flowers in her hair. The style became her trademark.

Kahlo's first solo art exhibition was held in New York, New York, in 1938. The following year, her work was shown in Paris, France. Not until 1953 was she honored with a show in her native country.

TOPICAL TIDBIT

Diego Rivera

Diego Rivera (1886-1957), a well-known artist, painted large, brightly colored murals (wall paintings) detailing industrial workers on the job. One of his most famous murals is on display at the Detroit Institute of Arts. Painted in 1932, it shows automobile workers making cars on the assembly line.

Kahlo's Legacy

Kahlo died in Coyoacán, Mexico, on July 13, 1954, at the age of 47. The cause of her death is uncertain. She may have died from problems resulting from her earlier injuries.

After Kahlo's death, two books of her personal writings were published—*The Diary of Frida Kahlo* and *The Letters of Frida Kahlo*. Diego Rivera donated Casa Azul to the Mexican people, as a tribute to his wife's life and work. It is now the Frida Kahlo Museum.

Kahlo's work is some of the most sought-after in the Western Hemisphere. In 1995, her painting "Self-Portrait with Monkey and Parrot" sold for $3.2 million. ◇

LIFE EVENTS

1907
Magdelena Carmen Frida Kahlo y Calderón is born in Coyocoán, Mexico.

1925
Frida Kahlo is involved in a serious bus accident that leaves her crippled and in pain.

Late 1920s
Kahlo expresses her pain through painting and shows her work to artist Diego Rivera.

1929
Kahlo and Rivera get married.

1938
Kahlo has her first solo art exhibition in New York City.

1953
Kahlo's work is exhibited for the first time in Mexico.

1954
Frida Kahlo dies.

Helen Keller
Activist for the Disabled
(born 1880 • died 1968)

Unable to see or hear, Helen Keller lived in a world of darkness. She wanted to communicate with others around her, but did not know how. With the help of special teachers, she climbed out of her lonely world and learned to read, write, and speak. Keller showed that a severely

> "Life is either a daring adventure or nothing."
> —Helen Keller

impaired person could overcome the limits of her disabilities. She became a strong supporter of the rights of the disabled.

Trapped in Darkness

When Helen Adams Keller was born on June 27, 1880, in Tuscumbia, Alabama, she could see and hear. When she was 19 months old, however, she got sick (perhaps with scarlet fever). The illness destroyed Helen's vision and hearing. Not knowing how to com-

Annie Sullivan (right) spells out the words of a book into Helen Keller's palm.

municate, Helen often became frustrated as a child. She would throw temper tantrums, kicking and screaming at those around her.

Some people thought that Helen was mentally disabled, too. Her parents knew otherwise. They had seen her try to communicate by touching people's lips and throats as they spoke. Helen could recognize people by touching their faces. She also felt people's hands as they were doing a task, then tried to do it the same way. She had even learned to milk a cow.

Despite her intelligence, Helen was wild. She could not tell people what she liked, disliked, or wanted to do. In her frustration, she would throw and break things, and hurl herself around the house.

When Helen was six, her parents hired a teacher for her. The teacher, Anne Sullivan, had been nearly blind before doctors were able to restore her sight. Sullivan knew the emotional pain of being trapped in darkness.

Amazing Breakthrough

Sullivan's work with Helen Keller was not easy. At first, Keller got angry with Sullivan, even kicked and bit her. Sullivan kept at it, however, and eventually got her pupil to understand sign language. Sullivan would make letters with her fingers that spelled out words. Since Keller could not see the signs, Sullivan spelled the words into the palm of Keller's hands. Keller then created special signs so that she could communicate with her family. She also learned how to read by using braille (patterns of raised dots representing letters).

Keller did not stop there—she learned to speak. She studied with Sarah Fuller, a teacher who helped many deaf people learn to speak. Keller learned to make certain sounds, as well as read lips, by touching a speaker's lips and throat.

A successful student, Keller went on to college. She graduated from Radcliffe College in 1904. Sullivan stayed at Keller's side, spelling out the lessons into her pupil's hands. In fact, Sullivan continued to help Keller until the teacher died in 1936.

Helen Keller's Influence

Keller became a writer, using a special typewriter. She wanted to tell the world what it was like to be blind. She wrote magazine articles as well as books. Her first book was an autobiography called *The Story of My Life*. Keller also spoke on behalf of the American Foundation for the Blind, which helped people with vision problems. With the help of an

TOPICAL TIDBIT

Super Man, Super Human

Actor and director Christopher Reeve, best known for playing Superman in a series of popular films, was paralyzed in a horse-riding accident in 1995. Reeve, who must use a wheelchair to get around and must struggle to speak, became a tireless activist. He works to increase public awareness about physical disabilities. Reeve reminds people that the disabled are capable of making great contributions to the world.

interpreter, she lectured in the United States, Egypt, South Africa, England, and other countries.

During her lifetime, Keller became interested in equality. She supported women's rights and civil rights, and worked to help the disabled. In her day, many disabled people were sent to mental institutions because their families did not know how to help or teach them. Keller showed that, with proper training, the disabled could lead successful lives.

Helen Keller died on June 1, 1968. During her life, she changed the way that people viewed the disabled. Keller continues to be an inspiration to others. In 1973, she was inducted to the National Women's Hall of Fame. She was also named one of the 100 most influential people of the 20th century by *Time* magazine. ◇

LIFE EVENTS

1880
Helen Adams Keller is born in Tuscumbia, Alabama.

1882
Keller contracts a disease—possibly scarlet fever—that leaves her blind and deaf.

1886
The Keller family hires Anne Sullivan to be Helen's teacher.

1903
Keller's auto-biography, *The Story of My Life*, is published.

1904
With the help of Sullivan, Keller graduates from Radcliffe College.

1968
Helen Keller dies.

Billie Jean King
Tennis Champion
(born 1943)

Armed with a tennis racket, Billie Jean King scored a huge victory for female athletes when she defeated male tennis pro Bobby Riggs in 1973. The highly publicized match, dubbed "The Battle of the Sexes," showed the world that female athletes are just as skilled and capable as male athletes. That was just one of many important victories for King throughout her career.

Finding Her Way

Billie Jean Moffitt was born on November 22, 1943, in Long Beach, California. She showed an interest in sports at an early age, and was a talented softball player. Her parents thought that tennis would be a better sport for her because it was more "ladylike." So Billie Jean took up tennis.

Billie Jean had a natural ability in tennis and she had the determination to succeed. In 1961, at 17, Billie Jean competed at Wimbledon in England—one

Billie Jean King goes for a shot during the opening match of the San Francisco tennis tournament in 1974.

of the largest tennis competitions in the world. Billie Jean and her teammate, Karen Hantz, won the doubles championship that year.

In 1965 Billie Jean Moffitt married Larry King.

(They have since divorced.) Billie Jean King kept winning tennis tournaments. In the 1960s and 1970s, she earned 20 Wimbledon titles, in both individual and doubles contests. She also participated in—and won—other major contests, including the U.S. Open, the French Open, and the Australian Open. She became one of the most successful female tennis players the world has ever seen. In 1967, she won the singles, doubles, and mixed doubles titles in the U.S. and at Wimbledon. She was the first woman to do this since Alice Marble in the late 1930s.

> "I think self-awareness is probably the most important thing toward being a champion."
> —Billie Jean King

Paving the Way

King's achievements had a much greater impact on sports than just a showing of athletic skill. King made it acceptable for girls to get more involved in sports. Before then, many girls were discouraged from participating in sports that required a lot of physical effort. Such activities were considered "boyish." King ignored that, however, and led the way for other girls to follow.

King made history in 1971, when she became the

first female athlete to earn more than $100,000 in a single year. Despite her successes, she often spoke out about the inequality between men and women in tennis. Up until this point, female athletes got paid less for winning the same tournaments as male athletes. King urged contest sponsors to offer equal prize money to male and female athletes. When she won the U.S. Open in 1972, she received $15,000 less than the male winner did. As a result, she refused to participate in the contest in 1973 unless the prizes were equal. The sponsors of the U.S. Open honored the request.

Billie Jean King's outspoken demands for equality in tennis came to the attention of player Bobby Riggs, and he challenged her to a match. He claimed that a woman could not beat him, even if he was 55 and she was 29. He admitted that he was a male chauvinist—that is, he truly believed that men are

TOPICAL TIDBIT

Tennis Before Mass

The game of tennis began hundreds of years ago. Historians trace its origins back to monks who played the game in monasteries—the religious centers where they lived, worked, and prayed. Apparently monks enjoyed the game so much that some church officials outlawed tennis at monasteries in 1245.

much more capable than women. He kept on challenging King until she agreed to meet him on the tennis court. Millions of television viewers watched as she proved him wrong in September 1973. In what is probably the most-watched tennis match in history, Billie Jean King beat Bobby Riggs by a score of 6-4, 6-3, 6-3.

No Stopping Billie Jean

King continued to help female tennis players by cofounding the Women's Tennis Association in 1974. She also helped establish World Team Tennis with Larry King, her ex-husband. Her other contributions are numerous, including founding the Women's Sports Foundation and *WomenSports* magazine. She also finds time to work with children who cannot afford to pay for tennis lessons.

LIFE EVENTS

1943
Billie Jean Moffitt is born in Long Beach, California.

1968
Billie Jean King turns professional.

1971
King becomes the first woman in tennis to earn more than $100,00 in a year.

1972
King wins the U.S. Open and refuses to return unless the women's prizes are equal to the men's.

1973
King beats Bobby Riggs in the "Battle of the Sexes" tennis match.

1974
King cofounds the Women's Tennis Association.

King's awards and honors include induction into the International Tennis Hall of Fame and the Women's Sports Hall of Fame. In 1990, she was also inducted into the National Women's Hall of Fame. She was named one of the 100 most important Americans in the 20th century by *Life* magazine, and continues to be involved in tennis as a coach and commentator.

Billie Jean King rose to the top of her profession when she was just a teenager. She worked hard to demonstrate that women athletes are just as talented as men. She opened the door for the many female athletes—in tennis and other sports—who have followed her inspiring example. ◇

Mary Leakey
Paleoanthropologist
(born 1913 • died 1996)

In 1978, Mary Leakey discovered human footprints that dated back more than 3.5 million years. At that time, she was already a noted paleoanthropologist *(PAY-lee-oh-an-thruh-PAHL-uh-jist)*—someone who studies early human life. She and her husband Louis Leakey discovered many fossils of early human and apelike creatures in eastern Africa.

> **"This motion, so intensely human, transcends time."**
> —Mary Leakey describing ancient fossilized footprints

Learning About the Past

Mary Douglas Nicol was born on February 6, 1913, in London, England. Her father was an artist. When Mary was a young girl, her family moved from town to town so that her father could paint. Since they were always on the move, Mary did not go to school. Instead, she learned from her father.

Mary Leakey *(right)* and her assistant hold plaster casts of the 3.5-million-year-old footprints that Leakey found in east Africa.

Mary did not pay much attention to her lessons until she was 11 years old. Then she visited caves in France where early humans had painted the walls. Mary was fascinated. She wanted to learn more about early humans—how they lived, what they ate, what tools they used. When Mary was older, she attended the University of London, taking classes in anthropology (the study of humans) and geology (the study of the earth), although she never graduated.

Mary began her career in anthropology by drawing ancient tools that had been found in England. Her drawings were published. In the 1930s, paleoanthropologist Louis Leakey saw her sketches and asked her to work with him.

In 1936, Mary Nicol and Louis were married. The following year, they moved to Kenya, a country in central Africa. They searched for stone tools used by early humans who had lived in Olduvai Gorge, a dried-up riverbed in Tanzania. Whenever they uncovered a tool, Mary would draw pictures of it while Louis figured out how it was used. They found many sharp stones, which they called "choppers." Used for hunting by ancient peoples, the choppers were made by striking two stones together, breaking off pieces until one stone became very sharp.

The Nutcracker Man

Popular belief at the time was that humans had first evolved in Asia. Louis and Mary Leakey, however, believed that humans evolved in Africa. They spent years there searching for signs of early human life. Often, they put their three children to work.

One morning in 1959, Mary noticed something glistening in the sun. As she bent down for a closer look, she saw that it was a skull. Mary carefully brushed away the dirt. She found and sketched more than 400 fragments, then collected them for further study.

After the Leakeys pieced the fragments together, the skull looked as if it might be human. It was very large, but the brain cavity was very small, unlike that of modern-day humans. Also, its teeth were very big. Mary called it "the Nutcracker Man" because of its large, strong teeth. She thought that it could easily

Olduvai Gorge, where Mary made most of her discoveries, is located in northern Tanzania.

have cracked the shell of a large nut. After further study, Mary and Louis Leakey realized that the skull belonged to an *Australopithicine*—an ancestor of early humans, dating back 1.75 million years. In 1962, Mary and Louis Leakey were awarded the Gold Hubbard Medal—the highest honor given by the National Geographic Society.

Footprints in the Rock

Television crews often recorded the Leakeys' research, spreading news of their discoveries to the rest of the world. The Leakeys received funding for their work from many groups, including the National Geographic Society. Mary, Louis, and their son, Richard, made several more discoveries. Many were featured on documentary programs sponsored by National Geographic.

TOPICAL TIDBIT

National Geographic Society

The National Geographic Society—a scientific group that explores Earth, its lands, oceans, people, and other living creatures—was founded in 1888. Since then, the society has sponsored more than 5,000 projects, including archaeological digs, underwater explorations, and mapping expeditions. The society publishes its findings in books, magazines, and videos.

Louis died in 1972, and Mary and Richard continued their work. In 1978, Mary made a remarkable discovery. While in Laetoli, Tanzania, she found footprints made by prehistoric humans. The footprints were made around 3.5 million years ago. Mary believed this was her most important find. The footprints, which were the oldest to date, showed that early humans walked upright nearly 3.5 million years ago.

Uncovering Our Past

Mary Leakey died on December 9, 1996, in Nairobi, Kenya. Throughout her life, she discovered many fossils that proved the existence of early humans. Her experiences have been recorded in television programs and articles, as well as in two books that she wrote—*Olduvai Gorge: My Search for Early Man* and *Disclosing the Past*. ◇

LIFE EVENTS

1913
Mary Douglas Nicol is born in London, England.

Early 1930s
Mary Nicol draws the finds from archeological digs for publication.

1936
Mary Nicol marries anthropologist Louis Leakey, for whom she was working.

1959
Mary Leakey finds the skull of an early human, which dates back 1.75 million years.

1972
Louis Leakey dies.

1978
Mary Leakey discovers footprints that were likely made by an early human 3.5 million years ago.

1996
Mary Leakey dies.

Annie Leibovitz
Photographer
(born 1949)

Annie Leibovitz is a world-reknowned photographer. She is known for her unique ability to capture the personalities of her subjects—often Hollywood celebrities. Leibovitz's color photographs contain bright and splashy tones. She also shoots in black and white, revealing her subjects through stark contrasts.

The Lens or the Brush?

Anna-Lou Leibovitz was born on October, 2, 1949, in Westbury, Connecticut. Her father was in the military, which meant that they had to move on occasion. As Annie grew up, she set her sights on becoming a painter. She enrolled at the San Francisco Art Institute.

When Leibovitz was about 20 years old, she lived on a kibbutz (farming community) in Israel. At the kibbutz, people lived and worked together, sharing food and other resources. The experience had a profound effect on Leibovitz.

Annie Leibovitz reviews photos of Hillary Clinton.

Leibovitz returned to her studies at the Art Institute and graduated in 1971. But her career plans had changed. She discovered that she loved taking pictures and developing the images in a darkroom. She began work as a freelance photographer even before she graduated.

Amateur photographers take their film to a store, where the pictures are developed by a technician. Professional photographers like Leibovitz, however, develop the negatives and make prints themselves. In the darkroom, they can experiment with the image, cutting out part of the background or adjusting the darkness of the image, for example.

Colorful Career

Leibovitz got her first big break when she sold a photograph to *Rolling Stone* magazine, which is a magazine devoted to the music industry. In 1970, Leibovitz was asked to join the staff of *Rolling Stone*. In 1973, she became its chief photographer.

While working for the magazine, Leibovitz took pictures of some of the most famous musicians in the world, including Bob Dylan, John Lennon, and

TOPICAL TIDBIT

Snapshots of History

American photographer Dorothea Lange (1895-1965) used her talents to record the tragic effects of the Great Depression in the 1930s. Her images of hungry and homeless men, women, and children helped draw the world's attention to the situation. This type of work is called documentary photography.

Mick Jagger. At first the magazine used black and white photos; it later switched to color. Leibovitz adjusted to the change with much success.

In 1983, Leibovitz left *Rolling Stone* to work for *Vanity Fair* magazine. Her more outrageous photos have stirred up controversy. One of Leibovitz's most famous photos is of actor Demi Moore. Leibovitz photographed a very pregnant Moore in the nude, and *Vanity Fair* put it on the cover. Some people thought that the photo was inappropriate. Many others loved it.

Leibovitz is one of the world's most successful photographers. She is well-known for her portraits of entertainers, athletes, politicians, and everyday people. On some assignments, she has spent several days with a subject in order to discover his or her unique personality, which she brings out in the photos she takes.

"The more I look at the work, the more I realize that one of the stereotypes I see it breaking is the idea of aging and older women not being beautiful. It's not true."

—Annie Leibovitz on her book of women's portraits, entitled *Women*

Focus on Women

In 1999, Leibovitz was praised for her book *Women*. The book features photographs of about 170 women in the United States. Leibovitz shows subjects from all walks of life, including artists, actors, showgirls, athletes, journalists, doctors, gang members, astronauts, politicians, singers, writers, models, miners, farmers, business people, military personnel, and abused women.

Leibovitz said that it was a difficult project because choosing which women to include was like trying to photograph the ocean—it is so large that there are endless possibilities.

Making Her Mark

Leibovitz's pictures have been included in books, magazines, and in print ads for companies such as the Gap, Honda, and American Express. In addition to all this, Leibovitz's work has also been displayed in museum exhibitions around the world.

LIFE EVENTS

1949
Anna-Lou Leibovitz is born in Connecticut.

1970
Leibovitz becomes a photographer for *Rolling Stone* magazine.

1971
Leibovitz graduates from the San Francisco Art Institute.

1983
Leibovitz begins to work at *Vanity Fair* magazine.

1991
Leibovitz's work is shown at the National Portrait Gallery in Washington, D.C.

1999
Leibovitz releases *Women*, a book of portraits of women—famous and not—from across the country.

Annie Leibovitz has helped define portrait photography in the late 20th century. Her images have set the standard for other photographers. She made history in 1991, when her pictures were displayed in an exhibition at the National Portrait Gallery in Washington, D.C. It was only the second time the facility had devoted an exhibition to the work of a living photographer. ◇

Maya Lin
Architect, Artist
(born 1959)

When she was just a 21-year-old Yale university student, Maya Lin entered a national contest to design a memorial for veterans of the Vietnam War. Lin's design beat out more than 1,400 other designs, including those submitted by professional artists and architects. Since then, Maya Lin has designed houses, sculptures, and other memorials. She is among the most successful artists today.

Combining Art and Architecture
Born October 5, 1959, in Athens, Ohio, Maya is the daughter of Henry H. and Julia Lin. Her parents fled from communist China in 1948 to seek freedom in the United States.

Although Maya is of Chinese descent, her parents encouraged her to live an American lifestyle. Both of her parents were professors at the University of Ohio. Her father taught art, her mother taught

literature. Both taught Maya to appreciate nature, art, and books.

Maya, who was a very bright child, went on to pursue architecture at Yale University. She also studied sculpture. To her, it was natural to combine those two fields of study. While at Yale, she took a course in funeral architecture, and her professor encouraged the class to enter a national competition to design a memorial that would honor U.S. veterans of the Vietnam War.

Vietnam

In 1961, the U.S. became involved in a civil war between North and South Vietnam in southeast Asia. The U.S. supported the South Vietnamese, who were trying to prevent the communist North Vietnamese from taking control. The involvement of the U.S. in the war bitterly divided Americans. Thousands of young Americans lost their lives in what many Americans saw as another country's problem. Many people held protest marches and rallies. Yet many other Americans supported the war effort. The war lasted until 1975, and 58,000 Americans were killed.

TOPICAL TIDBIT

Impressions of the Wall

People are often overwhelmed when they visit the enormous wall and see the seemingly endless list of names. Names are still being added today as more facts are uncovered. Some people leave items at the Wall, such as photos, flowers, and flags, to honor the memory of their loved ones.

When the soldiers returned from the war, many were treated harshly. It seemed that the American people blamed the soldiers for losing the war.

Over the years, a growing number of people realized that Vietnam veterans had been treated unfairly. In 1980, a committee was assembled to plan the building of a memorial to those who had died in Vietnam or remained missing in action. The committee held a competition to choose the design for the memorial.

"The Wall"

Twenty-one-year-old Maya Lin went to Washington, D.C., to see the site of the memorial. She picked her theme—one that incorporated the natural landscape of the area. Her proposal featured two long walls of polished black granite, in a V-shape, on which the names of the nearly 58,000 men and women killed in Vietnam would be carved. The wall would consist of 150 panels, each 40 inches wide. Each panel would

> "Some people wanted me to put the names in alphabetical order.
> I wanted them in chronological order so that a veteran could find his time within the panel. It's like a thread of life."
>
> —Maya Lin, on the Vietnam Veterans Memorial

have lines and lines of names.

Lin was one of more than 1,400 people to submit designs to the competition. Coming up with the right design was a challenge because the Vietnam War had so divided the country. During the judging, the contestants' names were withheld so that no committee member would know the identity of the artist until after they had voted. Lin's design was chosen by all the judges. Many were amazed to find out that the winner was a young, female student of Asian descent.

The Controversy

Some veterans and politicians did not like Lin's design because it was different. It did not contain the more traditional elements of a memorial, such as statues of men in uniform. Some critics called it a "scar in the earth." They

LIFE EVENTS

1959
Maya Lin is born in Athens, Ohio.

1981
A committee in Washington, D.C., chooses Lin's design for the Vietnam Veterans Memorial. Lin graduates from Yale University.

1982
The Vietnam Veterans Memorial opens.

1986
Lin gets her master's degree in architecture and opens her own design studio.

1989
Lin designs the Civil Rights Memorial in Montgomery, Alabama.

1993
Lin designs the Women's Table at Yale University.

criticized the judges for picking a design drawn by a woman. Others objected to Lin's youth and Asian heritage.

Lin refused to alter her vision, and the Vietnam Veterans Memorial—sometimes called the Wall—was built in 1982. To calm protesters, two more monuments, one featuring men and another featuring women, were placed near the Wall. Regardless of the controversy, people were deeply moved by the Wall. The impressive monument is now the most visited memorial in the country.

Carving out a Place for History

Lin went on to get a master's degree and open her own design studio. She has designed more monuments, including a civil-rights memorial in Montgomery, Alabama. The Civil Rights Memorial features water pouring over a granite table listing the names of people killed during the civil-rights movement. It includes a quote by Dr. Martin Luther King Jr.

Lin has also designed a women's monument at Yale University, the Langston Hughes Library in Tennessee, houses, sculpture, and furniture. She continues to combine her love of art and architecture in new and different ways. ◇

Belva Lockwood
Lawyer and Women's Rights Activist
(born 1830 • died 1917)

Women have been fighting for basic rights in the United States since the 1840s. Susan B. Anthony and Elizabeth Cady Stanton led the crusade for women's right to vote. Others paved the way for women to enter professions dominated by men. Belva Lockwood was the first female lawyer allowed to try a case before the U.S. Supreme Court. She helped open the legal profession to women.

The Road to Washington

Belva Ann Bennett was born in Royalton, New York, on October 24, 1830. She grew up on a farm and attended a country school in Niagara County, New York. Belva, who was was very intelligent, finished school early. She began teaching when she was just 15 years old.

In addition to teaching, Belva continued her studies

and graduated from Genesee College (now called Syracuse University) in 1857. After meeting Susan B. Anthony—one of the leaders of the women's suffrage movement—Belva realized how important it was for women to have equal rights to men's in the eyes of the law. The more she fought for women's rights, the more she wanted to study law.

Practicing Law

In 1866, Belva moved to Washington, D.C., where she opened a private school. In 1868, she married Ezekiel Lockwood, a minister and dentist. He helped run the school so that Belva could study law.

Belva Lockwood, now in her 40s, applied to some of the best law schools in the country. At first, she was refused because she was a woman. She kept trying, however, and was finally accepted into the law program at National University Law School in Washington. She earned her degree in 1873, then was admitted to the bar in the District of Columbia. At that time, however, the U.S. Supreme Court would not let her try cases because of "custom"—the Court recognized only men as lawyers.

> "The general effect of attempting things beyond us, even though we fail, is to enlarge and liberalize the mind."
>
> —Belva Lockwood

Lockwood was outraged that the U.S. legal system discriminated against women. She also was concerned by the economic status of women, who were not allowed to own businesses or run households on their own. They needed their husbands' permission to make transactions in real estate and finance. Business matters had to be conducted in the courts, yet women were not allowed to be part of the legal system. Lockwood thought that this was unjust, so she took it upon herself to change it.

First, Lockwood drafted a bill that required the U.S. government to pay female employees the same salaries as men who performed similar jobs. The bill passed in 1872. Next, Lockwood submitted a bill to Congress that would grant women the right to practice law before the U.S. Supreme Court. She spent five years lobbying for support. Eventually, the bill was passed. In 1879, Lockwood became the first woman allowed to try cases before the U.S. Supreme Court.

The Crusade for Women's Rights

Lockwood then turned her talents to woman's suffrage. Women had been demanding the right to vote since the 1840s, but each time a bill was submitted to Congress, it failed. Hoping to correct this situation,

TOPICAL TIDBIT

Married Women's Property Acts

Ellen S. Mussey and Belva Lockwood pushed a series of bills through Congress granting women the right to own and profit from businesses. They argued that women made business decisions while their husbands were away, so the government should not keep women from profiting from the decisions they made. The bills were passed into law, known as the Married Women's Property Acts, beginning in 1839.

Lockwood ran for president of the U.S. in 1884. She received more than 4,000 votes, but Grover Cleveland won with more than 4 million votes.

In 1903, Lockwood wrote amendments to the state constitutions of Arizona, Oklahoma, and New Mexico. These amendments gave women the right to vote in those states.

Fighting until the end, Lockwood died on May 19, 1917. Just three years later, in August 1920, the 19th Amendment to the U.S. Constitution was passed. It granted women the right to vote on a national level.

A Champion of the Law

Belva Lockwood is known as a champion of women's rights, especially in the legal system. She helped make it possible for women to have careers in law. in 1983, Lockwood was inducted into the National Women's Hall of Fame. ◇

LIFE EVENTS

1830
Belva Ann Bennett is born in Royalton, New York.

1872
Belva Lockwood writes a bill requiring equal salaries for men and women doing the same work.

1873
Lockwood gets her law degree.

1879
Lockwood becomes the first woman to try a case in front of the U.S. Supreme Court.

1884
Lockwood unsuccessfully runs for president.

1917
Lockwood dies.

1920
The 19th Amendment is passed, giving U.S. women the right to vote.

Dolley Madison
First Lady
(born 1768 • died 1849)

After the United States won its independence from Great Britain, Dolley Madison was there to help shape the new nation. As the wife of the fourth president of the U.S., Dolley entertained international politicians with her charm and hospitality. She is regarded as the first "First Lady."

Hello, Dolley!

Dolley Payne was born in New Garden, North Carolina, on May 20, 1768. She spent most of her childhood on her family's plantation in Hanover County, Virginia. Dolley's father owned slaves, who planted and harvested the crops.

Dolley's family was Quaker, believing that people should be kind to one another. Owning slaves was against Quaker beliefs, so Dolley's father sold the plantation and freed his slaves in 1783. The Payne family moved to Philadelphia when Dolley was 15.

While in Philadelphia, Dolley met a lawyer named

John Todd. They were married in 1790 and had two children—Payne and William. In 1793, tragedy struck when yellow fever claimed the lives of John and William. Although Dolley caught the fever as well, she managed to fight it off. She and Payne were spared.

Dolley and the Presidents

A year later, Dolley was introduced to James Madison, a member of the U.S. Congress. The two fell in love and were married in 1794. They moved to Madison's home, called Montpelier, in Virginia, where they raised Dolley's son together.

In 1801, President Thomas Jefferson appointed James Madison as Secretary of State. The Madisons packed up their belongings and moved to Washington, D.C., the nation's capital. Since President Jefferson's wife had died years earlier, Jefferson relied on Dolley to entertain the ladies of society. She held parties for the wives of U.S. cabinet members. She also led tours of women through the House of Representatives, so that women could learn about American government. Dolley became known as the hostess of Washington.

> "And now, dear sister, I must leave this house, or the retreating army will make me a prisoner in it, by filling up the road I am directed to take."
>
> —Dolley Madison, writing to her sister about the British attack on Washington in 1814

In 1809, James Madison was elected the fourth president of the United States. Dolley continued her role as hostess, inviting all of Washington to the first inaugural ball, held on the eve of her husband's swearing-in ceremony.

Dolley had a natural gift for entertaining. Dressed in gowns that were designed in Paris and turban headdresses with foot-long feathers, Dolley welcomed foreign officials and politicians to the White House. She offered public receptions on Wednesday evenings, encouraging everyone in Washington to attend—young and old, rich and poor. She treated everyone as if he or she were a friend.

Washington Burns

During Madison's presidency, the War of 1812 broke out. Although the colonists won the American Revolution years before, Great Britain refused to give up its remaining colonies in Canada. There, they had established trade routes along the Great

TOPICAL TIDBIT

Dolley Madison Cakes

When Dolley Madison held receptions every Wednesday evening, the White House was filled with laughter, not to mention tables overflowing with food. One of the dessert items—pastries filled with ice cream—became known as Dolley Madison cakes. Today, a brand of cupcakes is named for her.

Lakes. Great Britain attacked the U.S.

The war had been raging for two years when the British reached Washington, D.C., in 1814. They set fire to the whole city. Dolley managed to save many important documents, as well as a famous portrait of first U.S. president George Washington, before she fled the White House. She returned three days later to find that the White House had been burned to the ground. As Dolley Madison rolled up her sleeves and began to clean up the mess, other townspeople joined her.

The Americans won the war while James Madison was still president. When his term of office ended in 1817, James and Dolley moved back to Montpelier. Dolley remained in the spotlight, hosting many parties and entertaining guests until James's death in 1836. The following year,

LIFE EVENTS

1768
Dolley Payne is born in North Carolina.

1793
Dolley's first husband, John Todd, and one of their sons die of yellow fever.

1794
Dolley marries Congressman James Madison.

1809
Madison is elected president for the first of two terms. Dolley becomes First Lady.

1814
Dolley saves important documents from a burning White House during the War of 1812.

1836
James Madison dies.

1849
Dolley Madison dies.

Dolley moved back to Washington, D.C. She lived across the street from the White House until her death on July 12, 1849.

President Zachary Taylor spoke at Dolley's funeral, calling her the "First Lady"—and that she was. Dolley Madison was the first presidential wife to be so influential, and universally known and loved. ◇

Madonna
Singer, Songwriter, Actor
(born 1958)

Madonna is one of the most successful performers of the 20th century. In seven years, from 1984 to 1991, Madonna topped the music charts 21 times and sold more than 70 million albums. Since then, she has turned her talents into one of the most profitable businesses in the entertainment industry. Madonna has become one of the few women to achieve such a high level of power and success in the male-dominated music industry.

A Rising Star

Madonna Louise Veronica Ciccone was born on August 16, 1958, in Bay City, Michigan. Madonna's first love was dance. She received a scholarship to the University of Michigan to study dance. In the late 1970s, Madonna moved to New York City to study ballet. While in New York, however, Madonna kicked off her ballet slippers and joined the Alvin Ailey

Madonna sings at a concert, February 24, 1998.

American Dance Theater, one of the premier dance groups in the city. Later, she hooked up with the Patrick Hernandez Revue and traveled to Paris, France, performing disco numbers.

Madonna also liked to sing and wanted to be a rock star. After returning to New York City, she started a band, called Breakfast Club, with Dan Gilroy, her boyfriend at the time. Madonna played the drums and later became the group's lead vocalist. After a while, she left Breakfast Club to form a new band called Emmy, this time with a different boyfriend, Stephen Bray.

An executive at Sire Records heard Madonna sing, and signed her to a solo recording contract. In 1983, her first album, *Madonna*, was released and received good reviews from critics. In 1984, with the release of the song "Borderline," Madonna was on her way to stardom. She had 17 hits in a row, including "Crazy for You" and "Like a Virgin," which remained a number-one hit for six weeks.

> "I stand for freedom of expression, doing what you believe in, and going after your dreams."
>
> —Madonna

The Madonna Image

While her songs were climbing the charts, Madonna expanded her career and acted in the 1985 movie *Desperately Seeking Susan*. Later that year, she married actor Sean Penn and became the focus of intense media scrutiny. Girls around the world were copying her rebellious image, and would continue to do so for years to come.

In the next five years, Madonna released three more successful albums, starred in two movies that were box-office disasters, and divorced Sean Penn. In 1989, *Like a Prayer* was released; it is still one of Madonna's best-selling albums. The video for the title song sparked controversy because of its religious symbolism.

In 1990, Madonna embarked on her hugely successful Blonde Ambition Tour, in which she sang and danced in lavish costumes for audiences around the world. That same year, she acted in *Dick Tracy*, her first box-office success since *Desperately Seeking Susan*. More hit albums followed, and her bad-girl image seemed to soften after her appearance in the movie *A League of Their Own*.

In 1995, Madonna released *Something to Remember*, a compilation of love songs geared to a more mature audience. The release of this album coincided with Madonna's lobbying for the role of Eva Perón in the movie version of *Evita*. When

TOPICAL TIDBIT

The Other Madonna

As a pop star, Madonna has influenced fashion and music trends since 1984. However, her work behind the scenes may be more influential. She writes and produces her own music, which is something many singers do not do. She has collaborated with other musical innovators, such as Björk and Lenny Kravitz.

Madonna landed the role, she threw all her energy into the project. Although the movie was only a moderate success, Madonna's performance earned her the 1996 Golden Globe Award for Best Actress.

Soon after the film opened, Madonna gave birth to a daughter, Lourdes Maria Ciccone León.

Now a devoted mother, Madonna did not release another album until 1998. *Ray of Light* was yet another departure for the star, as it incorporated electronic and techno music. Critics and fans loved it.

The year 2000 was an exciting one for Madonna. In August, she gave birth to a son, Rocco, and by November was back onstage. She also released her thirteenth album, *Music*, and married British movie director and producer Guy Ritchie.

LIFE EVENTS

1958
Madonna Ciccone is born in Bay City, Michigan.

1983
Madonna releases her first album, *Madonna*.

1985
Madonna stars in *Desperately Seeking Susan* and marries Sean Penn. They divorce four years later.

1992
Madonna appears in *A League of Their Own*.

1996
Madonna wins a Golden Globe for her work in *Evita* and gives birth to a daughter, Lourdes.

2000
Madonna gives birth to Rocco Ritchie and marries Rocco's father, Guy Ritchie.

Not Just a Singing Star

Throughout her career, Madonna has successfully reinvented herself a number of times. She has earned the respect of her colleagues by proving that she is not just a passing fad. Not only does she sing, dance, and write songs, she also owns the production company Maverick Records, which produces albums for other recording artists as well. No other female pop star has had such a widespread influence on the music industry.

Despite controversy and criticism, Madonna always stays true to what she believes in. She also takes very good care of herself and, unlike other pop stars, doesn't drink or use drugs. Although she has been criticized by some people for lacking singing and acting talent, many others agree that she is a gifted songwriter, insightful innovator, and shrewd businesswoman. ◇

Margaret Mead
Anthropologist
(born 1901 • died 1978)

Margaret Mead was a pioneer in the field of anthropology (the study of people and their cultures). Anthropology first came on the scene in the early 1900s as people began to travel farther from home. As they traveled, they encountered new cultures—some similar to theirs, some very different. Margaret Mead dedicated her life to learning about new peoples and then using her wisdom to educate the world.

> "Never doubt that a small group of thoughtful, committed citizens can change the world."
>
> —Margaret Mead

A New Scientist

Margaret Mead was born on December 16, 1901. She was the first baby born in the newly opened West Park Hospital in Philadelphia, Pennsylvania.

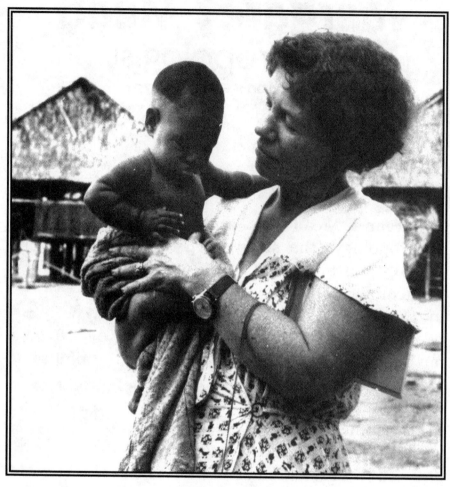

Margaret Mead holds a baby of the Manus Tribe, in Papua New Guinea, 1954.

Margaret was the daughter of Edward, a college professor, and Emily, a women's rights activist. The Mead family moved quite often between Pennsylvania, New York, and New Jersey. At times, Margaret went to school; other times, she learned at home.

Margaret went on to Barnard College in New York, and then received her doctorate degree from Columbia University. It was at Barnard that she developed her passion for anthropology.

Studying the Pacific Islanders

In 1925, at just 23 years old, Margaret Mead traveled 2,500 miles to American Samoa, a remote island in the South Pacific Ocean. She went there to study the culture of the Samoan people, who lived quite primitively. They hunted for food, had no electricity or running water, and were unaware of the technological changes going on outside their island nation.

In Samoa, Mead focused on adolescent girls going through puberty. She recognized that the girls in Samoa went through a difficult time in their early teens, just like girls in the U.S. Mead was fascinated to observe that young Samoan women struggled to find their place in society just as young women in America did—despite the vast differences in the two cultures.

A few years later, Mead traveled to the nearby nation of Papua New Guinea. There she further studied the impact that gender had on a person's place in society. She noted how young people can be shaped by the society in which they live. For example, treating girls as inferior is not something that children do automatically. The society in which the children live teaches them how to treat the people around them.

Mead observed this fact firsthand. She studied three different local cultures and observed that, in one group, men and women were equals. They hunted for food together and raised children together.

In another group, males were clearly the superior group. From birth, boys were taught to be aggressive and act superior to girls. It went so far as infanticide—unwanted baby girls were sometimes left to die.

In the third group, women were more aggressive than men. The men raised the children and took care of the household duties, while the women went in search of food.

TOPICAL TIDBIT

American Museum of Natural History

The American Museum of Natural History houses one of the world's finest collections of plants, animals, and fossils. Located in New York City, the museum was founded in 1869. It was one of the first museums to include exhibits on native cultures throughout the world—an effort largely pushed by Margaret Mead.

Mead compiled her observations into many books, including *Coming of Age in Samoa* and *Growing Up in New Guinea.*

Mead's Influence on Anthropology

In 1926, Mead took a job as an assistant curator at the American Museum of Natural History in New York City. Mead established herself as a driving force in the field of anthropology. By 1964, she was a curator at the museum and headed the division on race and culture. She established the museum's Hall of Pacific Peoples and contributed most of the artifacts on display. That exhibit would not exist if it not for Margaret Mead.

Throughout her career, Mead taught at colleges and universities. In 1973, she was elected president of the

LIFE EVENTS

1901
Margaret Mead is born in Philadelphia, Pennsylvania.

1925
Mead travels to American Samoa.

1926
Mead becomes an assistant curator at the American Museum of Natural History in New York.

1929
Mead travels to Papua New Guinea.

1964
Mead becomes a curator at the museum.

1973
Mead is named president of the American Association for the Advancement of Science.

1978
Margaret Mead dies.

American Association for the Advancement of Science. Mead was also very outspoken on women's rights issues, as well as such topics as nuclear war, drug abuse, and world hunger.

In 1976, Margaret Mead was inducted into the National Women's Hall of Fame. She died on November 15, 1978, in New York City. After her death, she was awarded the Presidential Medal of Freedom, one of the highest honors given in the United States. Mead's work in the field of anthropology will leave a lasting impression on anyone interested in other cultures. ◇

Catherine de Médicis
Queen of France
(born 1519 • died 1589)

Catherine de Médicis was queen of France between 1547 and 1559. When her sons became kings, she guided them and taught them to rule fairly. In a country torn by civil war, Catherine tried to bring peace to the French people, allowing them to pursue religious freedom.

The Queen Is Crowned

On April 13, 1519, in Florence, Italy, Catherine de Médicis was born into royalty. Catherine's mother was a princess and her father was a duke. Her uncle was Pope Clement VII—leader of the Roman Catholic Church.

Catherine's mother died while giving birth to her. Within several days, Catherine's father died as well. Baby Catherine was sent to live at a convent to be raised by nuns. In 1533, when Catherine was a

young girl, she learned that she was to be married to Henry, Duke of Orléans, who was to be the next king of France.

Catherine was amazed by all of the fuss about her marriage. A sum of 100,000 ducats (pieces of gold) was to be her wedding gift to her new husband. The wedding feast was scheduled to last 34 days. All of this made Catherine a little scared. She was only 14 years old and under five feet tall. She wanted to dazzle the French royalty, so she hired Italian dressmakers and shoemakers to create a new wardrobe for her. Catherine left for her wedding with jeweled gowns, furs, and high-heeled shoes. The shoes were designed especially to make Catherine look taller—never before had women worn high heels.

In 1547 Henry and Catherine were crowned king and queen of France, in a grand ceremony.

Religious Wars

During Henry's reign, France was in the middle of a civil war. Although many French people were Catholic, many others were Protestant. Each religious group wanted more power than the other in the French government. To make matters more complicated, the Catholic Church wanted all of France to be Catholic.

Henry supported the Catholics of France. During his reign, he did more and more to punish the Protestants. However, he also believed that all religious groups—Catholic or Protestant—should stay out of politics entirely.

> "I will do my best to hand [the kingdom] over to you entire and at peace so that you should not have to work for your greatness."
>
> —Catherine de Médicis, to her son, Henry III

During Henry's lifetime, Catherine had little power. Henry died in 1559 and their eldest son, Francis II, was king for a short time. In 1560, Catherine's second son, Charles IX, became king and appointed Catherine as regent (someone who will rule in the absence of the king). She was one of his closest advisers.

In 1560, Catherine issued an order of tolerance. This was to allow people to practice the religion of their choice, as long as they remained loyal to France. This restored peace for a while, but soon the country was at war again, as the different religious groups struggled for power. One of the greatest tragedies of the religious wars resulted in the deaths of thousands of Protestants. Called the Massacre of St. Bartholomew's Day, the revolt of Catholics against the Protestants took place in Paris in 1572. Catherine was blamed for the attack. The civil wars continued long after Catherine's death on January 5, 1589, in Blois, France.

TOPICAL TIDBIT

Important Heritage

Catherine de Médicis was the daughter of Lorenzo de' Medici, Duke of Urbino. Lorenzo, a patron of the arts, was instrumental in the career of Michelangelo (the world-famous painter and sculptor). Michelangelo immortalized Lorenzo de' Medici by creating a sculpture to adorn his tomb in the Church of San Lorenzo in Florence, Italy.

Catherine's Influence on the French

Italian-born Catherine had a tremendous influence on French culture. She hired Italian artists and musicians to teach the French new dances, and Italian cooks to instruct people about new dishes, such as cream puffs and cakes with icing.

Catherine also built several new palaces and buildings while she was queen. She designed the buildings herself, giving detailed maps and drawings to the architects. Catherine created the gardens and gallery at the Chateau de Chenonceaux. The gallery was built on a bridge that spanned a river near the palace. Catherine also commissioned the building of the Palais des Tuileries—an addition to the Louvre palace in Paris. Today, the Louvre and Tuileries are world-famous museums.

LIFE EVENTS

1519
Catherine de Médicis is born in Florence, Italy.

1533
Catherine marries Henry, Duke of Orléans

1547
Catherine becomes queen of France and Henry becomes Henry II, king of France.

1559
Henry dies.

1560
Charles IX becomes king and appoints Catherine regent.

1572
Catherine is blamed for the slaughter of thousands of French Protestants at the Massacre of St. Bartholomew's Day.

1589
Catherine dies.

Catherine de Médicis influenced history in many ways, including the separation of religion and politics. She built several monuments to French culture, such as the Chateau de Chenonceaux and the Tuileries. She was the mother of three kings of France: Francis II, Charles IX, and Henry III. ◇

Golda Meir
Prime Minister of Israel
(born 1898 • died 1978)

Golda Meir (meh-EER) dedicated 45 years of her life to government service, and became one of the first women in history to be elected leader of a nation. As Israel's fourth prime minister—from 1969 to 1974—Golda Meir shaped Israel into an international power.

Seeking a Homeland for the Jews

Goldie Mabovitch was born to Jewish parents on May 3, 1898, in Kiev, Russia (now part of Ukraine). When Goldie was eight years old, her family moved to Milwaukee, Wisconsin. She studied very hard and wanted to become a teacher, although her parents did not approve. Goldie was angry, so she moved to Denver, Colorado, to to live with her sister.

Eventually, Goldie's parents warmed to the idea of her teaching, so Goldie moved back to Wisconsin to attend Milwaukee Teachers' Training College. She graduated in 1917, but by that time, Goldie had

changed her mind. She no longer wanted to teach.
She believed that Jewish people should have their
own nation, and wanted to work toward finding a
place that the Jewish people could call their own.

Later that year, Goldie married Morris Myerson. In
1921, the couple moved to Palestine (now Israel) to
live on a kibbutz—a farm owned and operated by

many people. Life on the kibbutz was very hard. Goldie and her husband worked from sunrise to sunset, planting seeds and harvesting crops. They had two children, Sarah and Menachem. In 1924, Morris became ill, and the Myersons moved to the city of Tel Aviv. Goldie took a job with a labor organization called the Histadrut Trade Union. The Histadrut shared her dream of creating a homeland for Jewish people. She traveled throughout Europe and the United States raising money for a Jewish homeland in the Middle East.

Creation of the State of Israel

In 1948, in Palestine, the United Nations created the state of Israel. After 2,000 years of longing for a homeland, Jews finally had a place to call their own. However, many nations bordering Israel were unhappy because they were forced to give up land to the Jews. Since 1948, several nations have gone to

TOPICAL TIDBIT

What's in a Name?

Goldie Mabovitch Myerson changed her name to its Hebrew version, Golda Meir, in 1956, when she became Israel's foreign minister. *Meir* is a Hebrew name that means "to burn brightly."

war with Israel, trying to reclaim lands that are now part of Israel. Today, there is still unrest in the Middle East.

Becoming a World Leader

After the creation of the State of Israel, Goldie Myerson was appointed as one of its first ambassadors. In 1949, she was elected to Israel's government, called the Knesset. During the next 25 years, she held several government positions, including minister of labor and foreign minister. While

> "Those who don't know how to weep with their whole heart, don't know how to laugh either."
> —Golda Meir

in office, she encouraged Jews from all over the world to live in Israel. In 1950 alone, the population of Israel doubled in size.

In 1951, Morris Myerson died. Goldie continued working in the Israeli government. In 1956, she became Israel's foreign minister and changed her name to Golda Meir. In February 1969, she became prime minister. Meir was the world's second female prime minister (Sirimavo Bandaranaike, of Sri Lanka, was the first). Meir believed that peace was the answer to the land disputes that had troubled Israel since its creation in 1948. She tried to work with the leaders of other nations to end the conflict.

On October 6, 1973, Israel was attacked by several neighboring Arab nations. The war lasted only a few weeks, but many Israeli citizens were killed. Although Israel was victorious, many people blamed Meir for not being prepared for such an attack. She resigned as prime minister on April 10, 1974.

While in retirement, Meir wrote her autobiography, called *My Life*, which was published in 1975. She died of leukemia in Jerusalem, Israel, on December 8, 1978.

Golda Meir was one of the first women in history to be elected as the leader of a nation. For her work in creating a homeland for the Jewish people, she received the Freedom of Jerusalem award in 1971, one of Israel's highest honors. ◇

LIFE EVENTS

1898
Goldie Mabovitch is born in Kiev, Russia.

1924
The Myersons move to Tel Aviv, and Goldie works with the Histadrut Trade Union.

1948
The state of Israel is established in Palestine.

1949
Goldie Myerson is elected to the Knesset, the Israeli government.

1956
Goldie Myerson changes her name to Golda Meir.

1969
Meir becomes prime minister of Israel.

1974
Meir resigns as prime minister.

1978
Golda Meir dies.

Edna St. Vincent Millay

Poet and Playwright

(born 1892 • died 1950)

Edna St. Vincent Millay was the first American female poet to receive the Pulitzer Prize. Known mostly for her poetry, Millay also wrote plays and operas, one of which was performed at the Metropolitan Opera in New York City. The opera, called *The King's Henchmen*, was one of the most popular of the 1920s.

Becoming a Poet

Edna St. Vincent Millay was born on February 22, 1892, in Rockland, Maine. Her parents were divorced, and Edna was raised by her mother in Camden, Maine. Edna began writing poetry and stories when she was very young. Her mother thought that the poems were quite good and encouraged her to submit a sample of her writing to *St. Nicholas Magazine*, a magazine that published stories and

poetry written by children. When Edna was 14, her first poem was published in *St. Nicholas*. Several other poems were published in the magazine during the next few years.

In 1912, when Edna was 20, she entered her poem "Renascence" in a writing contest. She won fourth place in the contest and her poem was published in *The Lyric Year*. Literary critics praised "Renascence" (a variation of the word *renaissance,* meaning "rebirth" or "revival"). In fact, Edna had such talent that she was awarded a scholarship to attend Vassar College.

Burning the Candle at Both Ends

After graduating from Vassar in 1917, Edna issued her first book, *Renascence and Other Poems*. She moved to Greenwich Village in New York City with the hope of becoming an actor. To support herself, Edna wrote short stories and poetry for magazines, under the name of Nancy Boyd. She also wrote plays for the Provincetown Players, an acting group.

> "My candle burns at both ends/It will not last the night;/But ah, my foes, and oh, my friends—/It gives a lovely light."
>
> —Edna St. Vincent Millay, from her poem "First Fig"

In the early 1920s, Edna St. Vincent Millay published several poetry collections, including *A Few Figs from Thistles.* In the poem "First Fig," Millay wrote the line, "My candle burns at both ends." Many literary critics used this phrase to refer to Millay's generation—young people during the 1920s who were living life to the fullest, attending parties every night, and never worrying what tomorrow might bring.

Millay published other books of poetry to critical acclaim, such as *Second April* and *Fatal Interview*. In 1923, she published *The Harp-Weaver and Other Poems*, which earned her the Pulitzer Prize for Poetry—one of the highest awards given to writers in the U.S. Later that year, Millay married Eugen Jan Boissevain, a businessman from the Netherlands. They bought a farmhouse in upstate New York and called it Steeletop. They lived there the rest of their lives.

Political Causes

Throughout her life, Millay was involved in many social and political groups. She was a member of the National Women's Party, which fought for equality and women's right to vote. During World War II

TOPICAL TIDBIT

Millay Colony for the Arts

In 1973, Edna's sister, Norma Millay, opened the Millay Colony for the Arts in Austerlitz, New York, in honor of Edna. The colony allows artists, musicians, writers, and poets to leave the outside world behind them for a month or two so that they can focus their time on their craft.

(1939-1945), she wrote patriotic poetry and supported the
war effort.

In 1927, Millay wrote a
poem, "Justice Denied in
Massachusetts," about Nicola
Sacco and Bartolomeo
Vanzetti. Sacco and Vanzetti
had been tried and convicted
for the murder of two men in
Massachusetts. Although the
evidence in the case was
weak, Sacco and Vanzetti
were put to death. Many people, including Millay, thought
that the trial and sentencing
were unfair, possibly because
Sacco and Vanzetti were
Italian immigrants. When
Millay published "Justice
Denied in Massachusetts,"
she donated the money it
earned to help Sacco and
Vanzetti pay their lawyers.

Millay's Legacy

Millay's husband died in
1949. After his death, Millay

LIFE EVENTS

1892
Edna St. Vincent
Millay is born in
Rockland, Maine.

1912
Millay enters her
poem "Renascence"
into a competition.
She wins fourth
prize and
critical acclaim.

1917
Millay graduates
from Vassar College.

1923
Millay becomes the
first female poet to
win a Pulitzer Prize.

1927
Millay publishes the
poem "Justice
Denied in
Massachusetts" in
support of Nicola
Sacco and
Bartolomeo
Vanzetti.

1950
Edna St. Vincent
Millay dies in
Austerlitz, New York.

became very ill. She died a year later of heart failure, on October 9, 1950, in Austerlitz, New York.

Edna St. Vincent Millay was the first female poet to receive the Pulitzer Prize. She was one of the foremost poets of the 20th century and her poetry is read and enjoyed by a wide audience. Steepletop, the house where Millay and her husband lived in Austerlitz, New York, is a National Historic Landmark. ◇

Marilyn Monroe
Actor
(born 1926 • died 1962)

Although she died many years ago, Marilyn Monroe continues to be one of the most famous American actors ever. Her daring outfits and ditzy, funny characters made her a hit with audiences. Monroe, who died young, has become an American legend.

Troubled Beginnings

Norma Jean Mortenson was born on June 1, 1926, in Los Angeles, California. She was abandoned by her father and later took her mother's last name, Baker. Norma Jean's mother suffered from mental illness and was hospitalized, so Norma Jean was placed in foster care and, later, an orphanage.

During World War II (1939-1945), thousands of American women, including Norma Jean Baker, helped the war effort by working in factories. Norma Jean worked in an airplane factory. At age 16, she married a co-worker named James Dougherty.

Around the same time, a U.S. Army photographer asked her to pose for some pictures. Hoping that it would lead to an acting career, Norma Jean agreed.

Following that photo session, Norma Jean began modeling. In 1946, her dream came true when she signed a contract with 20th Century-Fox to make movies. She divorced James Dougherty and changed her name to Marilyn Monroe.

Becoming a Star

At first, times were tough in Hollywood. Monroe found it difficult to find acting work. Eventually, she was cast in a few movies, but she still got little attention.

Then people began to notice Monroe's beauty, innocence, and on-camera appeal. She played up her image, and audiences responded. Fans loved her silly characters, and Hollywood filmmakers realized that if they put Monroe in a movie, thousands of people would flock to the theaters.

> "I don't understand why people aren't a little more generous with each other."
>
> —Marilyn Monroe

Monroe appeared in more than 20 movies in the 1950s, including *Gentlemen Prefer Blondes*, *There's No Business Like Show Business*, and *How to Marry a Millionaire*. She was often cast as a glamorous blonde with more beauty than brains. In 1954, she continued to make headlines when she married—and then divorced—retired New York Yankees star Joe DiMaggio.

Monroe grew tired of critics noticing her charm and beauty, but questioning her acting ability. In 1956, she started taking acting lessons at the Actors' Studio in New York City. That year, she also started her own film production company and married playwright Arthur Miller. Her marriage to Miller lasted only a few years.

Troubled Endings

Monroe made several more films, and proved to audiences that she had talent as a comedic actor. In 1959, she starred in *Some Like It Hot*. Monroe portrayed a member of an all-girl band. Other band members included Tony Curtis and Jack Lemmon, disguised as women. Audiences loved the wacky comedy. *Some Like It Hot* is considered one of Monroe's best movies.

As her career soared, however, Monroe felt more and more alone. In public she appeared happy, but she suffered bouts of depression and started taking prescription drugs, sometimes combining them with alcohol. She would show up late for appointments and then try to joke about it. Some of the people who worked with her thought that she was spoiled, demanding, and unprofessional. She was fired from her last movie because she was late more often than not.

TOPICAL TIDBIT

Candles in the Wind

Singer-songwriter Elton John and lyricist Bernie Taupin paid tribute to Marilyn Monroe with his 1973 song "Candle in the Wind." In 1997, John adapted the song to describe Diana, Princess of Wales. Both women were known and loved throughout the world. Both women died tragically before their time.

Still Burning Bright

On August 5, 1962, at the peak of her fame, Monroe was found dead at her home in Los Angeles. She died of an overdose of sleeping pills. Some people believe that her death was accidental, while others claim that she had been murdered. Monroe was—and still is—mourned by millions of people around the world.

Although she was only 36 when she died, Marilyn Monroe had achieved more popularity during her short career than most actors do in a lifetime. Even today, she is one of the most famous American actors to have appeared on the silver screen. ◇

LIFE EVENTS

1926
Norma Jean Mortenson is born in Los Angeles, California.

1946
Norma Jean becomes Marilyn Monroe and signs a contract with 20th Century Fox.

Early 1950s
Monroe becomes one of the most popular actors in Hollywood.

1954
Monroe marries and divorces Joe DiMaggio.

1956
Monroe marries Arthur Miller. They divorce in 1960.

1959
Monroe stars in *Some Like it Hot*, proving her talent as a comedic actor.

1962
Marilyn Monroe dies.

Maria Montessori
Pioneer in Education
(born 1870 • died 1952)

Maria Montessori was a pioneer in modern education. Her methods and ideas—called the Montessori Method—are still used by educators throughout the world. Both privately owned Montessori schools and public schools use the Montessori Method to help children learn.

Scientist or Teacher?

Maria Montessori was born on August 31, 1870, in Chiaravalle, Italy. As a young girl, she attended a country school. During the late 1800s, girls usually studied to be teachers, or learned skills such as dressmaking. Maria did not want to become a teacher or a dressmaker, she wanted to become a doctor. However, women were discouraged from studying medicine. Many people believed that only men should be doctors. Despite her father's objections, Maria enrolled in the medical program at the University of Rome and graduated in 1894. She was

the first woman to receive a medical degree in Italy.

After she graduated, Maria Montessori worked with mentally retarded children. At first, she helped them as a physician. Later, she taught them how to care for themselves. She designed special activities to help the children with daily activities, such as brushing their hair or making their beds.

She used special tools like beads and blocks to help develop their coordination. Montessori noticed that as the children became self-reliant, they wanted to learn more.

Montessori was more of a scientist than a teacher. She allowed the children to teach themselves while she watched how they reacted. Montessori could see what worked and what did not. She said, "I studied my children, and they taught me how to teach them."

Children's House

In 1907, Montessori was chosen to run schools for poor children in parts of Rome. Called the Casa dei Bambini (Children's House), the schools were meant for young children without disabilities. The first class had nearly 50 children, two to five years old. Montessori used the same teaching style that she

TOPICAL TIDBIT

Open Classrooms

Maria Montessori liked the idea of the "open classroom." While teaching young children, she observed that students learned more quickly when seated on the floor or at tables instead of desks. Today, many schools in the U.S. are designed to include open areas.

had used with the mentally retarded children. The students taught themselves using activities that she designed.

Montessori showed the older children how to help her with the daily chores, such as tidying up. Soon the children were asking for more—they wanted to read and write. They wanted to know about the shape of the world and why things happened. Montessori created teaching tools for geography, science, and math.

"We discovered that education is not something which the teacher does, but that it is a natural process which develops spontaneously in the human being."

—Maria Montessori

The Montessori Method

Montessori's teaching style became known as the Montessori Method. This plan encourages students to be independent. Allowing children to do things that interested them helped them learn more quickly. The children could play with blocks, beads, and puzzles, which helped them develop coordination skills. Doing household chores taught the children to work together as a team. Some of the older children helped teach the younger students.

The program also helped teachers identify the

individual talents of each student. Some children worked better with beads, showing that they were good with their hands. Others showed a special talent for working with other children—in effect, becoming teachers.

A Continuing Influence

Maria Montessori's work in education led to teaching methods that are still used today. By focusing each child's studies on his or her areas of interest, and allowing the children to be independent, Montessori proved that children could learn to read and write at an earlier age.

Before her death on May 6, 1952, Montessori established training programs for teachers in Europe, the U.S., and India. She also wrote several books. She is remembered as a leader in modern education. ◇

LIFE EVENTS

1870
Maria Montessori is born in Chiaravalle, Italy.

1894
Montessori graduates from the University of Rome as the first woman in Italy to earn a medical degree.

1907
Montessori directs a number of schools for young children in Rome. She develops a unique style of teaching that becomes known as the Montessori Method.

1930s and 1940s
Montessori schools open in Europe, the U.S., and India.

1952
Maria Montessori dies.

Toni Morrison
Author, Teacher
(born 1931)

In such novels as *Beloved, Jazz,* and *Song of Solomon*, author Toni Morrison explores issues of race and gender in America. She fills her books with keen observations about the lives that African Americans and women have led in a country filled with racial and gender inequality. Toni has won many writing awards, including the Nobel Prize for Literature.

Growing up in Ohio

Toni Morrison was born Chloe Anthony Wofford on February 18, 1931, in Lorain, Ohio. She was one of four children. Before Chloe was born, her family lived in the South, where racism and discrimination were rampant. It was also the time of the Great Depression, when unemployment and homelessness were high, food was scarce, and the entire nation fell on hard times. The Woffords moved north in search of a better life.

Toni Morrison with a copy of her novel *Beloved,*
when it was first released in 1987.

During this time, many schools in the U.S. were segregated. This meant that white students went to different schools than black students. Chloe, however,
went to a school with both white and black children.

For a time, Chloe was the only black child in her class. At first, she did not feel discrimination toward her. As she got older, however, she saw the ways in which blacks were treated differently.

An Interest in Writing

Early in her life, Chloe showed an interest in reading. She loved novels by Leo Tolstoy, Gustave Flaubert, and Jane Austen. Later, she became interested in writing herself. After graduating from high school, she earned her bachelor's degree at Howard University in Washington, D.C., then received her master's degree from Cornell University in Ithaca, New York. While in college, she shortened her name to Toni (from her middle name, Anthony) because some people had difficulty pronouncing her first name, Chloe (*KLOH-ee*).

> "The purpose of freedom is to free someone else."
> —Toni Morrison

After graduation, Toni began a career as a teacher at Texas Southern University. After that, she joined the faculty of Howard University. There, she met Harold Morrison and the couple married in 1958. They had two sons. However, Toni was unhappy in her married life.

In 1964 the Morrisons divorced, and Toni took her sons back to Ohio. She got a job as an associate editor with Random House publishers and joined a writers' group. She wrote a short story for this group that became the key to her second career.

Finding Fame

In 1967, Random House transferred Morrison to New York, where she became a senior editor. She also took her short story and developed it into a novel, called *The Bluest Eye*. The book was published in 1970 to critical acclaim. *The Bluest Eye* is based on a girl Morrison once knew who had struggled to deal with the image of beauty in America—an image that was usually based on white features and characteristics. Seeking to be beautiful, the black character wants to have blue eyes.

TOPICAL TIDBIT

From Page to Screen

In 1998, actor and talk-show host Oprah Winfrey produced a screen adaptation of Toni Morrison's Pulitzer Prize-winning novel *Beloved*. Winfrey portrays Sethe, a former slave who is haunted by the ghost of her daughter, Beloved.

Toni Morrison receives the 1993 Nobel Prize for Literature, in Stockholm, Sweden.

Morrison followed with more novels, all of which were praised by critics, including *Sula* (1973), *Song of Solomon* (1977), *Tar Baby* (1981), and *Beloved* (1987). Morrison's characters experience and fight discrimination. She writes of prejudice against women and African Americans. In *Beloved*, Morrison tells the story of a slave who escapes, only to be caught and returned to her master. The slave takes desperate measures rather than have her children face a life of slavery.

Morrison's Mark

In 1993, Morrison made history by becoming only the eighth woman—and first black woman—to win the Nobel Prize for Literature. Since then she has published *Jazz* (1992) and *Paradise* (1998).

Morrison also enjoys teaching. She has said that she takes teaching just as seriously as she takes writing. She has held posts at Rutgers University, the State University of New York at Albany, and Princeton University.

Today, Toni Morrison is one of America's most popular and successful writers. A gifted storyteller, she presents characters who struggle to find themselves and maintain their identities in a world full of racial and gender prejudice. Readers recognize the strength and value of her stories. ◇

LIFE EVENTS

1931
Chloe Anthony Wofford is born in Lorain, Ohio.

1953
Toni graduates from Howard University.

1958
While teaching at Howard University, Toni Wofford marries Harold Morrison.

1964
The Morrisons divorce. Toni becomes an editor for Random House.

1988
Toni Morrison's fifth novel, *Beloved*, wins the Pulitzer Prize for fiction.

1993
Morrison becomes the first African American woman to win a Nobel Prize for Literature.

Grandma Moses
(Anna Mary Robertson Moses)
Painter of American Folk Art
(born 1860 • died 1961)

Grandma Moses had her own style of painting. It was simple and captured everyday life in the country. Today, this style is known as American Folk or American Primitive painting. Grandma Moses painted between 1,600 and 1,800 paintings—all after she was 70 years old.

Painting Without Paint

Anna Mary Robertson was born on a farm in Greenwich, New York, on September 7, 1860. As a young girl, she had very little education. She went to school during the summer so that she could help with planting and harvesting crops in the spring and fall. Anna liked to draw pictures. She colored them with berry juice, because she had no paint or crayons. When she was 12, she left home to work as a servant.

An 86-year-old Grandma Moses mixes colors for a painting in 1946.

In November 1887, Anna married Thomas Moses. They bought a farm in the Shenandoah Valley of Virginia. Later, they moved to upstate New York. Anna and Thomas had 10 children.

Anna Becomes a Grandma

After her husband died in 1927, Anna Moses moved to Bennington, Vermont, to live with one of her daughters and two grandchildren. When her daughter died two years later, she was left to raise her grandchildren, who called her Grandma Moses.

To pass the time, Grandma Moses embroidered pictures using yarn instead of thread. This type of embroidery is called crewel work. As Grandma Moses got older, her arthritis made it hard for her to thread needles. She turned to painting instead. At first, she copied prints of country scenes made by well-known artists Currier and Ives. Once she became comfortable painting, she sketched her own scenes, using the landscape around her home as the setting. She displayed her painted works at county fairs, where she also sold homemade jams.

> "Paintin's not important. The important thing is keepin' busy."
>
> —Grandma Moses

In 1939, some of her paintings were hanging in the window of a drug store in Hoosick Falls, New York, where she lived at that time. Louis Caldor, an art collector, saw them there while he was on vacation. He thought that they were remarkable, and should be on display in a gallery. Caldor set out to make it happen. Later that year, three of Grandma Moses's paintings were exhibited in the Museum of Modern Art in New York, New York.

Her first solo show, called "What a Farm Wife

Painted," appeared at the Galerie St. Etienne in New York City in 1940. The art world was impressed by Grandma Moses' paintings of country life. The paintings showed farm work, village feasts, and holidays, as well as landscapes of farm fields, pastures, and streams. Other scenes showed townspeople skating on frozen ponds, hunting, or harvesting crops. She used glitter in white paint to make the snow sparkle in her winter scenes.

Grandma Moses Day

As Grandma Moses got older, her arthritis got worse. She continued to paint, using her left hand only. Some critics said that the figures were not as detailed and the landscapes not as sharp, but people still admired her work. In 1950, a documentary film was made about her life.

TOPICAL TIDBIT

Unsolved Mystery of the Paintings

In 1984, Margaret Carr donated seven paintings by Grandma Moses to the Bennington Museum. The paintings were stolen before they reached their new home. In 1998, nearly 14 years after the paintings disappeared, they arrived back at the museum. The mysterious theft and recovery of the paintings has never been solved.

In 1960, Grandma Moses turned 100 years old. New York governor Nelson A. Rockefeller declared her birthday a holiday, calling it "Grandma Moses Day."

An American Treasure

Grandma Moses died on December 13, 1961, in Hoosick Falls, New York, at the age of 101. She never had an art lesson in her long life. She taught herself how to paint when she was in her 70s. The Bennington Museum in Vermont holds the largest collection of Grandma Moses' paintings. Many of her most famous works, including *Hoosick Falls in Winter*, *Catching the Thanksgiving Turkey*, and *Over the River to Grandma's House*, can be seen on greeting cards today. ◇

LIFE EVENTS

1860
Anna Mary Robertson is born in Greenwich, New York.

1887
Anna marries Thomas Moses.

1927
Thomas dies. Anna moves to Vermont to help care for her grandchildren.

1929
Grandma Moses begins to paint scenes from her life in Vermont.

1939
An art collector discovers Grandma Moses' work.

1940
An exhibit featuring Grandma Moses' paintings opens in New York.

1961
Grandma Moses dies at the age of 101.

Martina Navratilova
Tennis Champion
(born 1956)

Throughout her career, Martina Navratilova has shown skill, determination, and daring. She is one of the greatest female tennis players ever, and is known for her wit and honesty. She has proven her courage in all facets of her life, by leaving her native country, competing against the world's best tennis players, and telling the world that she is gay.

> "Just go out there and do what you've got to do."
> —Martina Navratilova

Tennis in Her Blood

Martina Subertova was born on October 18, 1956, in Prague, Czechoslovakia (now Czech Republic). Her parents soon divorced and Martina's mother remarried. Martina's name was changed from Subertova to Navratilova.

As a child, Martina watched her mother and step-father play tennis. Her grandmother, Agnes

Martina Navratilova defends her title at Wimbledon
in 1979.

Semanska, had competed in tennis matches when she was younger. Four-year-old Martina was given her grandmother's racket and taught how to hit tennis balls against a wall.

Martina was good at tennis, and she enjoyed playing.

She practiced with her stepfather, who was a tough but supportive coach. When Martina was nine, her stepfather took her to Czech tennis champion George Parma, who became her next coach. Parma put Martina in tennis competitions and she won most of them. In 1972, Martina Navratilova was the top-ranking tennis player in Czechoslovakia.

At that time, Czechoslovakia was ruled by a communist government. The government determined what the Czech people could and could not do, including leave the country. The Tennis Federation, which organized tournaments, was controlled by the government as well. In 1973, the government allowed Navratilova to travel to the United States to compete.

Feeling American

Once in the U.S., Navratilova saw, first-hand, what life in a democracy was like. She saw the freedoms that people enjoyed, such as freedom of travel and freedom of speech. Navratilova wanted to compete with the best players all around the world, but she felt that the Czechoslovakian Tennis Federation was stopping her. During this first trip to the U.S., Navratilova says, she "felt like an American." She wanted to play tennis her way, in the competitions she wanted to attend.

When she was 18, Navratilova was again allowed

to compete in the U.S. This time, she did not return to Czechoslovakia. Navratilova defected, staying in the U.S. against the demands of the Czechoslovakian government. This meant that she could not return home as long as the communists were in power. She asked the U.S. government to protect her from being sent back, which it did. She became a U.S. citizen in 1981.

Navratilova had a tough time at first, but she trained hard. Navratilova was one of the first athletes to train for tennis by playing other sports, such as basketball or running. (This practice is called cross-training.) She also worked with a nutritionist to be as healthy as she could. Although most athletes do this now, back then it was rare.

Navratilova soon became the number-one player in America. Her main rival was Chris Evert. The two women played very different styles of tennis,

TOPICAL TIDBIT

An Incredible Record

Over the years, Navratilova won more professional singles titles than any other player, male or female. She was ranked number one in the world seven times, and won nine Wimbledon titles, four U.S. Opens, three Australian Opens, and two French Opens. This makes her one of only a handful of players to win all four of those titles at least once.

but both were exceptional. Despite their fierce competition, they were—and still are—good friends.

Top Player

Navratilova was hard to beat in both singles and doubles competitions. During her career, Navratilova won the Wimbledon tournament title a record nine times. She took home 167 singles titles and 165 doubles titles. She won more than 1,400 matches and earned more than $20 million dollars in her career. In 2000, Navratilova was inducted into the International Tennis Hall of Fame.

It took American tennis fans some time to warm up to Navratilova, especially when, in 1991, she became the first professional athlete to announce that she was gay.

Navratilova's honesty and amazing talent have earned

LIFE EVENTS

1956
Martina Subertova is born in Prague, Czechoslovakia.

1972
At age 16, Navratilova is the top-ranked tennis player in Czechoslovakia.

1974
Navratilova defects to the U.S.

1981
Navratilova becomes a U.S. citizen.

1980s
Navratilova dominates women's tennis.

1991
Navratilova announces that she is gay.

2000
Navratilova is inducted into the International Tennis Hall of Fame.

her worldwide respect and kept her fans entertained for years. She retired from singles play in 1994, but made a comeback in doubles competition in 2000.

Navratilova has done more than play winning tennis. She is an outspoken supporter of gay rights, animal rights, and environmental issues. She has also written several books, both fiction and nonfiction. Her fiction novels are mysteries, featuring a tennis-playing detective. ◇

Nefertiti
Queen of Egypt
(about 1350 B.C.)

Throughout history, some women have been known for their extraordinary beauty. Nefertiti *(nef-ur-TEE-tee)* was one such woman. The word *Nefertiti* means "the beautiful one has come" in the ancient Egyptian language. Nefertiti was more than just a beautiful woman, however—she was queen of Egypt during the 14th century B.C. Ruling beside her husband, the pharaoh Akhenaton *(ahk-NAHT-un)*, Nefertiti brought religious, social, and cultural change to the land of the Nile.

Nefertiti and Akhenaton

Not much is known about Nefertiti and Akhenaton. Many historians believe that Nefertiti was born of royalty, but they are uncertain of her heritage. Some believe that she was a princess from the province of Mitanni, north of Egypt. Others think that she may have been Akhenaton's sister.

Akhenaton ruled Egypt from about 1353 to 1335 B.C.,

This is the most famous statue of Nefertiti.

during Egypt's 18th Dynasty. When Akhenaton came to power, most Egyptians believed in many gods, all of whom had equal power. Akhenaton, however, believed that the sun god, Aton, had more power and should be worshipped as the supreme ruler of the heavens. In fact, the pharoah gave himself the name *Akhenaton*—meaning "one useful to Aton"—to honor the sun god. (He was originally named Amenhotep IV.)

As was the custom, Akhenaton had many wives. Nefertiti was his head wife. Together, they had six daughters, two of whom became queens. Meketaten grew up to marry her father, Akhenaton. Ankhesepaaten married her cousin, Tutankhamen. Tutankhamen, commonly known as King Tut, became pharaoh several years after Akhenaton's death.

Nefertiti supported her husband's belief in the supreme power of Aton. She became a priestess, helping Akhenaton spread the new religion to the Egyptian people. As queen, she had a strong influence over the Egyptian people.

TOPICAL TIDBIT

King Tut's Tomb

In 1922, English archaeologist Howard Carter uncovered the burial tomb of Tutankhamen, who was pharaoh of Egypt during the 14th century B.C. Carter found the tomb in Egypt's Valley of the Kings, an area where many pharoahs were buried in places kept secret. Inside the tomb, Carter found hundreds of gold statues, pieces of jewelry, and the mummified body of Tutankhamen.

In honor of the new religion, Akhenaton built a new capital city on the eastern banks of the Nile River. It was called Akhetaten, which means "horizon of Aton." The city had a large temple and palace. Inside the palace were many rooms and apartments, and a place called the harem, where Nefertiti and the pharaoh's other wives lived. Akhenaton did not live in the palace. He lived in a separate house that was connected to the harem by a bridge.

"And the Heiress, Great in the Palace, Fair of Face, Adorned with the Double Plumes, Mistress of Happiness, Endowed with Favors, at hearing whose voice the King rejoices, the Chief Wife of the King, his beloved, the Lady of the Two Lands, Neferneferuaten-Nefertiti, May she live for Ever and Always."

—inscription found in Akhenaton's tomb

Few Known Facts

Most of what we know about Nefertiti and Akhenaton was found in the palace and temples of Akhetaten. Sculptures, paintings, and carvings show the pharoah and queen worshipping Aton, driving chariots, or relaxing with their daughters.

Other details of Nefertiti's life come from 400 ancient tablets discovered at the palace. The tablets are known as the Amarna Letters. Akhenaton wrote the letters to the officials of neighboring ancient countries, such as Syria, Mitanni, and Babylonia. The letters were "written" with a stylus, or penlike instrument, on stone or clay tablets. This form of early writing, called *cuneiform*, is one of the first examples of human record-keeping.

Nefertiti in Art

The cuneiform tablets were found at the palace during archaeological excavations in the early 1900s. Sculptures and paintings of Nefertiti were also found. Most show her wearing a crown and gold earrings. Many of these depictions show what life was like at the palace. The royal couple held banquets and feasts. One painting shows Nefertiti seated beside her future son-in-law, Tutankhamen.

Life at the palace was not always happy. Two wall paintings at the palace tell of the

LIFE EVENTS

About 1353 B.C.
Nefertiti becomes queen of Egypt when her husband, Akhenaton, becomes pharoah.

About 1335 B.C.
Akhenaton dies. Eventually he is succeeded by his nephew and son-in-law, Tutankhamen.

1922 A.D.
Tutankhamen's tomb is discovered in the Valley of the Kings in Egypt.

tragic death of Nefertiti's daughter, Meketaten. According to the painting, during the 12th year of Akhenaton's reign, Meketaten died giving birth to a child. A baby is shown being carried away from her mother's funeral table.

Only a few items remain to mark the life of Nefertiti, Queen of Egypt. The most famous is a colorful bust that shows the queen's beauty. Made of limestone and painted with bright colors that have withstood the test of time, the bust stands about 1.5 feet tall. Nefertiti, the beautiful one, wears a crown. ◇

Florence Nightingale
Founder of Modern Nursing
(born 1820 • died 1910)

If Florence Nightingale had followed her parents' wishes, she would have married a wealthy man instead of becoming a nurse. That would not have satisfied Florence Nightingale, however. She studied nursing and put her skills to use during the Crimean War. Although she tended to sick and wounded soldiers for only two years during that war, she became famous throughout the world for saving lives. She is known as the founder of modern nursing.

Different Ideas

Florence Nightingale was born in Florence, Italy, on May 12, 1820. Her parents, Frances and William Edward Nightingale, were a wealthy British couple. Florence and her older sister, Parthenope, were raised in England and schooled at home by their father. Florence enjoyed her studies, particularly

math. However, in the early 1800s, girls were supposed to be interested in subjects that prepared them to be good wives and mothers, such as cooking and sewing. Math was for boys.

Florence was different. She wanted to become a nurse, but her parents did not approve. In those days, nursing was not a job for wealthy, educated women like Florence. It was a job for working-class people, without much education.

That did not matter to Florence. She studied on her own and learned what she could about hospitals. Finally, her parents allowed her to go to nursing school. Her studies lasted only a few months—not like today's training. Florence believed that God had called her to help the sick and poor. She began caring for ill women in London in 1853.

Florence Helps the Wounded

In March 1854, England joined France and Turkey in a war against Russia. The fighting took place in Crimea (now Ukraine), so the conflict was called the Crimean War. It began when Russia invaded Turkish lands.

Wounded British soldiers were taken to Turkey for medical care. Many injured soldiers were surviving their injuries, but dying from infections and disease. In the 1850s, doctors did not know about germs. They did not realize that they could save lives by simply

"I think one's feelings waste themselves in words; they ought all to be distilled into actions and into actions which bring results."
—Florence Nightingale

keeping the soldiers and their surroundings clean.

However, some health care professionals like Florence Nightingale had noticed the importance of cleanliness. Although they did not yet understand why it worked, they realized that patients did better in clean conditions.

A war reporter sent news of the dying soldiers to British newspapers. People were alarmed. Nightingale wanted to help. She was appointed by Sidney Herbert, British Secretary of War, to take a team of female nurses to Turkey.

Nightingale and 38 nurses arrived at the military hospital in Turkey in November. They were shocked to find no supplies, no latrines (toilets), and little food. However, there were plenty of rats and bugs. Injured soldiers were lying on straw beds on dirty floors.

At first, the male doctors refused the nurses' help.

TOPICAL TIDBIT

Medical History

Doctors were only beginning to learn about germs around the time of the American Civil War (1861-1865). They did not realize the importance of sterilizing (cleaning thoroughly) their instruments after performing operations. If a soldier's wound showed signs of infection, they thought it was just part of the healing process.

After ten days, however, more wounded arrived and the nurses were put to work. They scrubbed floors, washed clothes, cooked meals, and insisted that latrines be built and kept clean. The nurses greatly improved conditions and saved many lives. Nightingale checked on the soldiers in the evenings, carrying a lamp to guide her way. The soldiers, thankful for her help, called her the "Lady of the Lamp."

The Hero Comes Home

In 1856, Florence Nightingale returned to England to find that she was a hero. The press had told the world about her success in saving lives. However, she was not feeling well and did not like to be in the public eye. She had an unknown illness and became too sick to leave the house.

Although ill for the rest of

LIFE EVENTS

1820
Florence Nightingale is born in Florence, Italy.

1853
Nightingale becomes a nurse in London.

1854
Nightingale and 38 nurses save lives in Turkey by keeping the hospitals and soldiers clean.

1856
Nightingale returns to England a hero.

1883
Queen Victoria honors Nightingale with the Royal Red Cross.

1907
Nightingale becomes the first woman to receive the Order of Merit, from King Edward VII.

1910
Florence Nightingale dies.

her life, Nightingale continued to improve medical practices. With donated funds, she set up the Nightingale Training School for Nurses at St. Thomas's Hospital in 1860. She wrote letters urging the government to improve hospital care.

The Lady of the Lamp Shines On

Florence Nightingale received many awards, including the Royal Red Cross from Queen Victoria of England in 1883. In 1907, the king of England, Edward VII, gave her the Order of Merit. She was the first woman to receive that honor.

Florence Nightingale died on August 13, 1910, in London. She continues to be a role model to young women who want to become nurses, and her work has had a lasting impact throughout the world. Nightingale's deeds during the Crimean War inspired the founding of the International Red Cross, which is still saving lives today. ◇

Annie Oakley
Sharpshooter
(born 1860 • died 1926)

One of the most famous women of the Old West was not from the West at all. Annie Oakley was from the backwoods of Ohio, where she learned how to hunt with a rifle. Little did she realize that her skill with a gun would lead her to a life as a famous performer.

Settling the Family Debt

Annie was born on August 13, 1860, in Darke County, Ohio, as Phoebe Ann Moses. (Some documents list her last name as "Mosey" or "Mozee." She took the stage name Oakley around 1882.) During her childhood, Annie learned to hunt, helping her family get enough food to eat.

Annie's father died in 1866, and the family fell on hard times. About two years later, eight-year-old Annie was sent to live at an orphanage. In her early teens, Annie returned home but found that her mother was still having money problems.

To raise money, Annie started hunting. She sold what she caught to hotel and restaurant owners. According to legend, when Annie was 15, she had saved up enough money to settle her family's debt.

"Little Sure Shot"

Annie's skills as a hunter had not gone unnoticed. In that era, it was unusual for a woman to earn a living with a gun. When expert marksman Frank Butler came to Ohio on a shooting exhibition, Annie entered a contest against him. She used the name Annie Oakley. Oakley beat Butler and proved that she was the best shooter around.

Oakley and Butler got to be friends. In time, the couple got married and performed together as "Oakley and Butler." In 1884, they toured with the Sells Brothers Circus. While performing with Butler, Oakley traveled west of the Mississippi River for the first time.

Oakley dazzled audiences by shooting rifles, shotguns, and pistols. Butler would throw a playing card into the air and Oakley would shoot a bunch of holes in it before it hit the ground. Resting a rifle on her shoulder, Oakley could look into a mirror and shoot an object out of the hand of someone standing behind her. While riding a horse, Oakley could pick off targets thrown by another rider. She

> "She possessed a rare modesty for a person that had followed the life she did, and was unaffected and sincere, and of charming personality."
>
> —from Oakley's obituary in the *Greenville Daily Advocate*, November 4, 1926

earned the nickname "Little Sure Shot." The name was given to her by Sioux Indian Chief Sitting Bull, who also adopted her as his daughter.

Buffalo Bill's Wild West Show

Oakley became a Western folk hero after joining Buffalo Bill's Wild West Show in 1885. Frank Butler became her manager. The show brought the Wild West to people around the world. Performers included cowboys, Native Americans, gunfighters, lawmen, sharpshooters, and rodeo stars. Acts included a stagecoach robbery, battles from the Indian Wars, trick riding, and shooting demonstrations.

Audiences loved Oakley. She wore fringed dresses and a cowboy hat with a star. When the show traveled to Europe, she met royalty. She was even asked to shoot a cigarette out of the hand of Crown Prince Wilhelm of Germany—and did so.

TOPICAL TIDBIT

Buffalo Bill

William F. Cody, or "Buffalo Bill," was born in Iowa, in 1846. During his lifetime, he was a Pony Express rider, buffalo hunter, guide, and scout. He led the popular Wild West Show from 1883 to 1913. He died in 1917. Renditions of the show are still being performed today.

Oakley spent 16 years with Buffalo Bill's Wild West Show. She left the show in 1901, after suffering injuries in a train wreck. After recovering, Oakley began performing with Butler again.

Oakley Lives On

Annie Oakley died on November 3, 1926, in Greenville, Ohio. During her career, she displayed grace and poise in addition to her skill with a gun. She showed the world that women could be skilled sharpshooters. Believing that women should be able to defend themselves, Oakley taught many women how to shoot. She also donated money to charities, orphanages, and to women seeking education.

Oakley won trophies and, in 1993, was inducted in the National Women's Hall of Fame. The musical *Annie Get Your Gun* is loosely based on her life and career. ◇

LIFE EVENTS

1860
Phoebe Ann Moses is born in Darke County, Ohio.

1875
Annie saves up enough money from shooting and selling game that she pays off her family's debts.

1884
Annie starts using the name Oakley and begins to tour with her husband, Frank Butler.

1885
Oakley joins Buffalo Bill's Wild West Show.

1901
Oakley leaves the Wild West Show.

1926
Annie Oakley dies.

Sandra Day O'Connor
U.S. Supreme Court Justice
(born 1930)

Women in the U.S. have struggled and fought for equal rights since the 1840s. Susan B. Anthony and Elizabeth Cady Stanton led the fight for women's suffrage. In 1879, Belva Lockwood became the first female lawyer to try a case before the U.S. Supreme Court. More than 100 years later, in 1981, Sandra Day O'Connor became the first woman to serve as a justice on the Supreme Court of the United States.

> "The power I exert on the court depends on the power of my arguments, not on my gender."
> —Sandra Day O'Connor

Cattle Ranching in Arizona

Sandra Day was born in El Paso, Texas, on March 26, 1930. Her parents, Harry and Ada Mae O'Connor,

owned a 155,000-acre cattle ranch in Arizona, where Sandra grew up. Sandra liked to go horseback riding and play tennis. She also helped out on the ranch, tending to the cattle. Since there were no schools nearby, she attended Radford School in El Paso, a boarding school for girls.

Sandra was an excellent student who studied very hard. Because of her good grades, she graduated from high school when she was only 16. Sandra then left home to attend college at Stanford University in California. After receiving her bachelor's degree in economics, Sandra joined the law program at Stanford. She graduated from law school in 1952, ranking third in her class of more than 100 students. While there, she served as the editor of the *Stanford Law Review*. After graduation, Sandra Day married one of her classmates, John J. O'Connor III.

A Seat in the Senate

Sandra and John O'Connor lived in Frankfurt, Germany, for a few years. John was a lawyer in the Judge Advocate General's Corps (JAG) of the U.S. Army. Sandra worked as a lawyer in the civilian quartermaster corps, drafting business contracts.

When the O'Connors returned to the U.S., they settled in Phoenix, Arizona. They had three sons, Brian,

TOPICAL TIDBIT

Race for the Cure

Sandra Day O'Connor is a survivor of breast cancer. She participates each year in the Race for the Cure—an annual running race that raises funds for research, education, and treatment of breast cancer. Runners and sponsors of the cause wear pink ribbons to show their support.

Jay, and Scott. While the boys were growing up, Sandra Day O'Connor worked part-time in her own law firm. She was appointed to the Arizona Governor's Committee on Marriage and Family. She worked her way up through the ranks of the Arizona legal system. In 1965, she became the assistant attorney general for the state of Arizona.

Sandra Day O'Connor addresses students at a college graduation.

In 1969, O'Connor was appointed by Governor Jack Williams to fill a vacant spot in the Arizona Senate. The following year, O'Connor was elected to the Senate on her own merits. She served two terms in that post.

The U.S. Supreme Court

In 1979, O'Connor was appointed to the Arizona Court of Appeals. In 1981, she spoke out regarding her belief that a state court's ruling on a case should be upheld—that is, the ruling should not be overturned by a federal court. O'Connor believed that state judges and federal judges should be equal in stature.

O'Connor's stance on the equality of judges gained her national recognition as a fair and impartial judge. In 1981, President Ronald Reagan nominated O'Connor to the U.S. Supreme Court. Upon her

LIFE EVENTS

1930
Sandra Day is born in El Paso, Texas.

1952
Day graduates Stanford Law School and marries John J. O'Connor.

1965
Sandra Day O'Connor becomes the assistant attorney general for the state of Arizona.

1970
O'Connor is elected to the first of two terms in the U.S. Senate.

1979
O'Connor is appointed to the Arizona Court of Appeals.

1981
President Ronald Reagan nominates O'Connor as a Supreme Court justice.

appointment, O'Connor became the first woman to hold the title of Supreme Court Justice since the founding of the national court, more than 200 years earlier.

Sandra Day O'Connor has ruled on hundreds of cases. Her hard work and fairness led the way for other women to serve at high levels in the U.S. court system. In an interview, O'Connor said, "Even more important than being . . . [the first woman to serve on the Supreme Court] is not being the last." In 1993, Ruth Bader Ginsburg—the second female justice—joined O'Connor on the bench. ◇

Rosie O'Donnell
Comedian, Actor, Talk Show Host
(born 1962)

When Rosie O'Donnell was a child, she spent hours watching television. She grew up to become a standup comedian known for her honest, clean humor. She's also an actor, parent, talk show host, and role model.

Surviving Loss

Roseanne O'Donnell was born on March 21, 1962, in Commack, New York. Rosie was raised on Long Island with her four brothers and sisters. Her mother was a homemaker, staying at home to raise the children. In 1972, when Rosie was only 10 years old, her mother died of cancer. It was an emotional time for Rosie as she struggled to learn how to live without her mother.

Rosie's father was often unable to give his children much attention. As a result, the O'Donnells grew up in a home without strict rules. Rosie got to watch as much television as she wanted. That is when she

developed a love for talk shows, which featured interviews with celebrities. She looked to movies and television to escape the sadness in her life, especially TV shows starring comedians Lucille Ball and Carol Burnett.

Rosie had a keen sense of humor. Naturally witty and funny, she was popular at school. She was elected president of her senior class and prom queen.

While in college, Rosie began performing stand-up comedy. Her career started to take off, so she left college without a degree.

From Stand-up Comic to Popular Actor

In 1979, Rosie O'Donnell started performing in comedy clubs. She found life on the road difficult, especially because she was one of very few female stand-up comedians. O'Donnell also saw some of the other comedians using drugs and alcohol, which was something that she did not do.

In the early 1980s, O'Donnell competed on the television show *Star Search*, which allowed the audience to choose their favorite perfomer. O'Donnell won Best Comedian five times.

TOPICAL TIDBIT

Rosie's Inspiration

Carol Burnett hosted her own comedy-variety show on CBS in the 1960s and 1970s. One of the funniest and most famous scenes from the show was a spoof of the movie *Gone With the Wind*. It featured Burnett as Scarlett O'Hara, wearing a new dress made from her mansion's curtains—complete with the curtain rod.

She got her big break in 1986, when she became a veejay for the VH-1 cable station. As a veejay, O'Donnell talked about music videos and sometimes interviewed musicians. Later, she hosted VH-1's *Stand-Up Spotlight*, a show that featured stand-up comedians. In 1992, O'Donnell co-starred with Tom Hanks, Geena Davis, and Madonna in the film *A League of Their Own*, which told the true story of female baseball players during World War II. After appearing in *A League of Their Own*, O'Donnell became a household name.

> "When you have celebrity in America, you also have a tremendous amount of power and influence, and you have to make a conscious decision about how you're going to use that power."
>
> —Rosie O'Donnell

"The Queen of Nice"

O'Donnell continued acting, landing roles in *Sleepless in Seattle* and *Beautiful Girls*. In 1994, she made her Broadway debut as Rizzo in the hit musical play *Grease!*

O'Donnell was thrilled with her success, but she also wanted to be a mother. In 1995, she adopted a son, Parker. Since then, she has adopted two more children, Chelsea and Blake. To balance her career and family, Rosie stopped touring.

In 1996, she premiered her own talk show called *The Rosie O'Donnell Show*. It allowed her to live in New York and raise her children. A huge nursery adjoins her office.

The Rosie O'Donnell Show became an instant hit. O'Donnell interviews celebrity guests, just like the talk shows she used to watch. In addition to movie and television stars, she features acts from Broadway. She often breaks into song—sometimes singing show tunes or old television theme songs. *Newsweek* magazine called her "the Queen of Nice."

O'Donnell has won several Emmy Awards for her show. She has also appeared in more movies, including *The Flintstones* (as Betty Rubble) and *Harriet the Spy* (as Golly).

LIFE EVENTS

1962
Roseanne O'Donnell is born in Commack, New York.

1972
O'Donnell's mother dies of cancer.

Early 1980s
O'Donnell becomes a five-time Best Comedian on *Star Search*.

1992
O'Donnell has her own short-lived TV series called *Stand By Your Man*.

1996
O'Donnell premieres her own talk show.

1998
O'Donnell provides the voice of Turk in Disney's animated feature *Tarzan*.

2000
O'Donnell launches *Rosie*, a magazine about celebrities and everyday heroes.

Not Just for Fun

A spirited, funny performer, Rosie O'Donnell delights audiences whether she is performing comedy routines, acting in movies, or hosting her television show. In addition to her humorous side, O'Donnell gets serious when fighting for the causes that are important to her. She supports various political and social causes, such as helping the homeless and funding charities for children. In 2000, she led the Million Mom March on Washington, which called attention to handgun control. ◇

Georgia O'Keeffe
Painter
(born 1887 • died 1986)

Georgia O'Keeffe saw beauty in the stark contrasts of nature—whether in the texture of a flower or the weathered bones of a cow's skull. Using bright colors, she painted what she saw, establishing herself as one of the most important artists of the 20th century.

Becoming a Painter

Georgia O'Keeffe was born on November 15, 1887, on a wheat farm near Sun Prairie, Wisconsin. She came from a big family—she had six brothers and sisters. Georgia dreamed of becoming an artist, so after graduating from high school, she left her family and moved to Illinois to attend the Art Institute of Chicago. In 1907, she headed to New York City. It was there that her dream came true. While attending the Art Students League, she received a prize for her still-life painting of a rabbit in a copper pot.

To earn a living, Georgia O'Keeffe took up teaching.

Georgia O'Keeffe stands with some of her work on display at the Whitney Museum of American Art in New York, in 1970.

In 1909, she accepted a teaching position in Texas. Later, she taught at Columbia Teachers College in South Carolina. In 1915, O'Keeffe accepted another teaching assignment—this time, she was to head the art department of West Texas State Normal College.

411

While in Texas, O'Keeffe painted colorful flowers and striking landscapes. She captured desert scenes of the Southwest like no one had ever before. She sent some of her work to a friend in New York, who showed them to Alfred Stieglitz, a noted photographer and owner of the 291 Gallery. Stieglitz exhibited O'Keeffe's paintings without her knowing about it. The fresh style of the paintings excited the New York art world, and a startled O'Keeffe

> "Before I put a brush to canvas I question, 'Is this mine? Is it all intrinsically of myself?'"
>
> —Georgia O'Keeffe

hurried to New York to see what was going on. She and Stieglitz met and fell in love. She moved to New York in 1918, and the two were married in 1924.

Painting New Mexico

Each year, O'Keeffe's paintings were displayed in Stieglitz's gallery. While living in New York, she painted giant flowers and views of the city. By 1928, she was famous for these paintings. When she received $25,000 for her painting of a calla lily, she proved to the rest of the world that a female artist could, in fact, earn a living by doing what she loves.

The following year, O'Keeffe traveled back to the Southwest—this time, to New Mexico. The wide, open spaces of New Mexico enchanted her. She could see for miles in the clear, dry air of the desert. Unfortunately, her life with Stieglitz was in New York City. So she bought a car—a Model A Ford, one of the first cars ever made. Each summer she tossed her canvases and paints in the back seat, and traveled to New Mexico.

O'Keeffe loved the New Mexico landscape—red, pink, yellow, and orange rock formations set against the blue sky. She would take long walks, noticing the bleached bones of long-dead cattle and other animals. She would paint these images and ship them back to New York and to a waiting world.

O'Keeffe Goes Home

Steiglitz died in 1946, and O'Keeffe moved to New Mexico. She bought a house near her favorite spot— Ghost Ranch. She painted the landscape that she loved, and other images from her life in New

TOPICAL TIDBIT

Dinosaurs Discovered at Ghost Ranch

In 1947, dinosaur bones were found in Ghost Ranch, New Mexico. The bones date back to the Triassic Period (about 220 million years ago). Scientists believe that the bones belong to the *Coelophysis* (*SEEL-uh-FYE-sis*) species of dinosaurs. *Coelophysis* averaged about nine feet long, with a long neck and a pointed head.

Mexico—mission churches, adobe houses, and cactus.

O'Keeffe's eyesight began to fail when she was 71. So she turned her talents to sculpting and pottery. O'Keeffe died in Santa Fe, New Mexico, on March 6, 1986. She was 98.

A Place in History

Today, Georgia O'Keeffe's paintings are exhibited in galleries and museums all over the world. A mural, titled "Sky Above Clouds IV," hangs in the Art Institute of Chicago, where she once attended school. In 1997, the Georgia O'Keeffe Museum in Santa Fe, New Mexico, opened to the public— a tribute to her work as one of the great American Modern artists. ◇

LIFE EVENTS

1887
Georgia O'Keeffe is born near Sun Prairie, Wisconsin.

1907
O'Keeffe wins a prize for a still-life.

1908
Alfred Steiglitz mounts an exhibition of European artists. It is many Americans' first exposure to Picasso, Matisse, and Cezanne.

1915
Steiglitz exhibits one of O'Keeffe's paintings.

1924
O'Keeffe and Steiglitz marry.

1946
Steiglitz dies and O'Keeffe moves to New Mexico.

1986
Georgia O'Keeffe dies at the age of 98.

Jacqueline Kennedy Onassis
First Lady
(born 1929 • died 1994)

Jacqueline Bouvier Kennedy Onassis spent her life in the public eye. She became First Lady of the United States in 1961, and captivated the world with her quiet intelligence and sophistication. She weathered hard times with grace, and remained a worldwide favorite until her death.

The Early Years

On July 28, 1929, in Southampton, New York, Jacqueline Lee Bouvier was born into a wealthy family. Jackie went to Miss Porter's School, where she learned math, reading, and writing. She was also taught foreign languages, proper manners, and how to behave in society.

Jackie loved to ride horses and study ballet. She also wrote poetry and stories, which she illustrated. When she turned 18, she became a debutante—a young lady who officially enters society. The debut, or "coming out" of debutantes, is celebrated with parties and dances. Jackie was "Debutante of the Year" in 1947-1948.

Jackie Bouvier attended Vassar College and George Washington University, spending her junior year at the Sorbonne, in Paris, France. Jackie graduated from George Washington University in 1951, and stayed in Washington, D.C. She spent the next two years working as a photographer for the *Washington Times-Herald*. On an assignment, she met a dashing young senator named John F. Kennedy.

> "Even though people may be well-known, they still hold in their hearts the emotions of a simple person for the moments that are the most important of those we know on Earth—birth, marriage, death."
>
> —Jaqueline Bouvier Kennedy Onassis

The Kennedy Years

John Kennedy was from Massachusetts. Known to his friends as Jack, or JFK, he was on the rise to political fame. He and Jackie got to know each other, and fell in love. They got married on September 12,

1953. In 1956, Jackie gave birth to a stillborn baby. The following year, a healthy daughter, Caroline, was born. While Jackie was expecting another baby in 1960, John was elected 35th president of the U.S. Their son, John Jr., was born in 1960, after the election.

In 1961, the Kennedys moved into the White House. Jackie restored several of the rooms with artwork and antiques from America's past. She turned the rooms of the White House into a museum of American art, history, and culture. No First Lady had done such a thing before. The following year, Jackie invited members of the press into the White House to give them a tour, which also had never been done. The tour aired on television, allowing millions of curious Americans to see inside the White House. Jackie introduced the nation to the historic significance of the White House. Jackie won an Emmy Award for the television special.

As First Lady, Jackie Kennedy acted as an ambassador to foreign officials when they visited the White House. She was a superb hostess and became known around the world for her intelligence, grace, and hospitality. Many American women looked to her as a role model.

TOPICAL TIDBIT

The Tragedy of John F. Kennedy Jr.

Jackie's son, John Kennedy Jr., was a handsome, friendly young man, a favorite of the media. He became a lawyer in the 1980s, then turned to magazine publishing in the late 1990s. In 1999, John, his wife, Carolyn, and her sister Lauren were killed when the plane John was piloting crashed into the Atlantic Ocean. The world mourned the loss of another Kennedy.

In early 1963, Jackie gave birth to a son, Patrick, who died two days later. Then, on November 22, 1963, President Kennedy was shot and killed while driving through Dallas, Texas. Jackie was at his side when he was shot. The nation mourned the loss of its president, and Jackie mourned the loss of her husband and the father of her children. The world watched her gracefully and quietly grieve.

The Later Years

Jackie Kennedy devoted her time to her children. After her brother-in-law, Robert F. Kennedy, was killed in 1968, she took Caroline and John to Greece. Later that year, Jackie married Aristotle Onassis, a tobacco and shipping tycoon. Onassis died in 1975.

After the death of her second husband, Jackie Onassis returned to New York and

LIFE EVENTS

1929
Jacqueline Lee Bouvier is born in Southampton, New York.

1952
Jackie meets John F. Kennedy. They marry the following year.

1960
Jackie becomes First Lady.

1963
President Kennedy is assassinated.

1968
Jackie Kennedy marries shipping tycoon Aristotle Onassis.

1978
Jackie Onassis becomes a book editor in New York.

1994
Jacqueline Bouvier Kennedy Onassis dies of cancer in New York City.

worked as an editor for Viking Press and Doubleday Books. Forever in the spotlight, Jackie maintained an air of grace and quiet intelligence. She died of cancer on May 19, 1994, in New York. Jackie was buried in Arlington National Cemetery beside her first husband, John Kennedy.

Grace and Dignity

Jacqueline Bouvier Kennedy Onassis had a style and manner that women around the world admired. She dictated fashion trends throughout her life—from pearls and pillbox hats to large sunglasses. But she influenced more than just fashion. She inspired Americans to take interest in the arts, she supported her children in their careers, and she showed the world how to survive tragedy with grace and dignity. ◇

Rosa Parks
Civil-rights Activist
(born 1913)

Rosa Parks made history in 1955, when she refused to give up her seat on the bus to a white man. Her actions sparked a bus boycott in Alabama, which influenced the course of history in the United States. By fighting a law that she thought was unfair, Rosa encouraged others to stand up for their beliefs.

> "My only concern was to get home after a hard day's work."
> —Rosa Parks

Rosa Faces Prejudice

Rosa Louise McCauley was born on February 14, 1913, in Tuskegee, Alabama. She was the daughter of a teacher and a carpenter, and the granddaughter of former slaves. Rosa attended a progressive school for girls. Her teachers encouraged her to work hard and build self-confidence. Later, she attended Alabama State University. She then moved to Montgomery, Alabama, with her new husband, Raymond Parks.

Living in the South was difficult for many African Americans in those days. Alabama was segregated, which meant that black people were allowed only in certain areas. In the 1950s, African Americans were often called "coloreds." White people dictated where blacks could sit, drink, eat, or swim. Laws were passed about what beaches African Americans could use, where they could sit in restaurants and buses, which water fountains they could use, and what schools they could attend.

White people always had better seats, schools, beaches, and the like. If a black person was found in a whites-only section, he or she could be arrested, jailed, and fined. Often, a black person was beaten for being in the wrong place. That was never the case if a white person wandered into a coloreds-only section.

A lot of tension existed between whites and blacks. As an African American, Rosa Parks faced discrimination every day. She believed that segregation was unfair and that all people should be treated as equals. Parks joined the National Association for the Advancement of Colored People (NAACP), an organization that sought to end racism, segregation, and discrimination.

Standing up by Sitting Down

Parks worked as a housekeeper and seamstress in Montgomery. She rode the bus to work. Because she was black, she had to sit in the coloreds-only section at the back of the bus. About 70 percent of Montgomery bus riders were black. They had to enter the bus in the front, pay their fare, exit the bus, then re-enter in the back because they were not allowed to walk through the white section.

On December 1, 1955, Parks got on the bus to head home after a long day of work. She sat in the coloreds-only section. As the bus picked up additional passengers, more whites entered the bus. There were not enough seats for them. So, the bus driver told Parks and other blacks to give up their seats. Parks thought this was unfair, so she said no. Parks was breaking the law, however, so the bus driver had her arrested.

Parks pleaded her case in court, but was found guilty. Montgomery's black citizens were outraged and organized a boycott of the town's bus system. The large black community no longer rode the bus—they walked or arranged car pools. This hurt the local ecomony and sent a message to racist lawmakers.

Civil Rights

The African American community was inspired by Parks's actions and came together. One of the boycott leaders was a young black minister named Dr. Martin Luther King Jr.

TOPICAL TIDBIT

King of the Civil Rights Movement

The Montgomery bus boycott thrust Dr. Martin Luther King, Jr. into the role of civil rights leader. When blacks were not allowed to register to vote in Selma, Alabama, he led marches in protest. He urged blacks to fight prejudice without violence. Despite his dedication to nonviolent protest, Dr. King was murdered in 1968.

Rosa Parks arrives at court on February 24, 1956, more than two months after sparking the Montgomery bus boycott.

Both Parks and King were threatened with violence for leading the boycott, and someone tried to blow up King's home. The boycott lasted more than a year, ending when the U.S. Supreme Court ruled that Montgomery's bus segregation laws were unconstitutional.

The Montgomery bus boycott became one of the

key steps toward racial equality in the U.S. It is often credited as being the start of the civil rights movement, a period of civil unrest and struggle for equal rights for African Americans.

Taking Pride

Rosa and her husband, Raymond, moved to Detroit, Michigan, in 1957. She worked for U.S. Congressman John Conyers Jr. for many years.

Wanting to inspire African American teens to build their self-esteem and take pride in their heritage, she started the Rosa and Raymond Parks Institute for Self-Development in 1987. She received the Congressional Gold Medal of Honor in 1999 for her civil rights work. *Time* magazine named Rosa Parks one of the 100 most influential people of the 20th century ◇

LIFE EVENTS

1913
Rosa Louise McCauley is born in Tuskegee, Alabama.

1955
Rosa Parks refuses to give up her seat to a white man. The Montgomery bus boycott begins.

1956
The bus boycott ends. Martin Luther King Jr. and Reverend Glen Smiley, a black and a white minister, share the front seat of the bus.

1957
The Southern Christian Leadership Conference creates the annual Rosa Parks Freedom Award.

1999
Parks receives the Congressional Gold Medal of Honor.

Eva Perón
Political Leader, Social Reformer, First Lady of Argentina
(born 1919 • died 1952)

As the wife of Argentine President Juan Perón (*pay-RONE*), Eva Perón rose to the top of Argentina's government. She was a powerful and influential leader, even though the government never officially recognized her as one. Eva led social reforms that improved the quality of life for poor and working-class people.

Humble Beginnings

On May 7, 1919, María Eva Duarte was born in Los Toldos, Argentina, to Juana Ibaguren and Juan Duarte. Eva started school when she was eight. She spent her childhood raising silkworms, collecting photographs of movie stars, and performing at make-believe circuses created by her brother and sisters.

At 15, Eva wanted to be an actor. Her mother thought that Eva was too young for an acting career,

Eva Perón (right) at a Paris reception in 1947. She sits with Argentine ambassador Julie Victoria Roca.

but realized that there was no stopping Eva. She was too headstrong. Mother and daughter boarded the train for Buenos Aires.

Eva's mother soon returned home, while Eva stayed in Buenos Aires with family friends. Eva toured with acting troupes and landed a starring role on a radio show, *Biographies of Illustrious Women.* The show detailed the lives of women in history, such as Queen Elizabeth I, Sarah Bernhardt, Isadora Duncan, and Catherine the Great.

A New Argentina

The 1940s were a time of political unrest in Argentina. Dictators had been in power for years, and the people of Argentina were ready for a change. They found hope in the form of Colonel Juan Domingo Perón, a man who believed in the rights of the working class, whom he called *descamisados*, meaning "shirtless ones" or laborers.

Eva Duarte met Juan Perón in 1944, while attending a charity benefit. They fell in love and were married on October 22, 1945. Eva and Juan shared the same beliefs regarding social reforms needed in Argentina. They worked together to unite the *descamisados* into a major political force. In 1945, the laborers chose Juan Perón as their presidential candidate. In 1946, he was elected president of Argentina.

> "I demanded more rights for women because I know what women had to put up with."
>
> —Eva Perón

Evita!

Evita, as Eva was called by the Argentine people, kept Juan informed of the needs of average citizens. She created the Eva Perón Foundation to help the poor find housing, medical treatment, and jobs. Evita was loved by the working-class. The upper class, however, hated her. They believed that she used her power to force them to donate money to her foundation. Regardless, the Eva Perón Foundation opened hospitals and schools, built houses for the poor, provided clothes and toys for children, and granted financial aid to senior citizens.

Evita helped earn Argentine women the right to vote in 1947. In 1952, when Juan was reelected, 29 women were voted into government service.

In 1951, Evita was chosen by the people to be Juan's vice president, but military leaders would not allow it. Also, at that time, Evita learned that she had cancer. She declined the nomination in a public address from the balcony of the Casa Rosada ("Pink

TOPICAL TIDBIT

The Eva Perón Hospital Train

Medical supplies were in short supply in remote areas of Argentina. The Eva Perón Foundation sent a "hospital train" into those areas. The special train carried medical services, doctors, and nurses to the people who needed them.

House"), a government office building. A crowd had gathered below, and was chanting "Evita! Evita!"

A Place in History

On July 26, 1952, Evita Perón died of cancer in Buenos Aires. Hundreds of thousands of people lined the streets to pay their respects. In 1955, Evita's body was stolen by military leaders who did not want her memory to live on in Argentina. It was finally returned in 1974. Evita is now buried in the Duarte family tomb in Recoleta Cemetery in Buenos Aires.

In 1979, Evita was immortalized in a Broadway show that chronicled her life. An audience favorite that later became a movie, it features the song "Don't Cry for Me, Argentina," sung from the balcony of the Casa Rosada. ◇

LIFE EVENTS

1919
María Eva Duarte is born.

1926
Eva's father dies, leaving the family poor.

1935
Eva moves to Buenos Aires to become an actor.

1946
Eva's husband, Juan Perón, is elected president. Evita becomes first lady.

1947
Evita Perón establishes programs to help the poor. She also fights for women's suffrage, which is granted.

1951
The Argentine people want Evita to run for vice president, but she cannot.

1952
Eva Perón dies of cancer.

Pocahontas
Native American Princess
(born about 1595 • died 1617)

For some historical figures, it can be difficult to separate fact from fiction. Such is the case with Pocahontas, a Native American princess who met some of the first British settlers in America. Whether she was eager to help the colonists, or forced to help them is debated. But this much is clear: as a young woman, Pocahontas influenced peaceful relations between Native Americans and British settlers.

"Playful One"

Originally named Matoaka, Pocahontas was born around 1595 near present-day Jamestown, Virginia. She was the daughter of Chief Wahunsonacock (also called Powhatan), who ruled more than 30 tribes in the area. The tribes were collectively called the Powhatan, sharing the chief's name.

Matoaka was an energetic and spirited child. She was a friendly girl and soon earned the nickname

This engraving of Pocahantas appeared in John Smith's *The Generall Historie of Virginia*, 1624.

Pocahontas, meaning "Playful One" or "Little Plaything."

The Powhatan lived in houses covered with mats of reeds or bark. Men and women worked together to make sure that their villages had enough food and supplies to survive, especially through the hard winters.

Men were hunters and warriors, protecting their villages from enemy groups who wanted to fight for food or land. Women tended crops, such as beans, squash, and corn. Although the Powhatan traded with other groups for food and supplies, their survival was based on how well they could provide for themselves.

The British Arrive

In 1607, Pocahontas and the Powhatan people faced a new threat to their survival—the arrival of British settlers. The British created the colony of Jamestown, named after their king. They wanted to make new lives for themselves, and many of them hoped to use the area's natural resources to make money.

The Powhatan and British ways of life were very different, so fighting sometimes broke out between the two groups. They did, however, try to maintain peace. When the colonists ran out of supplies, they traded with the Powhatan for corn.

> "She is the instrument to preserve this colony from death, famine, and other instruments."
>
> —John Smith on Pocahontas, 1616

Still, each group was suspicious of the other. In December 1607, John Smith, a British Captain, was captured by the Powhatan, who were going to kill him. According to legend, Pocahontas—then 12 years old—stepped in and begged her father to spare his life, which he did. However, some historians doubt that this really happened. Smith did not write of it until later in his life.

Living With the British

Pocahontas often visited Jamestown and was friendly with the colonists. After John Smith left the colony in 1609 to return to England, tensions between the groups increased. In 1613, Pocahontas was captured and held hostage by Captain Samuel Argall. The captain wanted to restore peace. He said that he would let the princess go in exchange for colonists being held by the Powhatan. Pocahontas was a prisoner for nearly a year. During that time, she became a Christian and took the name Rebecca.

TOPICAL TIDBIT

Separating Fact from Fiction

Moviemakers often change historical events if they think it will make a better story. In the 1995 Disney movie *Pocahontas*, the Powhatan princess is an adult when she saves John Smith. The movie shows her falling in love with Smith, not John Rolfe. Many people said that the true story of Pocahontas should have been filmed instead.

While living with the British, Pocahontas met colonist John Rolfe, a tobacco farmer. They married on April 5, 1614. About a year later, they had a son, Thomas. The union of the Powhatan princess and a British colonist helped restore peace.

In 1616, the Rolfes went to London, England, for a visit. Pocahontas was treated with respect and curiosity. Few British people had ever seen a Native American. She even met King James I.

A Life Cut Short

The Rolfes left England in March 1617 to head back to Virginia, but returned immediately to shore because Pocahontas was very sick.

She died soon afterward and was buried in Kent, England. She was 21. The cause of death was possibly smallpox, tuberculosis, or pneumonia. At that time, many Native Americans

LIFE EVENTS

1595
Matoaka is born to Chief Powhatan.

1607
British settlers arrive.

1613
Matoaka, now known as Pocahontas, is captured by the British.

1615
Pocahontas gives birth to Thomas, her son with her English husband, John Rolfe.

1616
The Rolfe family travels to London, where Pocahontas contracts smallpox or tuberculosis.

1617
Pocahontas dies.

1622
Rolfe is killed in a clash with Indians.

1635
Twenty-year-old Thomas Rolfe returns to the colonies from England.

died from diseases common in Europe but not in North America. Their bodies had not yet developed the ability to fight off such diseases. After Pocahontas' death and the death of her father, war broke out between the colonists and the Powhatan. In 1622, John Rolfe was killed.

Even if the legends that surround Pocahontas are untrue, she remains a powerful figure in American history. She worked to maintain peace and friendship at a time when tensions between two very different peoples were likely to erupt into war. ◇

Beatrix Potter
Author and Illustrator
(born 1866 • died 1943)

Beatrix Potter had her first book, *The Tale of Peter Rabbit*, privately printed in 1900. The story delighted many children, launching Potter into a literary career. Children still love reading about the adventures of Flopsy, Mopsy, Cotton-tail, and Peter.

Lonely Childhood

Helen Beatrix Potter was born on July 28, 1866, in South Kensington, Middlesex, England. Known as Beatrix, she was the daughter of wealthy parents. The family lived in a large house near London. Beatrix was a lonely child. Her parents were rarely around, and Beatrix was raised by nannies.

Beatrix's parents never encouraged her to have friends. She spent her time with the servants and pets. When she was six years old, her brother, Bertram, was born, and Beatrix finally had a friend.

By age nine, Beatrix showed great skill as an artist. She liked to sketch bugs, birds, flowers, and animals.

When her family vacationed in the Scottish country-side and the English Lake District, Beatrix developed a love of nature. This was also a perfect time for her to work on her painting.

At home, the Potter children had many pets, including rabbits, snakes, lizards, frogs, mice, fish, a dog, a pig, and a hedgehog. Beatrix would watch the animals carefully and study their actions and movements. Then she would paint them, using watercolors to create a realistic image of the animals and their surroundings.

Peter Rabbit and Friends

In 1893, when Beatrix Potter was 27, she wrote a letter that changed her life. Her friend's son was sick, and Potter wanted to cheer him up. So she sent him a story about the adventures of four rabbits—Flopsy, Mopsy, Cotton-tail, and Peter. She included drawings of the rabbits, modeled after her own pets. The child loved the story.

> "Now run along, and don't get into mischief."
>
> —from *The Tale of Peter Rabbit* by Beatrix Potter

Seven years later, Potter decided to have the story published. When no publisher was interested in the book, she had it printed herself. Once a few copies got around, the publisher Frederick Warne & Company saw the work and asked to publish more copies. The book was a success. Over the next 20 years, Potter wrote 22 more stories featuring such characters as Benjamin Bunny, Squirrel Nutkin, Jemima Puddle-Duck, and Mrs. Tittlemouse. Children loved reading about the animals' adventures and seeing the beautiful watercolor illustrations. Potter also made sure that the books were small—perfect for child-sized hands.

Beatrix Potter Finds Love

As Potter prepared books for Frederick Warne & Company, she fell in love with the publisher's son, Norman Warne. After Norman proposed to her, Potter was told by her parents that she should not marry him. She became engaged anyway in 1905, but never married Warne. He died suddenly a few months later.

Potter used some of the money from her book sales to buy a farm in the English Lake District. She called it Hill Top. It was Potter's way of gaining some independence from her parents. Potter took vacations at this country getaway, returning to London frequently to look after her aging parents.

Over time, and with the help of lawyer William

TOPICAL TIDBIT

Hill Top Farm

After purchasing Hill Top Farm in 1905, Beatrix Potter used its country setting in many of her books, including *The Tale of Samuel Whiskers*. When Potter left the farm and grounds to the National Trust in her will, the group turned the farmhouse into a museum and preserved the land.

Heelis, Potter bought more and more land near Hill Top Farm. Potter and Heelis got married in October 1913, despite her parents' objections. Around this time, Potter stopped creating children's books to tend to her farm. She and Heelis raised sheep and other animals. Potter was so good at raising sheep that she became president of a local sheep breeders' association—a rare honor for a woman at that time.

Still Pleasing Readers

Beatrix Potter died on December 22, 1943, in Lancashire, England. She is remembered for her richly illustrated picture books featuring lovable animals. For more than 100 years, her story of Peter Rabbit has delighted readers, young and old. ◇

LIFE EVENTS

1866
Helen Beatrix Potter is born in Middlesex, England.

1900
Potter privately publishes *The Tale of Peter Rabbit*, a story that she wrote and illustrated to entertain a sick child.

1902
The Tale of Peter Rabbit is published by a commercial company and is an instant success.

1905
Potter's fiancé dies. She devotes her time to writing and illustrating children's books, which are hugely popular.

1913
Potter marries William Heelis.

1943
Potter dies at age 77.

Jeannette Rankin
First Woman Elected to Congress
(born 1880 • died 1973)

In an era when few women in the United States were allowed to vote, Jeannette Rankin ran for the U.S. House of Representatives and won. During her career, she worked to get the right to vote for all American women, and she campaigned to improve working conditions. She was strongly opposed to war and never backed down from her beliefs, despite intense pressure to do so.

Votes for Women

Born on June 11, 1880, in Montana, Jeannette Rankin was the daughter of a rancher and a school-teacher. She was the oldest of seven children. Unlike most young women at that time who married early and had children, Jeannette attended college. She graduated from the University of Montana in 1902.

Jeannette Rankin tried various jobs after graduation, including teaching and sewing. In 1908, she

studied to become a social worker at the New York School of Philanthropy, then went to work in Seattle, Washington. Rankin, however, soon turned her attention to campaigning for women's suffrage (the right to vote).

During that time, women in the U.S. did not have

the right to vote in national elections. Many women, including Rankin, thought that this was unfair. Rankin worked tirelessly in the state of Montana to get women the right to vote. In 1914, Rankin had her first victory: Montana gave women the right to vote statewide. Rankin turned her efforts to convincing the rest of the country to do the same.

First Woman Elected to Congress

Rankin decided to run for Congress, seeking a Republican seat in the House of Representatives. In 1916, she won, becoming the first women elected to Congress. She was one of the first women elected to office anywhere in the world.

Her victory was short-lived, however. War had been raging in Europe since 1914, but the United States had kept out of the conflict. Many Americans supported "isolationism," meaning that they thought the U.S. should stay out of Europe's problems. As the war continued, however, President Woodrow Wilson asked Congress to allow the U.S. to enter the war.

> "You can no more win a war than you can win an earthquake."
>
> —Jeannette Rankin

Fifty-one representatives, including Rankin, voted against going to war. Rankin was a pacifist, someone who believes strongly in resolving conflict through peaceful means. Despite the efforts of Rankin and other pacifists, U.S. troops entered World War I in 1917. Although others had voted against war, Rankin became the center of attention because she was the only woman. Many people thought that she was being soft because she was female. They wanted her to resign from Congress.

Rankin was tough. She ran for re-election in 1918, but lost. She continued to work for women's suffrage and other causes. Her perseverence paid off. In 1920, the 19th Amendment to the U.S. Constitution was approved by the states, granting women the right to vote nationally.

Opposing Another War

Rankin worked with pacifist groups for several decades. She ran for Congress again in 1940, and

TOPICAL TIDBIT

Rankin's Pacifism

In voting against war, Jeannette Rankin said, "I want to stand by my country, but I cannot vote for war." She refused to send young men to fight when she, herself, could not do so. Once the war began, however, she supported the troops by selling Liberty Bonds, which raised money for the war effort.

won. This time, Europe was engaged in World War II. For a time, Americans did not want to get involved in the conflict, which had begun in 1939. When the Japanese bombed a U.S. naval base in Pearl Harbor, Hawaii, on December 7, 1941, however, the antiwar feeling changed for many Americans.

President Franklin D. Roosevelt asked Congress to declare war on Japan. When it came time to vote, Rankin stuck by her convictions and voted no. She was the only member of Congress to do so. Her stand was very unpopular and she was harshly criticized. She did not seek re-election.

Pacifist to the End

Rankin continued to work for peace for the rest of her life. In 1968, at age 87, she led a group of women, known as the Jeanette Rankin Brigade,

LIFE EVENTS

1880
Jeannette Rankin is born near Missoula, Montana.

1909
Rankin becomes a social worker.

1914
Rankin begins working for the National American Woman Suffrage Association. World War I breaks out in Europe.

1916
Rankin is elected to the U.S. House of Representatives. Her antiwar position loses her that seat two years later.

1940
Rankin is re-elected to the House of Representatives.

1968
Rankin leads an anti-war march in Washington, D.C. She dies in 1973.

in a march on Washington, D.C. The group called for an end to U.S. involvement in the Vietnam War.

Jeannette Rankin died in Carmel, California, on May 18, 1973. Although she was criticized for opposing World Wars I and II, today she is greatly respected for standing up for her beliefs. Rankin braved criticism as the sole woman in Congress and never wavered in her convictions. In 1993, she was inducted into the National Women's Hall of Fame. A bronze statue of her now stands in the Capitol building—the official home of the U.S. Congress—in Washington, D.C. ◇

Janet Reno
Attorney General of the U.S.
(born 1938)

In 1993, Janet Reno became the first woman to hold the office of Attorney General of the United States. Very outspoken against violent crimes, illegal drug sales, child abuse, and murder, Reno drafted and implemented laws to protect the citizens of America.

Alligators and Peacocks

Janet Reno was born on July 21, 1938, in Miami, Florida. Her parents, Henry and Jane, were both newspaper reporters. When Janet was eight, the Reno family moved to an area near the Everglades— a swampy, wilderness area in southern Florida, filled with birds, insects, snakes, and alligators. They built a large house and owned 20 acres of land.

Janet's mother was a local legend. She recited poetry, wrestled alligators, and kept snakes in the house as pets. The four Reno children helped their

mother raise peacocks, all named Horace. The children were encouraged to play outdoors, and Janet grew up riding horses, camping, sailing, swimming, and scuba diving.

Janet moved to Ithaca, New York, to attend Cornell

University and study chemistry. She later attended Harvard Law School, from which she received a law degree in 1963.

Rising to the Top

After law school, Janet Reno returned to Miami, but had a difficult time finding a job. At that time, few legal firms were willing to hire a woman. But that did not stop Reno. She kept trying, and finally became a lawyer with the law firm of Brigham and Brigham. By 1971, Reno had been named staff director of the Judiciary Committee of the Florida House of Representatives. In 1973, she was named assistant state attorney for Dade County, Florida.

In 1978, Reno was elected to the post of state attorney for Dade County. During the first year in her new position, she was responsible for more than 900 employees and oversaw more than 100,000 legal cases.

Reno was elected as state attorney five times. Over those 15 years, Reno helped reform the juvenile-justice system in Florida. She set up crime-prevention programs that helped keep young people away from drugs, gangs, and crime. She took action against fathers who did not pay child support. She also set up the Drug Court, which found new ways to punish nonviolent drug offenders and get them off drugs.

Janet Reno, U.S. Attorney General

Reno's hard work paid off. On March 12, 1993, she was sworn in as attorney general of the U.S. under President Bill Clinton. She promised to uphold the U.S. Constitution and to lead the U.S. Department of Justice, which is the legal administration for the entire country. Reno was the first woman to take this oath.

> "In 1960, when I graduated from college, people told me a woman couldn't go to law school. And when I graduated from law school, people told me, "Law firms won't hire you." Thirty years later, no one has ever told me I couldn't be attorney general."
>
> —Janet Reno

One of the main duties of the U.S. attorney general is to protect the rights of citizens and individuals within the United States. Sometimes, Reno used force to defend this right. At various times, she called in the National Guard, the Drug Enforcement Administration (DEA), or the Federal Bureau of Investigation (FBI) to carry out orders to protect citizens.

Sometimes, Reno found herself responsible for making difficult decisions that proved to be controversial. In 1993, for example, Reno ordered the FBI to investigate the Branch Davidian religious cult in Waco, Texas. A *cult* is a group of people who are devoted to a person or an idea. They are often extreme in their beliefs. The Branch Davidian religious cult was reported to have dangerous weapons. There were also reports that cult members were holding citizens, including children, against their will. After nearly two months of negotiations with the Branch Davidians, Reno ordered the FBI to seize the area. There were gunshots, and a huge fire broke out in the compound. In the end, 103 people, including FBI agents, cult members, and children, were killed. Reno expressed deep regret that the situation had not ended peacefully.

In 2000, Reno made another tough decision. Elián Gonzales was a young Cuban refugee who had illegally entered the country. Relatives in the U.S. wanted him to stay with them, but his father wanted him

TOPICAL TIDBIT

The Department of Justice Kids' Page

In order to help children learn more about the duties of the Department of Justice and the attorney general, Janet Reno sponsored a Web site just for them. Many topics were addressed on the site, including ways to prevent crime, how to recognize and fight prejudice and discrimination, and the history of civil rights in the U.S.

returned to Cuba. After weeks of negotiating with the family, Reno ordered the National Guard to get the boy and return him to his father in Cuba. Many people were upset by the use of force, but Reno believed that she had done the right thing in returning Elián to his father.

Proud of Her Work

Janet Reno served as U.S. attorney general until 2001. Throughout her term, Reno did what she believed was right to protect the rights of U.S. citizens, especially children. Some of the laws that she helped draft were against violence on television. In 2000, she was inducted into the National Women's Hall of Fame. Her work continues to inspire young men and women seeking careers in the legal profession. ◇

LIFE EVENTS

1938
Janet Reno is born in Miami, Florida.

1960
Reno enrolls at Harvard Law School, one of only 16 women in a class of more than 500 students.

1971
Reno is named staff director of the Judiciary Committee in the Florida House of Representatives.

1973
Reno becomes assistant state attorney for Dade County, Florida.

1978
Reno is named state attorney. She is elected to the post five times.

1993-2001
Reno serves as U.S. attorney general—the first woman to hold the job. She is the longest-serving attorney general since the early 1960s.

Sally Ride
First American Woman in Space
(born 1951)

Sally Ride soared to new heights in 1983 aboard the space shuttle *Challenger* as the first American woman in space. Through hard work, courage, and determination, this modern-day explorer broke barriers on her way to the top of the world.

Tennis or Physics?

Sally Kristen Ride was born in Encino, California, on May 26, 1951. As a young girl, Sally trained as an athlete, hoping to make professional tennis her career. Although she was good with a racket, she decided to explore other options. She enrolled at Stanford University to study literature and science. After receiving degrees in English and physics in 1973, she continued her studies. While working toward her doctorate degree in astrophysics, Ride accepted a job as a teaching assistant in laser physics at Stanford.

In 1977, the National Aeronautics and Space

Sally Ride and her fellow astronauts prepare to board the space shuttle *Challenger* at the Kennedy Space Center on June 18, 1983.

Administration (NASA) put out a call for scientists to join the space program. NASA was looking for technicians to conduct experiments in space, using advanced machinery. Ride fit the bill. She was just finishing her studies in astrophysics and wanted to become one of NASA's first female astronauts.

The *Challenger*

NASA received 8,000 applications from scientists for the space-shuttle missions; only 35 spots were available. Ride was one of six women selected for the program in 1978. First, she had to undergo training, including learning to fly high-speed planes. Once she had received her pilot's license and completed her astronaut training, she was given the title of Mission Specialist. Ride's duties included preparing the Space Transportation System (STS), commonly called the space shuttle, for flights into space.

The space shuttle was a new type of spacecraft at the time. Designed by NASA in 1981, the space shuttle was a reusable vehicle that carried people, scientific instruments, and satellites to space stations or other space vehicles orbiting Earth. Once the shuttle and its crew completed the mission, they returned to Earth. The shuttle was then refitted for the next

TOPICAL TIDBIT

Valentina Tereshkova

In 1963, Soviet cosmonaut Valentina Tereshkova became the first woman in space. Her flight lasted three days, during which she completed 48 orbits around Earth. Upon touchdown, Tereshkova was given a hero's welcome. She was awarded the Soviet Union's highest honor—the Order of Lenin—as the first woman in space.

flight. The shuttle that Sally Ride served aboard was called the *Challenger*.

The *Challenger's* fourth flight into space was scheduled for June 18, 1983. The crew's mission was to set up several satellites in orbit around Earth, then return six days later. Ride was selected as the crew's flight engineer. Reporters and camera crews flocked to the launch pad, waiting for the *Challenger* to take off. All of America watched and listened as the announcer called off the countdown: "Ten, nine, eight, seven, six, five, four, three, two, one. Liftoff!" Sally Ride became the first American woman in space.

> "You spend a year training just which dials to look at and when the time comes, all you want to do is look out the window. It's so beautiful."
>
> —Sally Ride, on traveling in space

Up, Up, and Away

In October 1984, Sally returned to space as part of the *Challenger's* crew on that shuttle's 13th flight. This mission was to take pictures of Earth using specially designed cameras.

The world was shocked in January 1986 when the *Challenger* exploded upon liftoff. The entire crew, including a schoolteacher, was killed. Ride was not part of that mission, but she participated in the investigation that followed.

Life After NASA

In 1988, Ride resigned from NASA. In 1989, she became the director of the Space Science Institute at the University of California, San Diego. Since then, Ride has written several books about space for children, including *The Third Planet: Exploring the Earth From Space*, *To Space and Back*, *The Mystery of Mars*, and *Voyager: An Adventure to the Edge of the Solar System*.

Sally Ride flew into history as the first American woman in space. She explored the regions of space known only to a handful of people. Her courage in facing the unknown makes her a hero to women and girls everywhere. ◇

LIFE EVENTS

1951
Sally Kristen Ride is born in Los Angeles, California.

1961
Alan Shepard becomes the first American in space.

1963
Cosmonaut Valentina Tereshkova becomes the first woman in space.

1978
Ride becomes one of six female astronaut candidates.

1983
Ride becomes the first American woman in space.

1987
Ride creates NASA's Office of Exploration.

1988
Ride becomes director of the California Space Institute.

Eleanor Roosevelt
Social Reformer and First Lady
(born 1884 • died 1962)

Eleanor Roosevelt was an important social activist and reformer, as well as First Lady. She was devoted to many social causes, including ending poverty and addressing race and women's issues. In many ways, she was ahead of her time in the issues she tackled, leaving an example for future generations to follow.

Overcoming Shyness

Anna Eleanor Roosevelt was born on October 11, 1884, in New York City. She was the niece of Theodore Roosevelt, who was president of the United States from 1901 to 1909. During Eleanor's childhood, both of her parents died and she was sent to live with her grandmother. Unlike her beautiful mother, Eleanor was a plain-looking girl. She was very shy and lacked self-confidence.

At 15, she was sent to a girls' school in England. There, Eleanor slowly overcame her shyness and

gained confidence. The school's principal thought that Eleanor had strong leadership qualities.

Three years later, Eleanor returned to New York. Interested in social issues, she taught exercise and dance classes to people living in the city's poor neighborhoods. In 1903, she became engaged to

Franklin D. Roosevelt (known as FDR), a distant cousin. They married on March 17, 1905.

Life with FDR

FDR devoted his career to public service. During the first 11 years of marriage, FDR and Eleanor had five children. They also got involved in politics as Democrats. In 1910, FDR became a senator from New York, and Eleanor assisted her husband with his political duties.

> "I could not, at any age, be content to take my place by the fireside and simply look on. Life was meant to be lived, and curiosity must be kept alive. One must never, for whatever reason, turn his back on life."
>
> —Eleanor Roosevelt

In 1918, during World War I, Eleanor worked with the American Red Cross and volunteered in Navy hospitals.

In 1921, FDR contracted polio, a crippling disease that affected his legs, making it difficult to walk. Encouraged by Eleanor, FDR continued in politics despite his disability. She often traveled around the country to see what was happening in different communities across the states. Then she reported her findings to FDR. In 1928, he was elected governor of New York.

Eleanor pursued her own interests too. She and some of her women friends—all of whom were activists—built a rustic cottage north of New York City. In 1926, they co-founded Val-kill Industries, a furniture factory, there. It was designed to give jobs to local youths and to keep the local economy strong.

Becoming the First Lady

In 1933, FDR became the 32nd president of the United States. At that time, many politicians' wives stayed in the background. Not Eleanor. She took up women's and civil-rights causes. She openly disagreed with FDR when she believed that she should speak out. Unlike other politicians, FDR truly respected his wife and her ideals. Even as president, he frequently asked Eleanor's advice.

FDR was reelected three times. During FDR's 12 years in office, he and Eleanor saw the nation through

TOPICAL TIDBIT

The Four-term President

Franklin Delano Roosevelt was the only U.S. president to be elected four times. In 1951, the 22nd Amendment to the Constitution was ratified. It states that no person can be elected to the presidency more than two times.

the Great Depression and World War II. During the Depression, FDR established work programs to keep people employed, and Eleanor made sure that women and minorities were included in those programs. During the war, the Roosevelts built morale for the American public and put women to work in jobs left by men who had been sent to the front lines.

Eleanor began holding press conferences at the White House. She was the first First Lady to do so. When she started inviting only female journalists to the press conferences, she forced many of the nation's top newspapers to hire female reporters for the first time.

A Continuing Influence

Eleanor Roosevelt continued to influence history. She wrote her own newspaper column, called "My Day," from 1935 until her death. She fought to end racial segregation laws, which created separate areas—such as beaches, parks, schools—for whites and blacks. At a meeting in Alabama in 1939, she caused a stir by sitting in the black section of seats instead of the whites-only section. With her help, segregation ended in the Army Nurse Corps in 1945.

When FDR died in 1945, Eleanor thought that her political career was over. However, the new president, Harry S. Truman, appointed her as U.S. delegate to the United Nations (UN). In 1947, she led the UN's Human Rights Commission in creating the Declaration of

Human Rights. In 1961, President John F. Kennedy appointed her as first chairperson of the President's Commission on the Status of Women.

Eleanor Roosevelt died on November 7, 1962, in New York City. She had always shown great sensitivity to others, and was respected and admired by people worldwide.

Many historians believe that Eleanor Roosevelt achieved more than any other First Lady. She furthered women's rights, human rights, and civil rights in the U.S. and abroad. She was inducted into the National Women's Hall of Fame, and named one of the most influential people of the 20th century by *Time* magazine. People can visit her cottage home, now called the Eleanor Roosevelt National Historic Site, in Hyde Park, New York. ◇

LIFE EVENTS

1884
Anna Eleanor Roosevelt is born in New York City.

1905
Eleanor marries Franklin Delano Roosevelt (FDR).

1933
FDR begins his first term as president.

1945
President Truman appoints Eleanor Roosevelt as a delegate to the United Nations (UN).

1948
Eleanor Roosevelt is a major contributor to the UN's Universal Declaration of Human Rights.

1958
On My Own, Roosevelt's autobiography, is published. She dies in 1962.

Wilma Rudolph
Track-and-Field Star
(born 1940 • died 1994)

Wilma Rudolph was a sickly child, often confined to bed. Childhood diseases had left her weak and without the use of one of her legs. Yet she was determined to overcome her disability. Rudolph learned to walk without a leg brace—then went on to become one of the fastest runners in the world.

Overcoming Obstacles

When Wilma Glodean Rudolph was born on June 23, 1940, in St. Bethlehem, Tennessee, she was a premature baby. She weighed only four and a half pounds. While still a child, she survived scarlet fever, pneumonia, and polio. Polio, which is a disease of the spinal cord, left Wilma unable to use one of her legs.

Wilma came from a large family, and her brothers and sisters tried to help her by massaging her leg. She also took physical therapy to make her leg work better. Wilma used a leg brace to help her walk. As she grew older, she got stronger and, eventually, she

Wilma Rudolph runs the last leg of a relay race.

could walk without help. By the time she was 11, she had started to play basketball.

Wilma played on the basketball team in high school and became a star athlete. Despite her successes, she still faced an obstacle: racial discrimination. As an

African American growing up in the South, she was treated as an inferior person. The South was segregated, which means that blacks and whites had to use separate public facilities. For example, there were separate beaches, parks, schools, bathrooms, and water fountains. The facilities for whites were better than those for blacks.

Running for the Gold

In high school, Wilma Rudolph got involved in track, and proved that the color of her skin had nothing to do with her ability as an athlete. At 5 feet, 11 inches tall, Rudolph had long legs and could run fast. She was so fast, in fact, that she qualified for the Olympics in 1956 and represented the U.S. at the Games in Melbourne, Australia. Rudolph participated in the 4-x-100-meter

TOPICAL TIDBIT

Overcoming Polio

Other famous people have battled polio and gone on to achieve their dreams. President Franklin D. Roosevelt was a polio survivor. He saw the country through World War II and the worst economic depression in history. The Mexican painter Frida Kahlo was also a polio survivor. She used bright colors on canvas to express her pain and struggle.

relay, a competition in which four team members each run one part of the race. She and her team won a bronze medal (third place).

Beginning in 1957, Rudolph attended Tennessee State University and continued to run track. In 1960, she set a world record for the 200-meter race at 22.9 seconds. That same year, she returned to the Summer Olympics, this time in Rome, Italy. Several other women

"Never underestimate the power of dreams and the influence of the human spirit. We are all the same in this notion: The potential for greatness lives within each of us."

—Wilma Rudolph

from Tennessee State joined her on the U.S. track team. Rudolph dazzled the crowds with her speed.

At the Olympics, Rudolph won three gold medals, becoming the first American woman to do so at one Olympic competition. She won both the 100- and 200-meter races. Her team also took home first place in the 4-x-100-meter relay.

After the Olympics, Rudolph continued to compete, and fans flocked to see her. Once, in Germany, a fan stole her shoes as a souvenir.

When Rudolph returned home to Tennessee, a parade was held in her honor. It was extra-special for Rudolph because it was the first nonsegregated parade held in her hometown. In the years that followed, Rudolph married and had four children. She worked with groups, such as Operation Champion, that helped inner-city children. She also set up the Wilma Rudolph Foundation, which provides athletic coaching and educational support for underprivileged children.

Into the History Books

Wilma Rudolph died of brain cancer on November 12, 1994, in Brentwood, Tennessee. Her courageous spirit and amazing talent still inspire people around the world. She was inducted into the National Track and Field Hall of Fame, the U.S. Olympic Hall of Fame, and the National Women's Hall of Fame. Her autobiography, *Wilma*, was made into a TV movie. Today, she is remembered as one of the fastest women who ever lived. ◇

LIFE EVENTS

1940
Wilma Glodean Rudolph is born in St. Bethlehem, Tennessee.

1956
Rudolph wins a team bronze medal at the Olympics.

1960
Rudolph sets a world record, and becomes the first female U.S. runner to win three gold medals at one Olympics.

1980
Rudolph is inducted into the International Sports Hall of Fame (and to two other Halls of Fame in 1974 and 1983).

1982
Rudolph founds the Wilma Rudolph Foundation.

1994
Rudolph dies.

Sacagawea
Interpreter and Explorer
(born about 1787 • died 1812 or 1884)

Sacagawea *(SAK-uh-juh-WEE-ah)*, a Shoshone Indian, helped lead explorers Lewis and Clark to the far west regions of the United States in the early 1800s. Hired as an interpreter and guide, Sacagawea joined the famous team on its journey in search of land and water routes to the Pacific Ocean.

Sacagawea Is Kidnapped

Sacagawea was born into the Shoshone tribe in Idaho around 1787. She was the daughter of a Shoshone chief. When she was 12 years old, she was kidnapped by warriors of the rival Hidatsa tribe and taken as a slave to their village along the Missouri River in North Dakota.

The Hidatsa sold Sacagawea as a bride to French-Canadian fur trapper Toussaint Charbonneau. In February 1805 Sacagawea gave birth to a son. They named him Jean Baptiste Charbonneau.

471

Sacagawea Becomes an Explorer

About the time that Sacagawea was kidnapped, people living in the eastern U.S. were curious about the vast, unexplored area between the Missouri River and the Pacific Ocean. President Thomas Jefferson sent a team of explorers, led by Meriwether Lewis and William Clark, to scout the area. Lewis's task was to study the plants and wildlife, while Clark was to make maps of the region. The expedition was called the Corps of Discovery.

On May 21, 1804, the explorers set out from St. Louis, Missouri. They set up camp for the winter in North Dakota, where they met Charbonneau and Sacagawea. The group knew that they would meet many native people along the way who did not speak English. Since Lewis and Clark spoke only English and one of the group's officers spoke French, they

TOPICAL TIDBIT

Bird Woman or Boat Launcher?

Sacagawea's name has been spelled with a *g* and with a *j*. *Sacagawea* means "bird woman" in Hidatsa. *Sacajawea* with a *j*, however, means "boat launcher" in Shoshone. This pronunciation, *sak-uh-juh-WEE-ah*, is the most common. In his journals, however, William Clark was very careful to point out that the name of his interpreter was pronounced *sah-kah-gah-WEE-ah*.

Sacagawea guides Lewis and Clark.

hired Sacagawea and her husband as interpreters. Sacagawea spoke Shoshone and Hidatsa; Charbonneau spoke Hidatsa and French.

The group left North Dakota in April 1805. Using horses and canoes, they made their way through the wilderness of Idaho, Montana, Oregon, and

Washington. As they roamed through the forests, Sacagawea collected nuts and berries for food, while carrying her infant son in a cradleboard (knapsack) on her back.

Once the expedition reached the Bitterroot Mountains of Idaho, they needed 30 horses to transport their supplies. They found a Shoshone tribe living nearby, so they asked Sacagawea to trade some goods for the horses. When she approached the tribal chief, she discovered that it was her brother Cameahwait *(kah-MAY-uh-wah-it)*. She had not seen him since she was kidnapped.

> "Sacagawea was sent for; she came into the tent, sat down, and was beginning to interpret, when in the person of Cameahwait she recognised her brother: She instantly jumped up, and ran and embraced him."
>
> —from the Lewis & Clark journals

After a tearful but joyous reunion, Sacagawea traded for the horses. She spoke with her brother in her native tongue of Shoshone and translated his response into Hidatsa. Charbonneau then translated the words from Hidatsa into French. The expedition's French-speaking officer translated the words into English so that Lewis and Clark and the other members of the group could follow the conversation.

The Explorers Return

The expedition reached the Columbia River in November 1805. The men built a shelter, which they named Fort Clatsop, to protect the team from the harsh winter weather. They stayed at the fort until spring, getting by with barely enough to eat.

When the snow melted, the group headed back to St. Louis. Sacagawea led the expedition through her homeland, following old Indian trails. When they reached the banks of the Missouri River in North Dakota, after traveling nearly 4,000 miles, Sacagawea and Charbonneau stayed; the team went on.

In 1812, Sacagawea had another baby, named Lisette. On December 20, later that year, Sacagawea

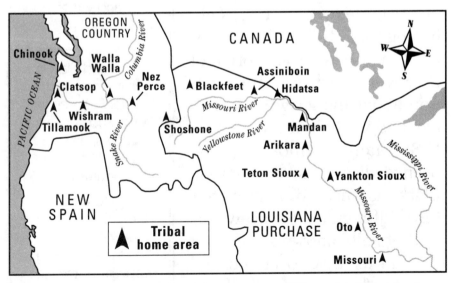

The Corps of Discovery encountered many different Native American tribes on its journey.

died. William Clark adopted both children. According to the Shoshone, however, Sacagawea did not die in 1812, but remarried and took the name Porivo. Porivo lived on the Wind River Reservation, and knew many details of Lewis and Clark's journey. She died on April 9, 1884.

A True American Hero

With Sacagawea's help, William Clark was able to map an uncharted wilderness, establishing trails and landmarks for later pioneers. The Corps of Discovery gathered information about the geography, people, and wildlife of the western U.S. Many memorials have been dedicated to Sacagawea. Clark also named a river after his skillful guide. Sacagawea is traditionally known as the first woman to travel overland and see the "great waters" of the Pacific Ocean. ◇

LIFE EVENTS

About 1787
Sacagawea is born.

About 1800
Sacagawea is kidnapped, sold to Mandan Indians, then to a French-Canadian fur trapper.

1804
Meriwether Lewis and William Clark start from St. Louis, Missouri, on their journey north and west.

1805
Sacagawea meets Lewis and Clark in what is now North Dakota. She, her husband, and baby son accompany the expedition. The team returns in 1806.

2000
The U.S. Mint issues new one-dollar coins. Sacagawea appears on the face of the coin.

Margaret Sanger
Founder of the Birth Control Movement
(born 1879 • died 1966)

Margaret Sanger was one of the first women to promote birth control and family planning—couples deciding when and if to have children. In a time when it was illegal to use contraceptives (birth-control methods), or even to talk about them, Sanger educated people about how to avoid unwanted pregnancies. She worked with the legal system so that doctors and nurses could be allowed to distribute contraceptives.

> "My fight is for the personal liberty of the women who work."
>
> —Margaret Sanger

A Big Family!

Margaret Louisa Higgins was born on September 14, 1879, in Corning, New York. She was the middle child of 11 children. Margaret's mother gave birth to 18 children in all,

but several died during childbirth. Margaret's mother also died at a young age. Margaret believed that her death had been caused by the stress placed upon her body through her many pregnancies and having to care for so many children.

As a young woman, Margaret attended Claverack College and later trained as a nurse. In 1902, Margaret married William Sanger and they eventually had three children. The Sangers moved to New York City, where Margaret worked as a nurse in a birthing center in a poor section of town. She saw women with many children, sometimes more than they could handle.

Margaret Sanger saw women die in childbirth, give birth to sick children, and live in poverty because they could not afford to take care of all their children. Sanger also cared for women who eventually died after trying to end a pregnancy. Sanger wanted to change this situation. She wanted to teach women how to avoid pregnancy.

"What Every Girl Should Know"

Sanger got a divorce in 1912, and devoted her time to educating women about birth control. On October 16, 1916, she opened the Brownsville Clinic with the help of two nurses—her sister, Ethel Byrne, and Fania Mindell. The clinic, located in Brooklyn, New York, was the first birth-control center in the U.S. The three women offered lectures on birth control and handed out pamphlets called "What Every Girl Should Know." The pamphlets explained how women become pregnant and how a woman can avoid it. More than 100 women and girls attended the lectures on the first day.

Many people thought that the pamphlet and lectures were too detailed. They told the police that the women were handing out "obscene" literature. Ten days later, the police closed the clinic and arrested Sanger, Byrne, and Mindell. The women spent the night in jail, but were released the next morning. This did not stop Sanger. She reopened the clinic in November, was arrested again, and spent 30 days in jail. That time, the clinic closed permanently.

Changing the Law

In 1921, Sanger founded the American Birth Control League, which, in 1942, became the Planned Parenthood Federation of America. In 1922, she married J. Noah H. Slee, the owner of a large oil company. He provided funds for Sanger to promote her ideas about birth control.

Sanger spoke in many cities across the country, teaching people about birth control and planning for

TOPICAL TIDBIT

Planned Parenthood Federation of America

Founded in 1942, the Planned Parenthood Federation of America (PPFA) educates people about birth control, abortion, and health-care issues. The PPFA operates family-planning counseling centers, and offers classes in sex education, prenatal care (care for babies not yet born), and care for new mothers and their infants.

parenthood. She also opened many neighborhood health-care clinics. Because of Sanger's determination, federal laws outlawing contraceptives were overturned. In 1936, new laws were put into place that allowed doctors and medical professionals to prescribe contraceptives for people wishing to avoid pregnancy.

Worldwide Influence

Margaret Sanger traveled to China and India and helped set up the Birth Control International Information Center, which distributed literature and birth-control devices throughout Europe and Asia. She also organized the International Planned Parenthood Federation, serving as its president until her retirement in 1959. She died on September 6, 1966. ◇

LIFE EVENTS

1879
Margaret Louisa Higgins is born in Corning, New York.

1902
Higgins, a nurse, marries architect William Sanger. They divorce in 1912.

1914
Sanger founds the National Birth Control League and opens the first U.S. birth-control clinic.

1921
Sanger founds the American Birth Control League.

1942
The Planned Parenthood Federation of America is formed.

1953
Sanger is the first president of the International Planned Parenthood Federation.

Elizabeth Cady Stanton
Women's Rights Leader
(born 1815 • died 1902)

During the 1800s, Elizabeth Cady Stanton and Susan B. Anthony led the crusade for women's rights in the U.S. United in the cause of women's suffrage—the right to vote—they worked together for more than 50 years to bring about change in the United States. A devoted wife and mother of seven children, Stanton wrote speeches for Anthony to present across the country, while she stayed at home to raise her children.

"I Wish You Were a Boy!"

On November 12, 1815, Elizabeth Cady was born in Johnstown, New York. She was one of six children, mostly girls. When Elizabeth's brother died, her father was very upset. He said to her, "Oh my daughter, I wish you were a boy!" Elizabeth tried to be like a son to her father. She studied very hard in

Elizabeth Cady Stanton *(right)* poses with Susan B. Anthony *(left)*.

school, learning math, philosophy, Greek, and Latin. She loved to go horseback riding and debate political issues—something that few girls ever did.

Elizabeth's father was a congressman and New York Supreme Court judge. Elizabeth spent hours studying law in her father's office. It was there that she learned about the unfair advantages that men had over women. She decided that she would work to make women equal to men in the eyes of the law.

"We Hold These Truths . . ."

In 1840 Elizabeth married Henry Stanton, a lawyer and abolitionist—someone who believed that slavery should be abolished (outlawed). They spent their honeymoon in London, England, so that Elizabeth could attend the World Anti-Slavery convention. Several women went to the convention, but were turned away because they were women. One of those women was Lucretia Mott. Elizabeth and Mott became good friends and, over the years, talked of women's rights issues.

On July 19-20, 1848, in Seneca Falls, New York, Stanton and Mott gathered together more than 100 women to discuss the issue of women's rights. The Seneca Falls Convention, as it is now called, was the beginning of the women's rights movement.

TOPICAL TIDBIT

Lucretia Mott

Lucretia Mott (1793-1880) believed that all people should be treated as equals. As one of the founders of the American Anti-Slavery Society, Mott devoted her energy to freeing African American slaves, including running a station on the Underground Railroad. Later, she worked with Elizabeth Cady Stanton to launch the women's rights movement.

At the meeting, Stanton read the "Declaration of Sentiments"—a document based on the Declaration of Independence. The opening lines of the declaration read: "We hold these truths to be self-evident: that all men AND WOMEN are created equal." The declaration states that women should be treated equally and fairly by the laws governing the United States. It also states

> "The prejudice against color, of which we hear so much, is no stronger than that against sex. It is produced by the same cause, and manifested very much in the same way."
>
> —Elizabeth Cady Stanton

that women should be allowed to vote, just like any other citizen in the country.

The Crusade for Women's Suffrage

A few years later, Stanton met Susan B. Anthony. For the next 50 years, the two worked together, crusading for women's suffrage. In 1869, they formed the National Woman Suffrage Association. Stanton served as president of the group until 1890.

Stanton was an excellent writer and lecturer. She wrote many articles for newspapers and magazines, and also wrote several books, including

The History of Woman Suffrage, with Susan B. Anthony and Matilda Joslyn Gage.

Stanton also drafted an amendment (change) to the U.S. Constitution, calling for the U.S. government to grant women the right to vote. Beginning in 1878, Anthony and other suffragists appeared before Congress each year to propose the amendment. When Stanton died, on October 26, 1902, the amendment still had not become law. Not until 1920 was the amendment, the 19th Amendment, finally added to the U.S. Constitution. Later that year, more than 8 million women voted for the first time in U.S. history.

Never to Be Forgotten

Elizabeth Cady Stanton devoted her life to women's rights issues. Although she

LIFE EVENTS

1815
Elizabeth Cady is born in Johnstown, New York.

1848
Elizabeth Cady Stanton and Lucretia Mott organize the world's first women's rights convention.

1851
Stanton meets Susan B. Anthony.

1869
Stanton and Anthony found the National Woman Suffrage Association.

1878
Stanton drafts an amendment to the Constitution that would grant women the right to vote. She dies in 1902.

1920
The 19th Amendment, granting women the right to vote, is ratified.

was never honored during her lifetime as one of the founders of the women's rights movement, she will always be remembered as such. A statue of Stanton, Anthony, and Mott stands in the U.S. Capitol in Washington, D.C. Stanton also has been inducted into the National Women's Hall of Fame in Seneca Falls, New York. ◇

Gloria Steinem
Journalist and Feminist
(born 1934)

"**A** woman without a man is like a fish without a bicycle," said Gloria Steinem, leader of the feminist movement. The point that Steinem was making with this statement is that women do not need to be dependent upon men for their survival. Women can make choices for themselves and should not be discriminated against because of their gender.

On the Road

Gloria Marie Steinem was born in Toledo, Ohio, on March 25, 1934, to Ruth and Leo Steinem. Gloria's father was an antiques dealer. Most of the year, the Steinem family traveled around the country in a trailer so that Leo could sell antiques. The family spent their summers in Michigan, where they owned a small resort. Gloria and her older sister, Susan, did not attend school like other children because the family moved from town to town. The girls were

taught by their mother, who had been a teacher.

When Gloria was 10, her parents divorced. Susan went off to college, while Gloria lived with her mother in Toledo. Ruth Steinem was very sick—she suffered from depression—and Gloria was left to take care of her. Gloria went to public school in Toledo and became very independent. It was up to her to clean, shop for groceries, and run the house.

Gloria excelled in school. She spent her senior year of high school in Washington, D.C., with her sister, while her father took care of Ruth. Gloria thrived. She was then accepted to Smith College, where Susan had gone.

At Smith College, Gloria studied government and politics. She spent a year in Geneva, Switzerland, as an exchange student. She also wrote articles for the college newspaper. As Gloria became more politically active, she realized that Ruth's illness was not always taken seriously because Ruth was a woman. Gloria decided to change things for women throughout the world.

> "I'm optimistic [about the future]. But I also know nothing will happen automatically. Change depends on what you and I do every day."
>
> —Gloria Steinem

Becoming a Feminist

In 1956, Gloria Steinem received a scholarship to study in India. When Steinem returned to the U.S. two years later, she published a book about her experience called *A Thousand Indias*. Steinem hoped that this would help her land a career in journalism.

However, many newspaper and magazine editors turned her down for jobs because she was a woman. They wanted a serious journalist, not a "pretty girl." Steinem was furious. Why did these men think that a woman could not be a professional journalist?

Steinem eventually became an editorial assistant for *Help!* magazine. She met people in the business and began writing freelance articles. In 1963, on an assignment for *Esquire* magazine, she went undercover as a "bunny" at New York's Playboy Club. Playboy bunnies were cocktail waitresses who wore skimpy outfits and bunny ears. Steinem's article, "I Was a Playboy Bunny," talked about sexual harassment and discrimination against women at the club. Steinem thought that it would be her ticket to serious journalism. She was wrong. The editors looked past her writing talent and saw her only as a Playboy bunny.

TOPICAL TIDBIT

Ms. Magazine

In 1972, a magazine published by women hit the newsstands. *Ms.* magazine, founded by Gloria Steinem and Dorothy Pitman Hughes, was dedicated to addressing the concerns of women throughout the world. Article topics include past and present political trends in the women's movement, women's rights, women's health issues, and social issues that face young and older women today.

Crusading for Women's Rights

Through hard work and determination, Steinem finally achieved her goal. In 1968, she became an editor for *New York* magazine. The job gave her the opportunity to choose her own assignments. She wrote about the assassination of Martin Luther King Jr., labor-union strikes, and women's liberation. In 1972, Steinem, along with Dorothy Pitman Hughes, founded *Ms.* magazine, where she served as editor for 16 years. Later that year, Steinem was named Woman of the Year by *McCall's* magazine.

As an outspoken, intelligent activist, Steinem was a leader of the women's rights movement. She founded many women's groups, including the Women's Action Alliance, the National Women's Political Caucus, and the Coalition of Labor Union Women. These

LIFE EVENTS

1934
Gloria Marie Steinem is born in Toledo, Ohio.

1958
Steinem's book about her experiences in India is published.

1963
Steinem publishes a feminist article on working at the Playboy Club.

1971
Steinem co-founds the National Women's Political Caucus. The following year she co-founds *Ms.*, a feminist magazine.

1973
Steinem helps found the Coalition of Labor Union Women.

2000
Steinem marries for the first time.

groups spoke out about women's issues, such as freedom of choice (legalized abortion), equal pay for equal work, and sex discrimination.

A Crusader for Rights

Throughout her career, Gloria Steinem has written books on the world of publishing and women's rights, including *Outrageous Acts and Everyday Rebellions*, *Moving Beyond Words*, and *Revolution From Within*. In 1993, Steinem was inducted into the National Women's Hall of Fame. She is one of the most famous and outspoken feminists of the 20th century, and remains a crusader for the rights of women. ◇

Martha Stewart
Home and Lifestyle Expert
(born 1941)

She can show you how to paint a room, make a Christmas ornament, plant a garden, or cook a meal for 15 guests. She can suggest what type of curtains would look best, how to fix a chair, or which cleaner to use to remove a stubborn stain. When it comes to teaching people how to fix up their homes and entertain guests, Martha Stewart has all the answers.

Learning Her Craft

Martha Kostyra was born on August 3, 1941, in Jersey City, New Jersey. She is the second oldest of six children in a Polish American family. Although many people think that Martha grew up in the country, she did not. She was raised in Nutley, New Jersey, a suburb near New York City.

During her childhood, Martha loved to read. One of her favorite authors is Jane Austen. Martha also loved to entertain her friends and family, and plan birthday parties. Along with the fun and games,

Martha was responsible for chores that helped keep the Kostyra household running smoothly. She learned how to cook, bake, sew, garden, and clean, among other things. Martha perfected her baking skills by making pies and cakes with her neighbors, an older couple who ran a bakery.

In her early teens, Martha worked as a model to raise money for college. Then she enrolled at Barnard College. At one time, Martha considered becoming a teacher. While in college, she met Andy Stewart. The two got married in 1961 and had a daughter, Alexis, in 1965.

Finding Her Gift

After obtaining her bachelor's degree from Barnard in 1962, Martha Stewart returned to modeling for a while. She was featured in ads for Clairol, Breck, and other products.

In 1967, Stewart went to work as a stockbroker on Wall Street. She was quite successful and, in 1973, she and her family moved to Connecticut. They bought an early 19th-century farmhouse and fixed it up together.

Several years later, Stewart quit Wall Street and started a catering company from her home. Stewart's knowledge of cooking, baking, and business helped her catering company take off. Word spread about Stewart, and she started writing articles for magazines, such as the *New York Times Magazine* and *House Beautiful*. Then, she began writing books and appearing on TV and radio shows. Stewart had finally found her gift—helping others with ideas on how to entertain guests and beautify their homes.

> "We pioneered a new media category which is called lifestyle. Nobody else ever did it before, and we did it, and we intend to really dominate this area for a very long time to come."
>
> —Martha Stewart

Sprucing It Up

Stewart was successful in business, but her marriage was breaking up. It ended in a bitter divorce in 1990. After that, Stewart began a monthly lifestyle magazine called *Martha Stewart Living*. She also started *Martha Stewart Weddings*, a magazine offering suggestions for brides and grooms.

Stewart issued more books, many reaching the best-seller list. In addition, she began an advice column called "Ask Martha." It appears in more than 200 newspapers around the U.S. A radio version of "Ask Martha" can be heard on more than 250 stations nationwide.

Stewart's following grew when she started appearing on television shows, including NBC's *Today* and *CBS This Morning*. She began a syndicated show called *Martha Stewart Living*, which deals with many home and gardening projects. In addition, Stewart

TOPICAL TIDBIT

Knowing the Answers

How does Martha Stewart know so much about so many topics? She reads a lot. Stewart, who was an avid reader as a child, continues to dig into books, magazines, and Web sites every day. She scours information to help with lifestyle advice to give in her columns, television shows, and radio broadcasts.

began selling her own line of products in K-Mart stores. You can find Martha Stewart brand sheets, paints, curtains, and bath items.

Big Business

Although Stewart has the image of a homemaker, she is also a highly successful businesswoman. She has helped millions of people by providing ideas on how to improve their homes and how to have entertaining parties. Although she is sometimes criticized for making things look too easy, she has created a huge business by helping others spruce things up. ◇

LIFE EVENTS

1941
Martha Kostyra is born in New Jersey.

1962
Stewart graduates from Barnard College.

1972
Stewart and her family move to Connecticut, where Stewart begins to focus on her interest in gourmet cooking.

Late 1970s
Stewart begins a catering business.

1991
Stewart begins publishing her magazine *Martha Stewart Living*.

1997
MarthaStewart.com debuts on the Internet, providing access to all of Stewart's books, magazines, and products.

Harriet Beecher Stowe
Abolitionist and Author
(born 1811 • died 1896)

When Harriet Beecher Stowe's novel *Uncle Tom's Cabin* was published in the 1850s, it caused a sensation in the U.S. The book spoke about the evils of slavery, which was still practiced in the South. Stowe's story made people think about whether

> "Women are the real architects of society."
> —Harriet Beecher Stowe

slavery was right or wrong. The book angered Southerners, who insisted on using slaves, as well as Northerners, who did not.

A Famous Family

Harriet Elizabeth Beecher was born on June 14, 1811, in Litchfield, Connecticut. Her father, a famous minister, had 13 children. Harriet was the

seventh. Many of her brothers and sisters became successful. Her sister Catherine started several schools for girls, while her brother Henry Ward was a popular preacher. The Beechers were one of the most well-known families in America.

The Beechers believed strongly in education. After Catherine started a girls' school in Hartford, Connecticut, Harriet enrolled there in 1824. She later taught at the school. As Harriet grew older, the U.S. was heading toward a civil war.

The country was divided on several issues, including slavery and states' rights. Many Southerners used slaves to plant and harvest crops on their large plantations. They believed that a state should decide whether slavery could be practiced there. Much of the North had outlawed slavery by that time. A movement was growing in the North to abolish (end) slavery in the entire U.S. Harriet Beecher was an abolitionist—someone opposed to slavery.

A River Apart

The Beechers moved to Cincinnati, Ohio, in 1832. Cincinnati is near the Ohio River, which provides a natural border between the states of Ohio and Kentucky. Ohio was a "free state"—it did not allow slavery. Across the river was Kentucky, a "slave state," where slavery was allowed.

Slaves were forced to work long hours with no pay. Many were treated terribly. They were insulted, beaten, whipped, even killed. Slave owners would break apart families by selling mothers, fathers, sisters, or brothers to different owners.

In Cincinnati, Harriet met fugitive slaves who had escaped, and she listened to their stories. She knew that the law permitted slave hunters to capture runaways and take them back to their masters. Harriet Beecher was outraged. She believed that it was wrong for one person to own another.

Uncle Tom's Cabin

Harriet began writing stories for magazines. In 1836, she married Calvin Ellis Stowe, a minister, and continued to work. She added motherhood to her list of accomplishments and eventually had seven children. In 1843, Harriet Beecher Stowe wrote a book about the Pilgrims and the *Mayflower*.

The Stowes moved to Brunswick, Maine, in 1850. In 1852, Stowe published what became her most famous novel, *Uncle Tom's Cabin; Life Among the Lowly*. She knew that Southerners were angry with Northern views about slavery, and that the South wanted to secede, or break away from the rest of the U.S. Stowe took the opportunity to put her anti-slavery thoughts together in a book.

In *Uncle Tom's Cabin*, Stowe told the story of slave owners and slaves. Through her characters, she

---

TOPICAL TIDBIT

The Stowe Sisters

Harriet teamed up with her sister Catherine to write a book about how to keep a clean and tidy house. Their book, *The American Woman's Home*, was published in 1869. Catherine, who worked hard to improve education for women, was nearly eleven years older than Harriet.

described the injustice of slavery. Stowe showed slaves as real people who experienced pain and suffering like everyone else. That was an important message, because many white Americans thought of slaves as workers whom they owned, like cattle or horses. The book became a best-seller and thrust Stowe into the limelight.

The Civil War

Stowe's book made people think long and hard about slavery. Most slave owners hated the book and used it to criticize the North's attitudes. Many Northerners supported the book's antislavery message and used it to condemn Southern practices.

Uncle Tom's Cabin added fuel to the already bitter debate between North and South. In 1861, the South seceded (withdrew) from the

LIFE EVENTS

1811
Harriet Elizabeth Beecher is born in Litchfield, Connecticut.

1832
Beecher begins to write sketches and short fiction.

1836
Harriet Beecher marries Calvin Ellis Stowe

1852
Uncle Tom's Cabin is published as a two-volume novel.

1850s
Stowe travels to Europe three times, befriending famous literary figures.

1869
Stowe writes *The American Woman's Home* with her sister Catherine.

1896
Harriet Beecher Stowe dies.

Union, an act that started the Civil War. When the war concluded in 1865, slavery was abolished throughout the U.S.

A Positive Influence on All

Although Stowe wrote other books, none was ever as popular as *Uncle Tom's Cabin*. Stowe died on July 1, 1896, in Hartford, Connecticut.

Harriet Beecher Stowe was one of the most important authors of her day. By writing and speaking about issues that were near to her heart, she influenced others to support basic human rights for all people. She was inducted into the National Women's Hall of Fame in New York. Her house in Connecticut is now a museum. ◇

Ida M. Tarbell
Investigative Reporter
(born 1857 • died 1944)

Ida M. Tarbell began a career in journalism in the late 19th century. She approached her work differently from most reporters of her day—she investigated her subjects thoroughly. Most journalists only touched the surface of a story, because getting it out first was more important than getting a full story. But Tarbell dug deep to uncover the truth. Tarbell's style of journalism became popular, and today she is recognized as one of America's first investigative reporters.

Early Influences

Ida Minerva Tarbell was born on November 5, 1857, in Erie County, Pennsylvania. Her father, Franklin, owned a small, independent oil company and her mother, Esther, was interested in furthering women's rights, such as the right to vote and the right to own property.

Ida was a curious child. She liked to explore, study,

Ida M. Tarbell poses with a statue of President Abraham Lincoln.

and read. Interested in her father's oil business, she learned about science and the natural world. She became aware of the problems that her father had in business. He worked independently, which meant that he was not part of a big business. As the oil industry boomed, big businesses began pushing out the independents, taking over their operations. Ida's father had a difficult time keeping his company going.

Despite the family's financial troubles, Ida went to college. In the 1870s, few teenage girls planned to attend college or start a career. They were expected to become good wives and stay at home and raise many children. Ida Tar-

> "Nobody begins or ends anything. Each person is a link, weak or strong, in an endless chain."
>
> —Ida Tarbell, from her autobiography

bell had other plans. She entered Allegheny College, which had just started to allow female students. She graduated in 1880.

Ida Becomes a Journalist

Ida Tarbell found work as a schoolteacher in Ohio, but left that position after two years. In 1883, she joined the staff of a small magazine. Eight years later, she did something that most women of her day would never dream of doing: She went to Paris, France, to live and study.

To support herself in Paris, Tarbell worked as a freelance writer. She returned to the U.S. in 1894 and began work as a reporter at *McClure's Magazine*.

The reporters at *McClure's* were among the first to take up investigative reporting. They wrote about social issues, and exposed corruption in government, politics, and big business. President Theodore Roosevelt called such reporters "muckrakers," because he believed that they would do anything—even rake through mud and muck—to dig up a story.

Tarbell's first assignments were biographies on such people as President Abraham Lincoln. She then began a long investigation into the Standard Oil Company, one of the big businesses that squeezed out smaller, independent oil companies, like her father's. Her series of articles was published as a book, *The History of the Standard Oil Company*, in 1904.

Tarbell's findings led to a government investigation of Standard Oil's illegal practices, and the case

TOPICAL TIDBIT

From Yellow to Muck

Before "muckraking" became a popular form of journalism in the U.S., many newspapers hired reporters who sensationalized stories. These reporters twisted and exaggerated the facts to make stories more appealing to readers. Such reporters wrote about sex scandals and violence, among other topics. This type of reporting was known as Yellow Journalism.

was brought to trial. In 1911, the U.S. Supreme Court ruled that Standard Oil had an unfair monopoly—it controlled too much of the oil business in the U.S. The Court ordered that the company be split into smaller, separate businesses.

Changing Attitudes

Tarbell's work made her a popular journalist. In 1906, she and several other *McClure's* writers left their jobs to start their own publication, *American Magazine.* Tarbell continued to write on social issues for the magazine until 1915. She also wrote books, including *The Business of Being a Woman* (1912).

As Tarbell grew older, her ideas about women and careers changed. She suggested that women avoid working outside the home.

LIFE EVENTS

1857
Ida Minerva Tarbell is born in Erie County, Pennsylvania.

1894-1906
Tarbell works as a staff writer for *McLure's* Magazine.

1904
Tarbell publishes *The History of the Standard Oil Company,* a critique of J. D. Rockefeller's business practices.

1906-1915
Tarbell writes and edits for *American Magazine,* which she helped found.

1912
Tarbell publishes *The Business of Being a Woman.*

1939
Tarbell's autobiography, *All in the Day's Work,* is published.

1944
Tarbell dies.

Tarbell no longer supported many women's rights issues, including a woman's right to vote. Some people thought that Tarbell was turning her back on the very movement that had helped her succeed in a man's world. Her new attitudes hurt her popularity.

A Journalist to the End

Tarbell continued to write into her eighties, penning her autobiography *All in a Day's Work*. She died on January 6, 1944, in Bridgeport, Connecticut. Despite her later ideas about working women, Tarbell had a successful career as an investigative reporter. She was one of the first women to excel in journalism. She was inducted into the National Women's Hall of Fame in 2000. ◇

Mother Teresa
Catholic Nun
(born 1910 • died 1997)

Mother Teresa was only a teenager when she devoted her life to God and became a Catholic nun. She felt destined to work with the homeless and the sick in India. She believed that all people needed to feel love, dignity, and compassion, and she opened centers to help those who were dying. She lived a humble life, with few possessions and without luxuries.

Becoming a Nun

Agnes Gonxha Bojaxhiu was born on August 27, 1910, in what is now Skopje, Macedonia. Her parents were Albanian, and Agnes's father was murdered when Agnes was just seven years old. At 18, Agnes went to Ireland to become a nun with the Sisters of Our Lady of Loreto. She worked in Ireland, then in India, as she studied to become a nun.

Often, when people devote their lives to God, they are said to "hear a calling." This means that

Mother Teresa blesses orphaned children at "Children's Home" in
Calcutta, India, in October 1979.

they believe God has called on them to do his work
on Earth, by helping the poor and sick, ministering
to others about religion, or helping those in great
need. Nuns usually live with few material
possessions.

In 1937, when Agnes Bojaxhiu was 27 years old,

she took the vow to serve God and became a nun. She took the name Teresa, after St. Teresa of Lisieux (1873-1897), the patron saint of foreign missionaries.

Teresa of Calcutta

Sister Teresa served as a teacher at St. Mary's High School in Calcutta, India. In 1944, she became principal. Then Sister Teresa became sick with tuberculosis. She had to take time out to rest and recover. During this time, she received a second calling from God. She believed that she was being called to work with the homeless, sick, and dying among the poor in India.

In Calcutta, Sister Teresa saw many people living a life of poverty, some in the slums of the city, others on the street. When she found a dying woman surrounded by rats in the street, Sister Teresa knew that it was her destiny to live and work with the poor. The local hospital did not want to help the woman because she had no money. Sister Teresa took some medical courses so that she could provide health care to the poor. Others soon joined her in this work.

> "Let us make one point, that we meet each other with a smile, when it is difficult to smile."
> —Mother Teresa

In 1948, Sister Teresa began a new order of nuns, called the Missionaries of Charity. As the head of the order, Sister Teresa came to be called Mother Teresa. In 1952, the order opened a center to help the poor who were near death.

Mother Teresa's Ministry Expands

In addition to the nuns and priests who worked at the center, many volunteers devoted time and money to the cause. In time, the Missionaries of Charity branched out to do its work in about 450 centers worldwide, including centers for AIDS victims in New York City and San Francisco.

The centers also include homes for disabled, orphaned, or adandoned children, as well as for lepers (people with leprosy, a life-threatening disease that causes deformities and paralysis). Mother

TOPICAL TIDBIT

The Little Flower

St. Teresa of Lisieux (1873-1897), Mother Teresa's namesake, was known as the "little flower." She wrote a short autobiography that many people have turned to in times of need. People have said that they were cured of their ailments after reading her book. Some people believe that seeing a rose—in a garden, in a picture, anywhere—is a sign that St. Teresa is working on their behalf.

Teresa sacrificed personal comfort to devote more money to her work. She believed that people should be able to live and die with dignity.

Spreading Peace

Mother Teresa served as an example of how much one person can accomplish. During her lifetime, she sought world peace and an end to human suffering. Among the awards she received were the Pope John XXIII Peace Prize (1971) and the Nobel Peace Prize (1979). True to her beliefs, Mother Teresa asked that the traditional Nobel Prize dinner not be held in her honor. She asked that the money for the dinner be devoted to her charity work, instead, so that hundreds of people could be fed for an entire year.

Mother Teresa died of a heart attack on September 5, 1997. ◇

LIFE EVENTS

1910
Agnes Gonxha Bojaxhiu is born in what is now Skopje, Macedonia.

1928
Bojaxhiu travels to India to teach at a convent school.

1937
Bojaxhiu takes her vows as a nun, becoming Sister Teresa.

1948
Sister Teresa leaves the convent to work independently in the slums of India, becoming Mother Teresa.

1979
Mother Teresa is awarded the Nobel Peace Prize.

1997
Mother Teresa dies.

Margaret Thatcher
Prime Minister of Great Britain
(born 1925)

In 1979, the United Kingdom of Great Britain and Northern Ireland announced that Margaret Thatcher had been elected prime minister. She was the first woman in history to be elected to the top governmental post of a major European nation. She made history again in 1987, when she became the first British prime minister in the 20th century to win three elections in a row.

A Life Full of Politics

Margaret Hilda Roberts was born on October 13, 1925, in Grantham, Lincolnshire, England. Her mother was a dressmaker and her father was a grocer involved in local politics. When Margaret was a child, she decided that she would become a member of the British Parliament, a governmental law-making body similar to the U.S. Congress.

516

Margaret, who was a bright child, went on to receive degrees in chemistry and law from Somerville College at Oxford University. In 1950, she campaigned for a seat in the House of Commons (similar to the U.S. House of Representatives), but lost.

She hoped to run for office again, but in the meantime, she worked as a chemist and later became a tax attorney. In 1951, Margaret married Denis Thatcher, the director of a paint-manufacturing company. In 1959, she ran for the House of Commons again and won.

The House of Commons and Beyond

As a member of the House of Commons, Margaret Thatcher headed the Ministry of Pensions and National Insurance. In the 1960s, she was the secretary of state in charge of science and education. In 1970, she was appointed to a cabinet position, to assist Prime Minister Edward Heath.

Like any person involved in a nation's politics, Margaret Thatcher had many critics. Some people thought that she was not concerned enough about Great Britain's poor. In 1972, a newspaper referred to her as "the most unpopular woman in Britain."

> "We want a society where people are free to make choices, to make mistakes, to be generous and compassionate. This is what we mean by a moral society."
> —Margaret Thatcher

Despite the criticism, however, Thatcher was elected prime minister in 1979. It was the first time in history that a woman had held the top government post in the United Kingdom. Thatcher had promised to reduce taxes and decrease government involvement in the nation's economy. When she took office, she tried to fulfill these promises. During Thatcher's time in office, the economy improved, but thousands of people lost their jobs or could not find work and hundreds of businesses were forced to close.

Running a Country

Throughout history, the United Kingdom has included colonies around the world. During Prime Minister Thatcher's three terms in office, some of the remaining colonies became independent nations.

In 1980, the African nation of Rhodesia was granted independence. Its name then changed to Zimbabwe. In 1984, Thatcher signed documents that would return

TOPICAL TIDBIT

The Empire Strikes Back

In 1982, Argentina invaded the Falkland Islands, a British colony located in South America, off Argentina's southeastern coast. Prime Minister Margaret Thatcher was quick to take action. She sent ships and soldiers. After 10 weeks of fighting, British troops successfully took back the island nation.

Hong Kong to China in 1997.

In the late 1980s, the European Economic Union (EEU) was formed. The EEU—or the Common Market, as it is called—is a group of European nations that work together to create a central economy. Each participating nation agreed to support European banks and businesses. Each nation also agreed to stop issuing its own currency (coins and paper money). Instead, the EEU issues currency that can be used throughout Europe.

The United Kingdom chose not to be part of the EEU. Thatcher was so harshly criticized for the decision not to become part of the EEU that she resigned from office in 1990.

A Mixed Review

Margaret Thatcher served her country as prime minister for 11 years. She was the first British prime minister in the

LIFE EVENTS

1925
Margaret Hilda Roberts is born in Grantham, England.

1950
Thatcher runs unsuccessfully for Parliament.

1959
Thatcher enters Parliament as a junior minister for pensions.

1970
Thatcher becomes education secretary.

1979-1990
Thatcher serves as prime minister of Great Britain.

1990
Margaret Thatcher resigns from her position as prime minister.

1992
Thatcher receives the title of Baroness Thatcher of Kesteven.

20th century to win three consecutive terms in office. She also was the country's longest-serving prime minister since 1827. As a result, Thatcher was awarded the Order of Merit—the highest honor given in the United Kingdom. In 1992, Thatcher was given the title of Baroness Thatcher of Kesteven when she became a member of Britain's House of Lords (similar to the U.S. Senate).

Along with the praise, however, comes criticism. Many of Britain's working-class people still have sour memories of the Thatcher years, due to the very high rate of unemployment. ◇

Sojourner Truth
Crusader for African American Rights
(born about 1797 • died 1883)

Standing six feet tall, Sojourner Truth had a powerful presence. As a freed slave, she traveled throughout the North preaching religion, abolition (ending slavery), and women's rights. She was a strong speaker, even though she had never been taught to read or write. In an era of limited opportunities for women, especially black women, Sojourner Truth was an inspiring activist.

A Slave in the North

Sojourner Truth's story is different from those of many others born into slavery. She was born around 1797 in Ulster County, New York. At that time, slavery was allowed in parts of the North, as well as in the South. Her name was Isabella. Like many slaves, she had no last name. Isabella was one of 10 children, but most of her brothers and sisters had been

sold and sent away to work for other families.

Unlike slaves in the South, most of whom worked on large plantations, Isabella tended to crops and housekeeping chores on a farm owned by a Dutch family. As a result, she spoke Dutch. People later remarked that she had an unusual voice because she spoke English with a Dutch accent. Isabella married a slave named Thomas and had five children. She was devastated when several of her children were sold to other slave holders.

The government of New York State ended the practice of slavery on July 4, 1827, and Isabella was set free. She began living with another family, the Van Wageners, and used their last name as her own.

Isabella went to court to try to free her young son, Peter, who was a slave in Alabama. She won her case and the two were joyfully reunited. Isabella and two of her children moved to New York City about 1829. Isabella worked as a housekeeper.

> "If the first woman God ever made was strong enough to turn the world upside down all alone, these women together ought to be able to turn it back, and get it right side up again! And now they is asking to do it, the men better let them."
>
> —Sojourner Truth, at the Women's Convention in Akron, Ohio, in 1851

A Religious Experience

Isabella was a deeply religious person and often preached on the streets of New York. Throughout her life, she said that she heard voices and had visions sent by God. In 1843, a voice told her to change her name to "Sojourner Truth," as she was to "walk in truth." Her name change signaled a new chapter in her life: She set out on the road to preach and sing about the gospel (God's word).

Sojourner Truth found a new home at the Northampton Association of Education and Industry in Florence, Massachusetts. It was a cooperative farm—a place where like-minded people lived, worked, and shared resources. Members of the community believed in equality, abolition, and other human rights. There, she met antislavery crusaders Frederick Douglass, William Lloyd Garrison, and Olive Gilbert. While at Northampton, Truth also took up the cause of women's equality.

Olive Gilbert helped Truth publish her first book. Since Truth could not read or write, she told her story to Gilbert, who wrote it down. The book was

TOPICAL TIDBIT

In the Shadows

Sojourner Truth had a limited income from her book sales, so she raised additional money by selling her photograph. Many speakers of the day did the same thing. In that era, photos were sometimes called "shadows." Truth's photo included the caption: "I Sell the Shadow to Support the Substance [herself]."

published in 1850 as *The Narrative of Sojourner Truth: A Northern Slave.* She supported herself with money from her book sales.

Truth also began lecturing about abolition and women's rights. She was a dynamic speaker who moved the audience with her wit and wisdom. At a women's convention in Akron, Ohio, in 1851, Truth gave what became her most famous speech. One by one, she knocked down reasons men often gave for why women were inferior to men. With each argument, she repeated "And ain't I a woman?" to prove her point.

The Work Continues

The Northampton Association broke up in 1846, and Truth remained in Florence before moving to Battle Creek, Michigan, in 1857. She continued to travel to support her

LIFE EVENTS

1797
Sojourner Truth is born a slave named Isabelle in Ulster County, New York.

1827
Isabelle is freed when New York State law abolishes slavery.

1850
Truth publishes *The Narrative of Sojourner Truth.*

1851
Truth becomes active in the suffrage movement.

1863
The Emancipation Proclamation is signed, freeing slaves in Confederate states.

1883
Sojourner Truth dies in Michigan.

causes. She even met with President Abraham Lincoln. During the Civil War (1861-1865), Truth raised money and supplies for black troops.

After the war, Truth asked Congress to set aside public lands to create a "Negro state." She also worked with former slaves to help them adjust to life as free individuals. She died on November 26, 1883, in Michigan, possibly from diabetes.

Sojourner Truth used her life experience to help others understand the important struggles facing the U.S. before and after the Civil War. Her work has been recognized in many ways, including induction into the National Women's Hall of Fame. Residents of Florence, Massachusetts, are building a statue in her honor. ◇

Harriet Tubman
Conductor on the Underground Railroad
(born about 1820 • died 1913)

Harriet Tubman risked her life to help slaves escape from the South before the Civil War (1861-1865). A former slave herself, Harriet faced jail, a return to slavery, or even death if she was caught. Regardless, she returned to the South again and again to lead others to freedom via the Underground Railroad. Tubman succeeded in helping many blacks find new, free lives.

Meager Beginnings

Harriet was born Araminta Greene around 1820 in Bucktown, Maryland. She later changed her name to Harriet, after her mother. Her parents, Harriet Greene and Benjamin Ross, were black slaves who were not allowed to marry. Laws in the South severely restricted what blacks could do. Slaves were treated like property, and white owners could sell them at

will, as a farmer might sell a cow or horse. Slave owners split up many black families that way. Marriage
was not allowed because owners did not want their
slaves to become too attached to one another.

As a slave, young Harriet worked the fields,
chopped wood, cleaned the master's house, and
toiled long hours without pay. She was sometimes
treated harshly by the man who owned her. Most

slaves, like Harriet, were not given any schooling, so they did not know how to read or write. Harriet faced a life of few opportunities.

Despite the law, Harriet secretly married John Tubman, a free black man, around 1844. She set her sights on escaping to the North, where slavery was outlawed. Any slave who escaped could be hunted down and sent back into slavery. That is why many slaves wanted to reach Canada—a place that did not recognize the slave laws of the U.S.

Leading Slaves to Freedom

Harriet knew the huge risk she was taking, but she still decided to leave. John did not support her, so she left without him. A white neighbor gave Harriet the name of a "conductor" on the Underground Railroad.

> "I had crossed the line. I was free; but there was no one to welcome me to the land of freedom. I was a stranger in a strange land."
>
> —Harriet Tubman

The Underground Railroad was not a railroad nor was it under the ground. It was a secret and illegal network of people who helped slaves escape to freedom. These people hid slaves, fed them, and told them where to go next.

The people involved in the Underground Railroad could be arrested or killed if they were discovered. To keep their plans secret, they talked about it in railroad terms. A guide, called a conductor, led slaves to safe houses, called stations. They walked and traveled by boat, horse, wagon, or train—mostly at night.

Harriet Tubman reached safety in Philadelphia,

There were many routes via the Underground Railroad. None would have been possible, though, without the help of brave conductors.

Pennsylvania. However, she felt the urge to go back to Maryland—not as a slave, but as a conductor—to lead other slaves to freedom. She returned to Maryland to help her parents and other family members escape. In all, she made 19 trips to the South to help slaves use the Underground Railroad. She helped about 300 slaves reach freedom and begin new lives.

People called Tubman "Moses," after the man in Biblical times who led the Hebrews out of slavery in Egypt. Slave hunters were aware of the new "Moses" who was helping slaves escape, and they put out a reward for Tubman's capture. However, they thought she was a man! They did not believe that a woman was capable of such dangerous activities. Tubman was never caught.

During the Civil War, which helped end slavery in America, Harriet worked for the Union Army. Not

TOPICAL TIDBIT

"Follow the Drinking Gourd"

Slaves used songs to help them travel to safety in the North. One song was "Follow the Drinking Gourd." It contained code words to guide the way. The "drinking gourd" was the Big Dipper in the night sky. By following the gourd, they would find the "promised land" of Canada.

only was she a cook and a nurse, but a spy and scout, too. She helped slaves seek safety with the Union Army.

Courage and Compassion

After the war, Tubman continued to devote her life to others. She started a home for orphaned children and the elderly in Auburn, New York. She died on March 10, 1913, in Auburn.

Rising above her status as a slave in the South, Tubman showed that one woman could change the fate of many others. Her contributions have been honored in many ways, including statues, paintings, and, in 1973, induction into the National Women's Hall of Fame. Harriet's former home in Auburn, New York, is open for tours, allowing people to see how the "Moses of her people" lived. ◇

LIFE EVENTS

1820
Araminta Greene is born in Dorchester County, Maryland.

1849
Tubman escapes to Pennsylvania alone.

1850s
Tubman is a conductor on the Underground Railroad.

1863
The Emancipation Proclamation is signed, freeing slaves in Confederate states.

1908
Tubman opens the Harriet Tubman Home for Aged and Indigent [poor] Colored People.

1913
Harriet Tubman dies in Auburn, New York.

Victoria
Queen of the United Kingdom
(born 1819 • died 1901)

Queen Victoria ruled the United Kingdom for more than six decades. During her reign, many changes took place in the world. Railroads were built to span continents, the camera was invented, and steel hit the marketplace for the first time. The era was also marked by a rise in family values and strict morals. Because Victoria was one of the most influential people in the world during this period of British History it is known as the "Victorian Era."

Long Live the Queen!

Alexandrina Victoria was born on May 24, 1819, in Kensington Palace, in London, England. Victoria, as she was called, was the only daughter of Edward, Duke of Kent. She was third in line to inherit the throne of the United Kingdom.

Edward died when Victoria was a baby, and she was raised by her mother at Kensington Palace.

Tutors came to the palace and taught Victoria to speak, read, and write in English, French, and German. She studied geography and history; she also learned how to paint and to play the piano. She was 10 years old when she learned that she would one day be queen.

When Victoria's uncle, King William IV, died on June 20, 1837, 18-year-old Victoria became queen. Her coronation (official crowning ceremony) was held one year later, on June 28, 1838.

Victoria and Albert

In October 1839, Queen Victoria met her cousin, Prince Albert of Saxe-Coburg-Gotha (now part of Germany), for the first time. She wrote in her diary, "Albert really is quite charming, and so extremely handsome . . . [that] my heart is quite *going*." She proposed to him five days later. On February 10, 1840, they were married. Together, they had nine children—five girls and four boys.

The royal family often spent time away from the

TOPICAL TIDBIT

Great Exhibition of 1851

Prince Albert sponsored the Great Exhibition of 1851. Held in London, England, the exhibition was one of the first World's Fairs. Booths and displays showing the latest technology, agricultural products, and riches of the British Empire were housed in the Crystal Palace—a huge glass building built for the fair.

---

palace in London. They spent time in Scotland and on the Isle of Wight, which is in the English Channel. Victoria liked to go to the circus and see the waxwork shows. She spent a lot of time reading, especially the stories of Charles Dickens. According to Albert, Victoria liked "sitting up at night and sleeping late into the day."

In 1861, Albert died of typhoid. Victoria was heartbroken. She suffered from depression and withdrew from the public eye. She would see no one and did not fulfill her royal duties. Her popularity suffered. Then, after nearly 10 years in mourning, Victoria returned to public life.

The Building of an Empire

As queen, Victoria devoted much of her time to ceremonial duties, such as opening hospitals, schools, and museums or visiting wounded soldiers. Officially, she had no political power. In the United Kingdom, the real power was in Parliament, a governing body that is similar to the U.S. Congress. The queen did, however, have great influence on the men in Parliament who had power.

> "We are not interested in the possibilities of defeat; they do not exist."
> —Victoria, Queen of England

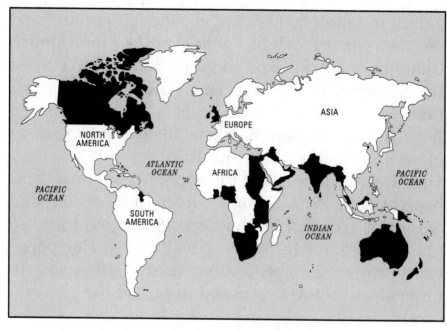

During Queen Victoria's reign, the British Empire consisted of the nations shown in black above.

During her reign, Victoria persuaded government officials to increase the size of the United Kingdom. Those officials then began to build the "greatest empire on earth," taking control in faraway places to form colonies in Australia, Canada, Cyprus, India, New Zealand, and the Falkland Islands. The British also purchased the Suez Canal in Egypt to better control the colonies in Africa. Victoria used her influence to build schools, hospitals, and museums throughout the empire.

A Place in History

Victoria's full title was Queen of the United Kingdom of Great Britain and Ireland and Empress of India. She remained on the throne for 63 years, the longest reign in the history of the United Kingdom.

On January 22, 1901, the queen died on the Isle of Wight. She was 81 years old. Her oldest son, Albert Edward, became King Edward VII. Many of Victoria's nine children married rulers or children of rulers of other European countries, including Germany, Norway, Romania, Russia, Spain, and Sweden. Victoria became known as the "Grandmother of Europe." ◇

LIFE EVENTS

1819
Alexandrina Victoria is born in London, England.

1838
Victoria is crowned Queen of England.

1840
Victoria marries her cousin, Prince Albert of Saxe-Coburg-Gotha.

1851
Prince Albert sponsors the Great Exhibition in London. It was one of the first World's Fairs.

1861
Prince Albert dies. A devastated Queen Victoria withdraws from public life.

1901
Queen Victoria dies. She is succeeded by her son, Edward VII.

Sarah Breedlove Walker

(Madam C. J. Walker)
Business Executive
(born 1867 • died 1919)

Sarah Breedlove Walker (also known as Madam C. J. Walker) showed that, through hard work and determination, anyone can rise above poverty and become a successful businessperson. Walker was one of the first women of any race to become a self-made millionaire. She never forgot her roots and often donated large sums of money to African American causes.

The Daughter of Former Slaves

Sarah Breedlove was born on December 23, 1867, on the Burney plantation near Delta, Louisiana. Sarah's parents were former slaves who had become sharecroppers, planting and harvesting crops for a farmer who owned the land. The family lived in a

small cabin. Despite working hard, they had little money and Sarah received little schooling.

When Sarah was seven years old, her parents died. As an orphaned African American girl growing up in the South, Sarah had few opportunities. So she worked in cotton fields with her sister.

When Sarah was 14, she married Moses McWilliams. They had a daughter, A'Lelia, several years later. In 1887, when Sarah was just 20, her husband died. Sarah knew that she would have to make her own way in life. She once said, "I got my start by giving myself a start." In order to support herself and her daughter, she moved to St. Louis, Missouri, and took a job as a washerwoman. She also attended night school.

Inventing a Hair Treatment

Sarah worked hard at her job for 18 years. Then, in 1904, her scalp started bothering her and her hair began falling out. No treatments seemed to work, so she developed her own. In addition to soothing her scalp, the formula took some of the kinks out of her hair.

In 1905, she left St. Louis for Denver, Colorado. There she went into business with Charles Joseph (C. J.) Walker. They got married in 1906, and she became known as Madame C. J. Walker.

> "I am a woman who came from the cotton fields of the South . . . I promoted myself . . . I have built my own factory on my own land."
>
> —Sarah Breedlove Walker

The Walkers began selling Sarah's hair treatment door to door. One of the products was called Madam C. J. Walker's Vegetable Shampoo. To drum up business, Sarah Walker gave demonstrations in homes, local churches, and clubs.

Walker's products were successful among African American women who wanted to condition their scalps and straighten their hair. In the era before beauty shops, women looked for products that they could use at home. Walker's formula helped women whose only other option for straightening their hair was to use an iron. Walker's treatment was known as the "Walker System" or "Walker Method."

The Business Expands

As her business grew, Walker hired other women to sell her products. Walker called them "hair culturists"

TOPICAL TIDBIT

Josephine Baker

The Walker Treatment's success in Europe was helped by Josephine Baker, a famous and glamorous African American dancer who used the formula. For a time, Baker lived and performed in Paris, France. During World War II, she helped the French Resistance fight the Nazis. In the U.S., she fought for civil rights.

or "scalp specialists," and dressed them in white blouses and long black skirts. At one time, Sarah had some 3,000 employees. In 1908, she opened a second branch of her business in Pittsburgh, with her daughter, A'Lelia, as its manager.

Two years later Madame Walker moved the business to Indianapolis, Indiana. There, the Walker College of Hair Culture and the Madame C. J. Walker Manufacturing Company grew and continued to succeed. Walker even expanded to Europe. Her hard work and determination paid off. Sarah Walker became the first African American self-made millionaire.

Walker also found time to support social causes. She donated money to scholarships for African Americans and youth program, homes for the elderly, and organizations that provided food for the poor. Walker also encouraged

LIFE EVENTS

1867
Sarah Breedlove is born in Delta, Louisiana.

1887
Breedlove moves in with her older sister's family and works as a domestic.

1906
Sarah Breedlove marries Charles Joseph Walker and begins selling hair-care products.

1908
Madame Walker opens Lelia College for hair culturists.

1913
Walker moves to New York City to open a company base.

1919
Madame Walker dies.

her employees to give back to the community. In fact, she awarded prizes to her workers who contributed their own time and money to community projects.

Proof that Women Can Do It All

Sarah Breedlove Walker died on May 25, 1919, at her estate in New York. Her family continued to operate the business for many years.

Seeking to improve "cleanliness and loveliness" among her clients, Walker had helped countless other women improve their hygiene and self-esteem. Despite little schooling, she built and ran a major enterprise, showing the world that African American women could design and operate highly successful businesses.

Sarah Breedlove Walker was inducted into the National Women's Hall of Fame. In 1998, the U.S. Postal Service issued a Madam C. J. Walker first-class stamp. ◇

Barbara Walters
Television Journalist
(born 1931)

In the early days of television news programs, women held only minor positions. Men reported the important news stories, while women were left the trivial topics. Women were often chosen for their looks, not their reporting skills. The role of women journalists began to change with reporters like Barbara Walters. She helped show the world that women could present important news in an intelligent and creative manner.

"The Daughter of Lou Walters"

Barbara Walters was born on September 25, 1931, in Boston, Massachusetts. Her father was a night-club owner named Lou Walters. As a child, Barbara met many celebrities who performed at her father's clubs. She quickly learned that entertainers were just as human as anyone else. Unlike many other people, Barbara was not awestruck by celebrities—a

fact that benefited her later when interviewing world leaders and popular movie stars.

Because of her father's job, Barbara rarely saw him. This made her feel lonely as a child. When she visited his clubs, she was often referred to as the "daughter of Lou Walters." She became determined to establish an identity of her own.

In 1953, Barbara Walters graduated from Sarah Lawrence College and later joined the publicity department of New York City's local NBC television station (WNBC-TV). After building her skills as a writer and producer there, Walters then worked at CBS for a time.

Changing Attitudes

Walters returned to NBC in 1961 as a writer for the *Today* show, which aired in the morning. She also gained some experience as a reporter on the show. Three years later, she became the "Today Girl." Her role, however, was not to report news or interview people, it was to add chitchat to the show and read commercials.

That was not enough for Walters. She began researching major stories and urged her producers

TOPICAL TIDBIT

Diane Sawyer

Diane Sawyer also furthered the role of female journalists in the U.S. Born in Kentucky, she worked for President Richard Nixon in the 1970s and helped him write his autobiography. After a stint at CBS News, she joined *ABCNEWS* and has since co-anchored *PrimeTime Thursday* and *Good Morning America*.

to allow her to report them on air. Finally, they did. Audiences liked Walters. About 10 years after beginning work with *Today*, she joined Hugh Downs as co-host, becoming the first woman to host the program. She also hosted *Not for Women Only* for five seasons.

Still, Walters wanted to do more. She had become a popular reporter and was widely admired by the viewing audience. In 1976, in a move that shocked other journalists, she accepted a handsome offer from ABC to join its evening news program, *ABC-NEWS*, as a co-anchor. Her contract came with a hefty salary of $1 million each year. That made Walters the highest-paid journalist—male or female—of the day. By comparison, some other veteran news anchors were making about half as much.

> "I was the kind nobody thought would make it. I had a funny Boston accent. I couldn't pronounce my *R*s. I wasn't a beauty."
>
> —Barbara Walters, on her success as a TV journalist

After two years with *ABCNEWS*, she left the show. She joined *20/20*, a television news magazine, in 1979. She continued to develop, investigate, and report timely stories. She also began *Barbara Walters Specials*, occasional special programs that gave her the opportunity to interview actors, musicians, directors, and other celebrities.

Barbara Walters's View of the World

Over the years, Walters has interviewed important political leaders such as British Prime Minister Margaret Thatcher and U.S. President Bill Clinton. She made journalism history by bringing Middle East leaders Menachem Begin of Israel and Anwar Sadat of Egypt together for a joint interview in the 1970s.

Walters has also interviewed some of the world's most popular entertainers, including Harrison Ford, Julia Roberts, Ricky Martin, and Audrey Hepburn. Despite a slight lisp, Walters perfected a frank and engaging interviewing style, which draws revealing answers from her subjects.

In 1984, Walters became co-

LIFE EVENTS

1931
Barbara Walters is born in Boston, Massachusetts.

1961
Walters begins work at NBC, researching and writing for the *Today* show.

1972
Walters is chosen as part of a core press group to travel to China with President Richard Nixon.

1976
Walters moves to ABC and launches the first *Barbara Walters Special*.

1984
Walters signs a contract to do *20/20* full time.

2000
At $12 million a year, Walters becomes the highest-paid news host in history.

host of *20/20*, and became its sole anchor in 1999. In 1998, she took on co-executive producer and co-host duties on *The View*, a new talk show on which five women of various backgrounds and ages discuss current events. In addition to her career, Walters has been married several times and has a daughter.

Barbara Walters overcame obstacles to become one of the late-20th century's most popular and respected journalists. She has won several Emmy Awards and received major journalism honors. In 1990, she was inducted into the Academy of Television Arts and Sciences Hall of Fame. Walters has paved the way for other women who want to become serious journalists. ◇

Ida B. Wells-Barnett
Antilynching Crusader
(born 1862 • died 1931)

Ida B. Wells-Barnett saw terrible tension between whites and blacks in Mississippi after the Civil War. African Americans had just been freed from slavery, and many Southern whites resented them. Wells-Barnett was discriminated against not only because of her race, but also her gender. She devoted her life to improving the treatment of African Americans and women in the U.S.

Always a Fighter

Ida Bell Wells was born during the Civil War on July 16, 1862, in Holly Springs, Mississippi. She had to be tough. Her parents were slaves who were freed after the war ended in 1865. Times were difficult for blacks in the South as they tried to adjust to life as free men and women. Most slave owners had denied slaves any schooling, so many former slaves could not read or write. It was hard to start businesses or farms on their own because they had

little money. They had worked for years as slaves, and received no payment.

Ida had the opportunity to go to school. She was very bright, and became a teacher herself at age 14, after her parents died. In 1884, she went to

Tennessee to teach at a country school while attending Fisk University. In Tennessee, Ida experienced prejudice firsthand.

One incident occurred in 1887, when she was thrown off a train for sitting in the whites-only section. The train had separate seating for white passengers and black travelers, but Ida refused to change seats when asked. She sued the railroad because it had not provided equal facilities. She won the case in local court and was awarded $500. Later, however, the Tennessee Supreme Court reversed the decision.

A Target of Hate

Ida B. Wells continued to stand up to injustice. She wrote articles about the poor quality of black schools, especially when compared to white schools,

TOPICAL TIDBIT

The Origins of Lynching

Lynching became popular in the U.S. during the American Revolution, under the direction of Charles Lynch, a planter and patriot from Virginia. He led a group that punished people who remained loyal to Great Britain. The practice became known as *lynching*, and continued for more than 150 years. Between 1882 and 1951, 1,293 whites and 3,437 blacks were lynched in the U.S.

which were far superior. Wells lost her teaching job because of these articles so, in 1891, she started a newspaper called the *Memphis Free Speech*. In her articles, she called for an end to discrimination and violence against blacks.

Wells spoke out most passionately against lynching, which was occurring throughout the South. Lynching was when angry mobs of white men hunted African American men and women and dragged them

> "One had better die fighting against injustice than die like a dog or a rat in a trap."
>
> —Ida B. Wells-Barnett

from their homes or jobs. The mobs would beat their victims, then hang them—often for no reason other than the color of their skin. The police, who were white, ignored the murders.

Several of Wells' friends were lynched in the early 1890s. Her newspaper instructed blacks to boycott (refuse to use) white businesses in protest. She became a target herself, and her office was destroyed. Wells was warned to stay away or be killed.

Wells moved to New York and continued her work. In 1895, she married Ferdinand Lee Barnett. Wells kept her maiden name as part of her married name, and became Ida Wells-Barnett. Although this is relatively common today, it was rare, even shocking, in

1895. Also in 1895, Wells-Barnett published a book about lynching called *A Red Record*. Three years later, she went to the White House to urge President William McKinley to take government action to end lynching.

A Nonstop Activist

Wells-Barnett's fight did not end with African American issues. She also fought for women's rights. Wells-Barnett was proof that a woman could be a journalist, activist, wife, and mother of four children. She tried to combine race and gender issues, but some leaders of the women's movement were not very supportive. They feared that adding race to the mix would take away interest and support from the women's movement.

Wells-Barnett started many groups to address social causes, including the Negro Fellow-

LIFE EVENTS

1862
Ida Bell Wells is born a slave in Holly Springs, Mississippi.

1887
Wells is forced to sit in third class on a train, even though she had bought a first-class ticket. She sues the train company.

1891
Wells establishes the newspaper *Memphis Free Speech*. She writes articles that call for an end to violence against blacks.

1895
Ida B. Wells marries Ferdinand Lee Barnett and moves to Chicago.

1931
Ida B. Wells-Barnett dies.

ship League and the Alpha Suffrage Club. She was one of the founders of the National Association for the Advancement of Colored People (NAACP) in 1909. The NAACP is an organization that works toward establishing equal rights for African Americans. Wells-Barnett died on March 25, 1931, in Chicago, Illinois.

Ida B. Wells-Barnett described her struggles in her autobiography, *Crusade for Justice*. Although lynching continued in the 20th century, Wells-Barnett fought courageously in the face of death threats. She brought the issue before the eyes of the world and encouraged others to work toward ending injustice. ◇

Laura Ingalls Wilder
Author
(born 1867 • died 1957)

Laura Ingalls Wilder wrote children's stories about growing up on the prairies of America. Like other pioneers, Wilder's family traveled by covered wagon to places like Nebraska, Minnesota, and North Dakota, hoping to make a new life on the prairie. Wilder's "Little House" books tell of the hardships and joys her family encountered along the way.

Life on the Prairie

Laura Elizabeth Ingalls was born to Charles and Caroline Ingalls on February 7, 1867, in a farmhouse near Pepin, Wisconsin. Laura had four sisters and one brother. Laura and her older sister, Mary, attended the Barry Corner School, learning to read and write. Life was simple but hard. For an evening's entertainment, Charles often played the fiddle while Caroline taught the girls to cook and sew.

When Laura was seven, the family traveled by covered wagon to Walnut Grove, Minnesota, to start a

farm. When they first arrived, they did not have any-place to live, so Charles Ingalls built a "dugout" sod house—a hole carved into the side of a hill—on the banks of a creek. Then he built a house of wood. Laura and Mary helped him plant wheat in the fields.

Life on the prairie was often hard. Many times, the crops failed due to droughts or blizzards. In 1874, swarms of grasshoppers invaded the crop fields. Farmers tried to save their crops from the hungry insects by setting fire to straw and manure, hoping that the smoke would kill the grasshoppers. It took two years to rid the land of the jumping insects. In 1879, the Ingalls family moved to De Smet, Dakota Territory, so Charles could work for the railroad.

Through all the difficulty, Laura continued her studies. She was an excellent student and was interested in literature and history. When Mary was struck by fever and blindness, Laura stayed by her side, helping her with schoolwork and household chores.

Laura worked very hard and received her teaching certificate when she was 15. She took a job as schoolmistress of the Bouchie School, 12 miles from home. Since it was too far to walk each day, she lived with a local family. Laura's friend, Almanzo "Manly"

TOPICAL TIDBIT

Sod Houses

American pioneers traveled west, often settling in the plains where there were few trees. Instead of using lumber to build homes, the pioneers used sod, mud, and clay. They made the roofs from straw and branches. Sometimes, the houses were built into the side of a hill; these were called "dugouts."

Wilder, drove her home each weekend in his horse-drawn wagon, so that she could spend time with her family. In 1885, Laura and Almanzo were married. They lived on a farm near town. The following year, they had a daughter, named Rose.

A Career in Writing

Laura Ingalls Wilder lived in many places over the course of her life. Then, in 1894, she, Manly, and Rose settled in Mansfield, Missouri, in the Ozark Mountains. They built a farm called Rocky Ridge, which remained home. In addition to tending to her home and raising her daughter, Wilder wrote articles for the *Missouri Ruralist* and *McCall's Magazine.* She told Rose about her childhood—about growing up on the prairie and moving from place to place by covered wagon.

When Rose was a young woman, she begged her mother to write down those stories of her childhood—about Laura, the young girl who had grown up on the prairie. Rose helped her mother write the stories that were later published as *Little House in*

> "I am beginning to learn that it is the sweet, simple things in life which are the real ones after all."
> —Laura Ingalls Wilder

the Big Woods, the first in a series of "Little House" books.

After the success of the first book, Wilder wrote several others, including *Little House on the Prairie*, *On the Banks of Plum Creek*, and *On the Way Home*. Wilder received the Newbery Award—one of the highest honors given to an author of children's books. In fact, Wilder's books were so popular that, in 1954, the American Library Association created the Laura Ingalls Wilder Award for children's authors. Three years later, on February 10, 1957, Wilder died. She was 90 years old.

Laura Ingalls Wilder captured the hearts of children throughout the world with her "Little House" books. In the 1970s, her stories were turned into a television series called *Little House on the Prairie*. In many places, the shows are still being aired on cable stations. ◇

LIFE EVENTS

1867
Laura Elizabeth Ingalls is born in Lake Pepin, Wisconsin.

1882-1885
Ingalls teaches in the Dakota Territory.

1885
Laura Ingalls marries Almanzo Wilder.

1894
Laura Ingalls Wilder begins writing for the *Missouri Ruralist*.

1935
Wilder writes *Little House on the Prairie*, based on her experiences as part of a pioneer family.

1954
The Laura Ingalls Wilder Award for children's literature is created.

1957
Laura Ingalls Wilder dies.

Oprah Winfrey
Talk-show Host, Actor, Humanitarian
(born 1954)

One of the most successful African American women today, Oprah Winfrey uses her fame to help others. She hosts a talk show that millions of people watch, and she covers topics that help viewers learn more about themselves. Winfrey has inspired millions of people—especially women—to make their lives, and the world, a better place.

The Preacher

Oprah Winfrey was born January 29, 1954, in Kosciusko, Mississippi. Her parents were unmarried teenagers, and Oprah spent the first six years of her life with her grandmother. Her parents had given her the Biblical name Orpah, but misspelled it.

Oprah learned to read the Bible when she was about three. At that time, she also began to recite Bible verses and speeches at church. Later, she

sometimes repeated sermons at school, so her classmates started to call her "Preacher." Even at such a
young age, Oprah became known for her
ability to speak well and captivate an audience.

When Oprah was six years old, she went to live
with her mother in Milwaukee, Wisconsin. There,
she was physically abused by several male relatives.

Oprah, who blamed herself for the abuse, often got into trouble and tried to run away.

When Oprah was a teenager, she was sent to Nashville, Tennessee, to live with her father, who was very strict. He set curfews for her and assigned her many book reports, encouraging her love of reading. Oprah began to settle down and slowly turn her life around.

When Oprah was 19, she began work as a radio reporter. She switched to television reporting while a student at Tennessee State University. In 1977, she took a job as a TV news anchor in Baltimore, Maryland. She remembers trying to act like noted journalist Barbara Walters. However, Oprah Winfrey had difficulties as a reporter. She could not remain unaffected by the news stories she read. Sometimes she laughed when a story was funny, or cried when it was sad, which an anchor is not supposed to do. She feared that she would lose her job. Instead, the station assigned her to an early-morning talk show called *People Are Talking*. The format of the show was more casual than reporting the news. Winfrey made the show a success. She believed that she had found her calling in life.

> "Think like a queen. A queen is not afraid to fail. Failure is another stepping-stone to life."
> —Oprah Winfrey

Talking Her Way to the Top

In 1984, Winfrey moved to Chicago to host a talk show called *A.M. Chicago*, which later became *The Oprah Winfrey Show*. In 1986, when the show was broadcast nationwide, Winfrey rose to the top of her profession. By the late 1990s, more than 20 million people were tuning in to see her show every day. Since 1994, Winfrey has vowed to present only helpful or uplifting programs, unlike many other talk shows that present trashy topics.

Eventually, Winfrey started her own production company, Harpo Productions. She took control of *The Oprah Winfrey Show*. She also tried her hand at acting. In 1985, she appeared in Steven Spielberg's film *The Color Purple*. In 1998, she produced and starred in *Beloved*, a film based on a Pulitzer Prize-winning novel by Toni Morrison.

Winfrey has won several Emmy Awards for television and a Peabody Award, which honors achievement

TOPICAL TIDBIT

Oprah's Book Club

Oprah Winfrey encourages people to read by sponsoring a book club. She gives her television audience time to read each book. Then she arranges for a few viewers to meet the author to discuss the work. Winfrey has recommended books by many writers including Maya Angelou and Toni Morrison.

in broadcasting and cable. *Time* magazine named her one of the most influential people of the 20th century.

Winfrey's success has made her one of the richest women in America. However, she strongly believes that people should give back to their communities, so she makes large contributions to charity. Winfrey also worked to get Congress to pass the National Child Protection Act to help abused children. The bill became law in 1993.

Making a Difference

Oprah Winfrey brings important issues to light, especially problems faced by African Americans and women. Winfrey's ability to relate to the experiences of her guests and share her own personal stories has allowed her to help many people improve their lives. ◇

LIFE EVENTS

1954
Oprah Winfrey is born in Kosciusko, Mississippi.

1977
Winfrey moves to Baltimore.

1984
Winfrey hosts *A.M. Chicago*, which becomes *The Oprah Winfrey Show*.

1985
Winfrey appears in the movie *The Color Purple*. She is nominated for an Academy Award for Best Supporting Actress.

1998
Winfrey produces and stars in the movie *Beloved*.

2000
Winfrey launches *O: The Oprah Magazine*.

Babe Didrikson Zaharias
Athlete
(born 1911 • died 1956)

When sportscasters are asked to name the top female athlete of all time, the answer is usually Babe Zaharias. Standing 5 feet, 5 inches tall at the height of her career, Zaharias excelled in sports like no other female athlete. From playing basketball to jumping hurdles to throwing a javelin, Zaharias set many speed and distance records before turning her talents to golf, where she won every major women's title at least once between 1936 and 1954. She was truly a pioneer in the field of women's sports.

Becoming an Athlete

Mildred Ella Didrikson was born on June 26, 1911, in Port Arthur, Texas. After a hurricane flattened the city in 1914, her family moved to Beaumont, 17 miles inland from the sea.

As a young girl, Mildred loved all types of sports,

Babe Didrikson boxes to keep in shape (1933).

including swimming, diving, tennis, bowling, football, cycling, figure skating, handball, and volleyball. After hitting five home runs during a school baseball game, her classmates started calling her "Babe," after Babe Ruth. Babe's parents were very supportive of her athletic abilities. They encouraged her to try out for the basketball team. She played on the All-American girls' basketball team from 1930 to 1932.

Heading for the Olympics

On July 16, 1932, Didrikson competed at the Olympic trials in Evanston, Illinois. She competed in 10 track-and-field events and won 8. By the end of the day, Didrikson was a member of the U.S. Olympic Team.

The 1932 Olympics were held in Los Angeles, California. Didrikson qualified for five events, but because she was a woman, she was only allowed to compete in three. She set world records for the javelin toss (143 feet, 4 inches) and the 80-meter hurdles (11.7 seconds). She also broke the world record for the high jump but was disqualified because her head went over the bar

> "Before I was even in my teens, I knew exactly what I wanted to be when I grew up. My goal was to be the greatest athlete who ever lived."
>
> —Babe Didrickson Zaharias

before the rest of her body. (This is known as the "Western Roll" and is now acceptable in high-jump competition.) Didrikson won two gold medals (for the javelin and 80-meter hurdles) and one silver (for the high jump).

The World of Golf

In 1935, Didrikson turned her attention to golf. Believing that practice makes perfect, she would practice for eight hours straight, hitting more than 1,000 golf balls each day. Didrikson could take a swing and hit the ball more than 250 yards, landing it where she wanted it to go.

Didrikson played golf for the next 20 years. In 1946 and 1947 alone, she won 17 out of the 18 tournaments in which she played. In total, she won 41 tournaments, including the U.S. National Women's Amateur Championship (1946) and the British Ladies' Amateur Championship (1947). She also won

---

TOPICAL TIDBIT

Ladies' Professional Golf Association

Babe Didrikson Zaharias was one of the founders of the Ladies' Professional Golf Association (LPGA). The LPGA is now one of the top professional golf organizations in the world. Some of the other founding members were Patty Berg, Helen Dettweiler, Opal Hill, Betty Jameson, and Louise Suggs. Some of today's stars include Nancy Lopez, Se Ri Pak, and Annika Sorenstam.

Babe Didrikson Zaharias tees off at the Women's British
Amateur Championship in Scotland, 1947.

the U.S. Women's Open three times—in 1948, 1950, and 1954. She was one of the founders of the Ladies' Professional Golf Association (LPGA).

In 1938, Didrikson met George Zaharias when they were paired at a golf tournament. Zaharias was a pro wrestler called the "Weeping Greek from Cripple

Creek." They were married later that year. George became Babe's manager.

Gone too Soon

In 1953, Babe Zaharias was diagnosed with cancer. She had surgery in 1953 and again in 1956, but the cancer spread quickly. Babe died of cancer on September 27, 1956, in Galveston, Texas. She was only 42.

Babe Didrikson Zaharias has earned as many honors in death as she did in life. The Associated Press named her Woman Athlete of the Year many times. *Sport's Illustrated* magazine called her the Female Athlete of the Century in 1999. She has also been memorialized in other ways—the Babe Didrikson Zaharias Memorial Center in Beaumont, Texas, is a museum dedicated to her career in sports. The Babe Zaharias Foundation raises money for cancer research. ◇

LIFE EVENTS

1914
Mildred Ella Didrikson is born in Port Arthur, Texas.

1931
At the National Women's Amateur Athletic Union (AAU) track meet, Didrikson wins first place in eight events.

1932
Didrikson breaks three world records in track and field events at the Olympics.

1950
Babe Didrikson Zaharias is named Athlete of the Half Century by the Associated Press.

1954
Zaharias wins the U.S. Women's Open in golf for the third time.

1956
Zaharias dies of cancer.

Addams • Madeleine Albright • Louisa May Alcott • Marian A
on • Sarah Bernhardt • Mary McLeod Bethune • Shirley Temp
ë and Emily Brontë • Rachel Carson • Mary Cassatt • Cather
• Diana, Princess of Wales • Emily Dickinson • Isadora Dunc
ne Frank • Betty Friedan • Indira Gandhi • Judy Garland • A
• Fannie Lou Hamer • Dorothy Hamill • Lillian Hellman • Au
• Helen Keller • Billie Jean King • Mary Leakey • Annie Leib
therine de Médicis • Golda Meir • Edna St. Vincent Millay •
tilova • Nefertiti • Florence Nightingale • Annie Oakley • S
dy Onassis • Rosa Parks • Eva Perón • Pocahontas • Beatrix
olph • Sacagawea • Margaret Sanger • Elizabeth Cady Stante
r Teresa • Margaret Thatcher • Sojourner Truth • Harriet Tub
ngalls Wilder • Oprah Winfrey • Babe Didrikson Zaharias • J
ngelou • Susan B. Anthony • Jane Austen • Lucille Ball • Cla
eth Blackwell • Nellie Bly • Margaret Bourke-White • Charlot
opatra VII • Hillary Rodham Clinton • Nadia Comaneci • Mar
t • Elizabeth I • Ella Fitzgerald • Margot Fonteyn • Dian Fos
Goodall • Martha Graham • Ella Grasso • Florence Griffith J
Holiday • Mae Jemison • Joan of Arc • Mother Jones • Frid
• Belva Lockwood • Dolley Madison • Madonna • Margaret
e • Maria Montessori • Toni Morrison • Grandma Moses • M
nnor • Rosie O'Donnell • Georgia O'Keeffe • Jacqueline Bou
tte Rankin • Janet Reno • Sally Ride • Eleanor Roosevelt •
inem • Martha Stewart • Harriet Beecher Stowe • Ida M. Tar
ia • Sarah Breedlove Walker • Barbara Walters • Ida B. Wells
dams • Madeleine Albright • Louisa May Alcott • Marian And
on • Sarah Bernhardt • Mary McLeod Bethune • Shirley Temp
ë and Emily Brontë • Rachel Carson • Mary Cassatt • Cather
• Diana, Princess of Wales • Emily Dickinson • Isadora Dunc
ne Frank • Betty Friedan • Indira Gandhi • Judy Garland • A
• Fannie Lou Hamer • Dorothy Hamill • Lillian Hellman • Au
• Helen Keller • Billie Jean King • Mary Leakey • Annie Leib

va Angelou • Susan B. Anthony • Jane Austen • Lucille Ball •
abeth Blackwell • Nellie Bly • Margaret Bourke-White • Charl
Cleopatra VII • Hillary Rodham Clinton • Nadia Comaneci • N
hart • Elizabeth I • Ella Fitzgerald • Margot Fonteyn • Dian F
• Jane Goodall • Martha Graham • Ella Grasso • Florence Grif
• Billie Holiday • Mae Jemison • Joan of Arc • Mother Jones
n • Belva Lockwood • Dolley Madison • Madonna • Margaret
e • Maria Montessori • Toni Morrison • Grandma Moses • Ma
onnor • Rosie O'Donnell • Georgia O'Keeffe • Jacqueline Bo
ette Rankin • Janet Reno • Sally Ride • Eleanor Roosevelt •
inem • Martha Stewart • Harriet Beecher Stowe • Ida M. Tarb
• Sarah Breedlove Walker • Barbara Walters • Ida B. Wells-Bar
Madeleine Albright • Louisa May Alcott • Marian Anderson •
ah Bernhardt • Mary McLeod Bethune • Shirley Temple Black
Emily Brontë • Rachel Carson • Mary Cassatt • Catherine the
a, Princess of Wales • Emily Dickinson • Isadora Duncan • An
nk • Betty Friedan • Indira Gandhi • Judy Garland • Althea G
Lou Hamer • Dorothy Hamill • Lillian Hellman • Audrey Hepl
n Keller • Billie Jean King • Mary Leakey • Annie Leibovitz • /
ine de Médicis • Golda Meir • Edna St. Vincent Millay • Maril
ova • Nefertiti • Florence Nightingale • Annie Oakley • Sandr
Onassis • Rosa Parks • Eva Perón • Pocahontas • Beatrix Pot
a • Sacagawea • Margaret Sanger • Elizabeth Cady Stanton •
eresa • Margaret Thatcher • Sojourner Truth • Harriet Tubmar
a Ingalls Wilder • Oprah Winfrey • Babe Didrikson Zaharias •
Angelou • Susan B. Anthony • Jane Austen • Lucille Ball • Cl
abeth Blackwell • Nellie Bly • Margaret Bourke-White • Charl
Cleopatra VII • Hillary Rodham Clinton • Nadia Comaneci • N
rhart • Elizabeth I • Ella Fitzgerald • Margot Fonteyn • Dian F
• Jane Goodall • Martha Graham • Ella Grasso • Florence Grif
• Billie Holiday • Mae Jemison • Joan of Arc • Mother Jones
n • Belva Lockwood • Dolley Madison • Madonna • Margaret